Carl Henry—Theologian for All Seasons

Carl Henry—Theologian for All Seasons

An Introduction and Guide to
God, Revelation, and Authority

G. WRIGHT DOYLE

PICKWICK *Publications* • Eugene, Oregon

CARL HENRY—THEOLOGIAN FOR ALL SEASONS
An Introduction and Guide to *God, Revelation, and Authority*

Pickwick Publications
An Imprint of Wipf and Stock Publishers
199 W. 8th Ave., Suite 3
Eugene, OR 97401

www.wipfandstock.com

ISBN 13: 978-1-60899-073-3

Cataloguing-in-Publication data:

Doyle, G. Wright.

Carl Henry—theologian for all seasons : an introduction and guide to God, Revelation, and Authority / G. Wright Doyle.

xiv + 236 p. ; 23 cm. Includes bibliographical references and indexes.

ISBN 13: 978-1-60899-073-3

1. Henry, Carl F. H. (Carl Ferdinand Howard), 1913–2003. 2. Evangelicalism. I. Title.

BR1640 .A25 .D75 2010

Manufactured in the U.S.A.

It gives me great pleasure to dedicate this book to my esteemed colleague and good friend Dr. John Wong, Professor of Theology at China Evangelical Seminary. Dr. Wong proofread the entire text of the Chinese edition of the first four volumes of God, Revelation, and Authority, *has taught graduate courses on Henry's theology, and is a very fine theologian.*

Contents

Acknowledgments / ix
Introduction / xi

PART I

1 The Life and Character of Carl F. H. Henry / 1
2 The Recent Neglect of Carl Henry among Evangelicals / 13
3 Twentieth-Century Theologian / 21
4 The Reformed Theology of Carl Henry / 38
5 Doctrine of Revelation / 51
6 Apologist for the Twenty-first Century / 65
7 Prophet for the Twenty-first Century / 79
8 Carl Henry and His Critics I / 92
9 Carl Henry and His Critics II / 105
10 Carl Henry and His Critics III / 115
11 Carl Henry: Twentieth-Century Augustine / 130

PART II

Theological Index to *God, Revelation, and Authority* / 149
Macro Index to *God, Revelation, and Authority* / 151
Outline of *God, Revelation, and Authority* / 156

Bibliography / 223
Index of Names / 229
Index of Subjects / 232

Acknowledgments

Laura Philbrick read the entire manuscript several times, editing, proof-reading, and formatting. Her careful eye and insightful suggestions have greatly improved the text. My brother, the Reverend Dr. Peter R. Doyle, who studied with Karl Barth, has provided me with invaluable theological guidance for more than forty years. Dr. D. A. Carson kindly offered helpful advice, which increased the value of the book. The Right Reverend John Rogers, my systematic theology teacher in seminary, imbued me with a love for the subject and showed me the necessity of reading authors from a variety of viewpoints. My wife Dori has encouraged me in all stages of this project, as she has with my other books. Without her I would be able to do very little. Special thanks go to Chris Spinks of Wipf and Stock Publishers for his meticulous and expert editorial guidance. All deficiencies in this volume must be charged to my ignorance and inability, any merits to the help I have received from others and from God himself, to whom alone be the glory.

Introduction

- Carl F. H. Henry has been widely acclaimed as the leading evangelical theologian of the twentieth century. Roger Olson calls him "the dean of evangelical theologians."[1] For decades, he helped to lead evangelicalism as a movement, not only in the United States, but around the world.

Today, however, he receives much less attention than he did two decades ago. Indeed, he is largely ignored outside certain circles. I think this is a loss to the church worldwide. To rectify the situation, I have undertaken in this book to introduce the wide-ranging learning of Carl Henry to a new generation of readers and perhaps prod a few people my age and younger to delve into his magnum opus: *God, Revelation, and Authority*.[2] This six-volume work is a major contribution to Christian theology, covering a broad range of subjects, but hardly anyone reads it.

God, Revelation, and Authority possesses value not only as a monumental statement of evangelical theology in the last quarter of the twentieth century. In it Dr. Henry has also dealt with almost all the major theological challenges now facing us, and with admirable profundity and clarity. He not only lays out a clear statement of biblical teaching, but also answers questions that thinking people have asked about Christianity.

Nevertheless, Carl Henry has been not only neglected, but seriously misrepresented by influential commentators on modern theology. Major handbooks and introductions to theology, not to mention works by widely read evangelical theologians, have so distorted Henry's thought that his contribution, which could be of considerable help to us in the twenty-first century, has been largely lost. I realize that this is

---

1. Olson, *Westminster Handbook*, 41 and often.
2. Abbreviated as *GRA* in the notes of this book.

a serious charge, and shall try to provide adequate evidence to explain why I believe it is warranted.

Since I am not a specialist in systematic theology, and especially not an expert on modern theology, I hesitated to undertake this project. During and immediately after my seminary years I did concentrate upon systematic theology. After graduating from seminary and pastoring three small churches for two years, I pursued graduate studies in the Classics department of the University of North Carolina at Chapel Hill. My aim was to gain familiarity with the Greco-Roman world so that I could later teach New Testament in seminary. After preliminary studies that included Hellenistic philosophy, I wrote a dissertation on St. Augustine's sermons on the Gospel of John. In 1980, following several years of Mandarin Chinese language study, I joined the faculty of China Evangelical Seminary in Taipei, Taiwan, where I taught Greek and New Testament. For almost ten years, I eschewed systematic theology in favor of the Bible and its proper exegesis.

Since there was no modern Greek-Chinese lexicon of the New Testament, at the urging of Chinese colleagues I supervised a team of my students in translating an abridgment of the *Greek-English Lexicon* of Bauer, Arndt, and Gingrich into Chinese. That project took five years and much energy. I was looking forward to a respite from any other large undertakings.

Meanwhile, however, Dr. Henry had come to Taiwan to lecture at our seminary. I knew who he was, of course, but had not met him personally until that time. He was introducing us to the material that would come out in later volumes of *God, Revelation, and Authority*. I purchased volume 1, which he kindly signed for me. Eager to learn from him, I began the book. The first few chapters captured my attention, but then my lack of background in modern philosophy slowed me down as Henry moved into the deeper waters of his apologetics. I put the book down.

After about a year, the editor of the seminary press was telling me how few people were able to understand the Chinese translation of the first four volumes of *God, Revelation, and Authority*. As we talked, we agreed that the set needed to be abridged for Chinese readers. But who had the time or the ability to make such an abridgment? He turned to me and said, "You must do this!"

At first I objected. As I said above, I wanted to rest from such intensive work. Gradually, however, I sensed that this was a task that I must assume, and so arrangements were made with another publisher, Campus Press, to produce a shorter version of the Chinese edition. That was in 1986. Over the next several years, working from the English but with constant reference to the Chinese translation (which had been ably done by a Chinese scholar), I reduced Henry's work to about half its original length, adding an internal outline to make the flow of the argument clearer, with study questions for Chinese readers at the end of each chapter.

The first four volumes of that abridgment were published in Chinese by Campus Press. After much deliberation, and in the absence of a translator for the last two volumes, Dr. Henry agreed that we could simply produce a translation of my abridgment of them. As I write these lines, two capable men in Taiwan are working on my abridgment of volumes 5 and 6. Readers from all over the Chinese world have expressed appreciation for the way that Carl Henry answers their pressing questions, and how the shorter version is much easier to understand.

It goes without saying that to make such an abridgment, with the accompanying internal outline, I had to go through the work very carefully more than once. As I did, I began to delight in it. Now I pick up *God, Revelation, and Authority* and read it for pleasure, as I do Augustine, to whom I compare him (see the chapter "Carl Henry: Twentieth-century Augustine"). I am on my fourth journey through the set now.

After a while, however, we realized that even knowledgeable evangelical theologians were not aware of the riches of *God, Revelation, and Authority*. Its length and complexity make the set hard to use, and few will read it straight through. Furthermore, as I have said, many evangelicals under the age of fifty do not know about Carl Henry, and are dissuaded from getting acquainted with his thought by the criticisms of people whom they respect. Liberal and European theologians may know who he is, but pay him even less attention than he receives among evangelicals in North America.

At the suggestion of several people on both sides of the Pacific, therefore, I decided to write an introduction to Carl Henry's theology as he expressed it in *God, Revelation, and Authority*. In the process, I have learned to appreciate Henry all the more, partly because I have in recent years returned to my initial love of systematic theology. I have taught this subject for China Evangelical Seminary–North American Campus and for Reformed Theological Seminary–Washington DC, as well as taking private students twice through Bruce Demarest and Gordon Lewis's excellent *Integrative Theology*.

For this guide to *God, Revelation, and Authority*, I have tried to familiarize myself with the basic contours of modern theology, but I cannot in any way claim to be an expert, so I ask for criticisms from those who know far more than I.

The following chapters have two goals: To introduce new readers to *God, Revelation, and Authority*, and to dispel the myths perpetrated about Henry's theology, so that his erudition, illuminating insights, and simple faith may assist us as we face the challenges of the twenty-first century.

This introduction and reader's guide is divided into two parts: The first discusses Carl Henry from a variety of perspectives and responds in some detail to criticisms that have been directed towards Henry's point of view. The exposition and defense of Carl Henry's theology ends with a comparison of him with Augustine of Hippo. Most of these chapters, though related to all the others, can be read by themselves; as a consequence, there is a fair bit of repetition in them. The second part provides helpful outlines and indices to allow you to easily access the contents of *God, Revelation, and Authority*.

Since Bob Patterson has already penned a very accurate introduction and survey to *God, Revelation, and Authority*, I make no attempt to duplicate his work here, but direct interested readers to his most helpful book.[3]

---

3. Patterson, *Carl F. H. Henry* (1983).

PART I

ONE

The Life and Character of Carl F. H. Henry

Early Years[1]

Carl Ferdinand Howard Henry was born the son of German immigrant parents in New York City on January 22, 1913. He grew up on Long Island where, during his high school years and afterwards, he worked as a reporter for several newspapers, including the *New York Times* and the *New York Herald Tribune*. Later, he became for a while the editor of a major Long Island weekly paper.

He was baptized as an infant and brought up in the Episcopal Church, but lived as a pagan until his conversion in 1933. God used a variety of factors in this transformation, including the witness of friends and a violent thunderstorm. He committed himself unreservedly to follow Christ wherever he was commanded to go, and began to seek the Lord's will for the rest of his life.

Reflecting on this period later, he wrote:

> I have always been open to some so-called mystical aspects of the Christian life, if in fact mysticism is really a term appropriate to the New Testament. Too many theologians have hastily dismissed the apostle Paul's teaching on 'union with Christ.' . . . God has revealed his nature normatively to the inspired prophets and apostles as set forth in Scripture. That does not mean, however, that he enters into no significant relations today. New truth about God there is not. . . . But when God becomes

---

1. Carson and Woodbridge, eds., *God and Culture*, contains a brief curriculum vitae of Henry and a selected chronological bibliography of his works.

my God, when divine revelation penetrates not only the mind but rather the whole self, when the Spirit personally illumines the believer, dynamic fellowship with God opens possibilities of spiritual guidance in which the Holy Spirit personalizes and applies the biblical revelation individually to and in a redeemed and renewed life.[2]

Sensing God's leading to pursue higher education, he applied in 1935 to Wheaton College. Then he confronted several obstacles: His father, who had for years been unfaithful and had divorced his mother, left her with a large debt, which Carl Henry then paid. Two weeks before he was to matriculate at Wheaton, he was stricken with acute appendicitis, for which his doctor urged immediate surgery.

But Henry believed that God wanted him in Chicago in less time than full recovery from major surgery allowed, so he asked the surgeon whether he could wait one night while asking God to work a miracle. He and his friends prayed for healing, and the next morning the physician declared him healed. Henry reflected later:

I knew there was a healing power of nature, for the cosmos owed its source and sustenance to a providential Creator. I respected the healing power of doctors and the marvels of medical science. . . . I knew there was a healing power also of mind over matter, and that a patient's will to recover is sometimes half the battle. But I knew something more, that the great God who is sometimes glorified by the courageous and victorious bearing of one's thorn in the flesh is, on other occasions, equally glorified in the direct healing of the body no less that of the soul. I left for college in good time, reassured that God would and could supply every need.[3]

Education

With his meager financial resources, Henry had to work his way through college. While still in New York, he had sensed that God would provide two means of income: "Teaching typing" and "Newspaper work."[4] For the next several years, he supported himself as a journalist, writing

2. Henry, *Confessions of a Theologian*, 53.
3. Ibid, 58–59.
4. Ibid., 52.

for both the college and community newspapers, while majoring in philosophy. Henry gratefully acknowledges the influence that Gordon Clark had upon him, praising Clark for his wide knowledge and careful thinking.

After graduating with a BA *cum laude*, he began working toward a BD (now called MDiv) from Northern Baptist Theological Seminary and an MA in theology from Wheaton. Living at the seminary, he writes:

> I would for some years focus on biblical languages, church his-
> tory and theological concerns. In my solitary room I explored
> New Testament Greek, stretched my prayers around the world,
> and at times sank to my knees and wept, entreating God before
> an open Bible to forgive my sluggish spirit, redeem the failings
> of a religious life, and make me a worthy witness to his grace.[5]

In due time, he earned the MA from Wheaton, BD from Northern, and a ThD from Northern. During the summers, he attended classes at the Winona Lake School of Theology which, though unaccredited, attracted many fine teachers. He also took graduate courses on Roman Catholic theology at the University of Chicago, Loyola University, and the University of Indiana.

During and after earning his doctorate at Northern, Henry served on the faculty there, teaching systematic theology and philosophy of re-ligion. During the summers of the late 1940s, he also taught at Gordon College while pursuing a doctorate in philosophy at Boston University. He spent these years also studying the class syllabi of Cornelius Van Til, the influential professor of theology and apologetics at Westminster Theological Seminary.

Let us pause for a moment to ponder both the unusual diligence of this young man and his devotion to the knowledge of God. Clearly gifted with a first-rate mind, he applied his mental powers to the Scriptures, theology, and church history for a full dozen years, toward the end of which he broadened his scope to include philosophy. Even a casual skimming of *God, Revelation, and Authority*—especially the last five volumes—will testify to the depth and breadth of Carl Henry's familiarity with the Bible and with Christian theology, both Protestant and Roman Catholic. With no fewer than four advanced degrees in

5. Ibid, 89.

theology, Henry had laid a solid foundation for his later defense and exposition of scriptural teaching.

Preaching, Teaching, Writing

Though fully occupied with study and teaching, Henry preached on Sundays in different churches and spoke on Saturday nights at Youth for Christ rallies.

He received the PhD in philosophy with a dissertation on Augustus S. Strong's theology, which had been influenced by personal idealism philosophy. From the beginning, therefore, Henry was critical of theologians who allowed alien philosophical ideas to influence their interpretation of Scripture.

In 1947, he was asked by Harold Ockenga to join the founding faculty of Fuller Theological Seminary in Pasadena, California. He had already helped to found the National Association of Evangelicals, and his short book *The Uneasy Conscience of Modern Fundamentalism* had made a powerful impact upon the conservative theological world. This "tract for the times" marked Henry as a leader in the movement that soon came to be known as neo-evangelicalism, or simply evangelicalism.

Carl Henry, Harold Ockenga, Billy Graham, E. J. Carnell, and others sought to adopt a more balanced, irenic, and inclusive stance towards mainline churches, modern biblical criticism, and science than had the fundamentalists they criticized. They also sought to engage both secular society and the academy in ways that fundamentalists had eschewed. As Albert Mohler comments, the evangelical movement "would combine a stalwart defense of the orthodox faith, buttressed by solid academic underpinnings, with careful attention to the application of the gospel message."[6] Mohler adds:

> Evangelicalism would embody the mood of engagement with broader theological movements and a recognition of the social and cultural dimensions of the gospel. . . . [It would avoid] the excessive preoccupation on eschatology, spirit of separatism, and lack of engagement common to fundamentalism.[7]

6. Mohler, "Carl F. H. Henry," 283.

7. Ibid., 284.

For almost ten years Henry taught at Fuller, where he also served briefly as dean. His courses included theology, philosophy, and ethics— the major areas of research and writing that he would pursue for the rest of his career. While at Fuller, he kept up the pace of his prolific writing, which has made him so influential, not only in America, but around the world, where his works have been translated into a number of languages. These publications include *Remaking the Modern Mind, Giving a Reason for Our Hope, Fifty Years of Protestant Theology, The Drift of Western Thought, Christian Personal Ethics, Basic Christian Doctrines, Christian Faith and Modern theology,* and *Jesus of Nazareth: Savior and Lord.*

Editor of *Christianity Today*

A new and decisive turn in his life came in 1965, when he accepted the invitation to become editor-in-chief of the new evangelical journal *Christianity Today*. Designed as a conservative counterpart to *The Christian Century,* this magazine soon became a powerful rallying point for evangelicals in both independent and mainline churches. Henry's editorials addressed the major issues of both church and society, and were marked by solid scholarship and profound thought. He also contributed columns on modern theological trends, which I, as a student in a liberal seminary, found both helpful and hard to read! For many of us in denominations that were dominated by liberal theology, *Christianity Today* provided inspiration and nourishment for the mind.

Carl Henry always tried to major on the fundamentals of the faith, and avoided controversy over secondary matters like eschatology and ecclesiology. He sought to apply biblical truth to the complex challenges of modern society, usually espousing positions that were thought too "conservative" by some, but which reflected the realistic view of human nature and thus of political programs that Henry found in the Bible. However, critics on the right considered him too soft on the World Council of Churches and its support of revolutionary movements, and not sharp enough in his exposures of the errors of non-evangelical theologians.

Never losing his passion for the worldwide spread of the gospel, he organized and led the Berlin Conference on Evangelism in 1966, of which Billy Graham was honorary chairman. The gathering high-lighted his concern for united efforts by all those who take the Bible as the Word of God, and led to openings for him to address scholars and church leaders on the Continent. Henry also edited a volume of papers presented at the conference—only one of many symposia that he produced.

In Full Stride

In 1968, Henry was forced to resign as editor of *Christianity Today*. Reading his account of the trying events that led to his departure from the magazine, one is struck by the tangle of miscommunication, vary-ing perceptions of the same events, and even political maneuvering that can so easily bedevil groups of even the most dedicated and godly Christians.

In hindsight, however, shedding himself of the myriad responsi-bilities that fall to the editor's lot, Henry gained God-given space to concentrate upon study and writing, and to compose his magnum opus, *God, Revelation, and Authority*. During a sabbatical year at Cambridge University in England, he worked on this tome while also becoming acquainted with British theologians and scholars of all schools.

Returning to the United States, he taught at Eastern Baptist Theological seminary from 1969 to 1974, after which he became lec-turer-at-large for World Vision International (1974–86). At the peak of his intellectual powers, he completed *God, Revelation, and Authority* in six thick volumes, penned numerous articles, and spoke at dozens of churches, universities, and seminaries in more than thirty-five coun-tries. As I said above, I first met him in Taipei, to which he had come from Seoul, where he taught annually for several years. Besides lectur-ing all over the world, Carl Henry offered courses at Trinity Evangelical Divinity School in Deerfield, Illinois, influencing hundreds of younger scholars and pastors.

Henry was heartened to witness the growing impact of evangeli-cals and the resurgence of evangelical biblical and theological scholar-ship, for which others give him a great deal of credit. Especially in his later years, however, he frequently expressed dismay at the lack of unity among evangelicals, their pragmatism and anti-intellectualism, and the tendency of leading evangelical theologians (like Donald Bloesch and Bernard Ramm) to succumb to the charm of Karl Barth's dialectical theology, with its ambiguous view of Scripture and love of paradox. Though aware that much about God remains unknown to us, he believed that the Bible is the Lord's inerrant Word to us, which can be largely understood with the help of the Holy Spirit and careful study.

In 1989, he and Kenneth Kantzer (formerly president of Trinity Evangelical Divinity School) sponsored a conference on "Evangelical Affirmations," which issued a compendium that Henry edited. *Evangelical Affirmations* forcefully states what Henry and the other contributors considered to be the key doctrines of Scripture, while refuting objections and aberrations that had been voiced by both evangelical and non-evangelical thinkers.

His growing apprehension about the cultural decline of the West and of the United States in particular, never absent from his writings, found expression in *Twilight of a Great Civilization: The Drift Towards Neo-Paganism*, published in 1989 and marked by the powerful, penetrating, and pictorial style that makes him one of the most eloquent writers in recent Christian history.[8]

Keenly aware that most people would not take the time to read the full *God, Revelation, and Authority*, he published his Rutherford Lectures, given in Edinburgh also in 1989, in *Toward a Recovery of Christian Belief*. This little book clearly and succinctly summarizes the main points of the larger set, but is no substitute for reading the original six volumes.[9]

Character

In 1993, a *Festschrift* for Carl Henry was published, in which men who knew him well offer glimpses of him as a man and a Christian.[10] His close friend and colleague, Kenneth Kantzer, describes a most winsome person. In their time together at Boston University, a number of evan-

8. This is one reason I compare him with Augustine of Hippo. See chapter 11 in this volume.

9. Sadly, it seems that even the highly influential historian of theology Roger Olson bases his critique (which almost amounts to caricature) of Henry almost solely upon this précis of *GRA*.

10. Carson and Woodbridge, eds., *God and Culture*.

gelicals who would go on to lead the movement theologically gathered regularly to discuss their specialties. Kantzer said, "Though Henry did not know as much in each field as specialists in that field knew . . . on all crucial points, he knew enough to argue intelligently with any of us."[11]

On his intellectual curiosity: "He was never afraid of new ideas. He constantly searched for new ways of presenting the Christian message to the world of the mid-twentieth century. He rigorously sought to discard the extraneous chaff from what is central to a truly biblically grounded Christianity."[12]

In the last two-thirds of the twentieth century, "he has been acknowledged by almost all as the dean and outstanding theological representative of the conservative evangelical movement."[13]

Kantzer draws attention to Henry's lifelong devotion to the training of ministers, "preparing them in quality ways to penetrate their community effectively through the pulpit and through the use of the resources of the church. He was also seeking to penetrate the non-evangelical religious world by defining Christianity accurately and removing some of the false stereotypes that carried such wide acceptance in intellectual and prestigious circles of the day."[14] Unlike many who criticize him, "He strove, above all, to interpret his theological opponents fairly."[15]

In the same volume, John D. Woodbridge notes, however, that "as a teacher, he paid most attention to the top ten percent of the students."[16]

Still, what Henry treasured most, as he said himself, was "Jesus Christ as personal Savior and Lord." He was a man of prayer, but he did not live as an isolated believer. "The local church loomed very large in his life."[17]"His love for his wife was evident. He cared for her. He always spoke of her with respect and deep appreciation." Helga Henry was his constant companion and indispensable colleague, especially as her fluency in German enabled him to keep up with the latest German

11. Kantzer "Carl Ferdinand Howard Henry," 371. Quotes without notes in this section are taken from this chapter.

12. Ibid, 372.

13. Ibid.

14. Ibid., 373.

15. Ibid., 374.

16. Ibid.

17. Ibid.

theological speculations.[18] He "was also a family man" who shared in the rearing of their children, of whom he was immensely proud. "He loved his home." He was a handyman in the home, and, in his youth, an amateur magician.[19] The Henrys were hospitable, as countless guests discovered over the years.

As you might expect, Carl Henry's intellect saw the incongruous, tenuous temptations of the Christian life. One close associate tells of walking back to the *Christianity Today* offices in Washington after lunch one day, passing by a very attractive woman. Henry's comment was, "There is a fine line between appreciation and lust." That same colleague notes that Henry sought to make the most of his time, and commented after a meeting with one not particularly intelligent person that, "With him, the yield is low."[20] But note that he continued to spend time even with someone whose company was not especially rewarding.

Though he insisted upon rigorous study, he believed firmly that "all Christian learning must be for the sake of worship and service of God in the world."[21] His friend Kantzer observed, "He prizes more than anything else his walk with the Lord."[22]

Though I spent only a few hours with Dr. Henry on two of his visits to Taiwan, I can verify that he comported himself as a true Christian gentleman, with graciousness and kindness. He took our little girl Sarah into his arms when she was a baby, as if he missed his own grandchildren. He encouraged me to make the abridgment of the Chinese edition of *God, Revelation, and Authority*, and provided funds for its translation and later publication in simplified script for readers within China.

Towards the end of his long life, in what was to be my last telephone conversation with him, I expressed my profound appreciation for the contribution he had made to the worldwide church through *God, Revelation, and Authority*. His reply, in a faltering voice, was characteristic: "I couldn't do it now."

"Well, you did it then, and we are all grateful," I answered.

18. Ibid., 375.
19. Ibid., 376.
20. Richard Ostling, in a telephone conversation with the author.
21. Henry, *Confessions of a Theologian*, 76.
22. Kantzer, "Carl Ferdinand Howard Henry," 377.

Reading Henry's autobiography, I was repeatedly impressed by the extent of his productivity, his incessant travel, and tireless writing. Afflicted with debilitating migraine headaches and chronic pain from an injury in his youth, Carl Henry pressed on, day after day, year after year, decade after decade, seeking to be a good steward of the abilities and energy God had so munificently bestowed upon him.

In closing, allow me to quote the balanced evaluation of Carl Henry's significance penned by Timothy George:

> Henry's stature within evangelicalism rivals that of Karl Barth in neo-orthodoxy and Karl Rahner in Roman Catholicism. Henry is the only theologian who has served as president of both the Evangelical Theological Society (1967–1970) and the American Theological Association (1979–1980). The world evangelical movement owes much to his legacy of personal devotion to Christ, strategic evangelistic thinking, cultural and ethical engagement and theological consistency and faithfulness across several generations.[23]

23. George, "Carl Henry," 297–300.

TWO

The Recent Neglect of Carl Henry among Evangelicals

Widespread Recognition

Carl Henry was a leader among evangelicals for more than fifty years. As founding editor of *Christianity Today*, charter member of the National Association of Evangelicals, organizer of the Berlin Congress on Evangelism, member of the original faculty of Fuller Theological Seminary, cofounder of the Evangelical Theological Society, prolific writer, ubiquitous lecturer, teacher at several seminaries, itinerant speaker, and friend to hosts of scholars, theologians, and pastors, he exerted profound influence in America and overseas.

His contribution did not go unrecognized. Prominent leaders from across the theological spectrum hailed his importance as a thinker.

TIME Magazine's Richard Ostling said of *God, Revelation, and Authority* that it "establishes Henry as the leading theologian of the nation's growing evangelical flank."[1] Kenneth Briggs in the *New York Times* labeled it "the most important work of evangelical theology in modern times."[2] He was one of two evangelical theologians discussed in *20th Century Theology*, by Roger Olson and Stanley Grenz, and the only evangelical treated in the series *Makers of the Modern Mind*, in which Bob Paterson himself, editor of the series, wrote the volume on Henry.

Elsewhere, Roger Olson has called him "the Dean of evangelical theologians"—a title few would challenge.[3] In another place, he

---

1. From the dust jacket of *GRA*.

2. Ibid.

3. Olson, *Westminster Handbook*, 41. Note, however, that Olson incorrectly says that *GRA* is a seven-volume work, confesses that "few persons, if any, could claim to

has written that "Most observers of postfundamentalist, conservative Evangelicalism . . . would agree that Henry ranks as its most influential thinker between World War II and the end of the twentieth century."[4] "Carl Henry's influence on post-World War II conservative Protestant theology in North America can hardly be overestimated."[5]

According to theologian Timothy George, "The two most formative shapers of [the evangelical] movement are (Southern Baptists): Billy Graham and Carl F. H. Henry."[6] R. Albert Mohler Jr. asserts, "His influence, extended through his voluminous writings and public exposure, has shaped the evangelical movement to a degree unmatched by any other evangelical theology of the period."[7] He concludes: "[Henry] has been recognized by evangelicals and nonevangelicals as the premier theological representative of the evangelical movement in the last half of the twentieth century."[8]

Despite a couple of rather curious characterizations of Henry's theological method in the opening chapter, Gordon Lewis and Bruce Demarest regularly cite *God, Revelation, and Authority* in their own superb *Integrative Theology*, as does Millard Erickson in his popular *Christian Theology*.[9] Wayne Grudem gives references to Henry along with other theologians at the end of almost every chapter of his *Systematic Theology*.

Carl R. Trueman, in a review article in *Themelios*, called Henry "the central intellectual figure of American evangelicalism this century," and quoted Gabriel Fackre's assessment: "If the twentieth century 'evangelical renaissance' in North America has produced a Michelangelo, that exemplar is surely Carl Henry."[10]

---

have read all of it," and immediately characterizes Henry's thought as rationalistic (a point to which we shall return).

4. Olson, "Carl Henry," 489.

5. Ibid., 492.

6. George, "New Dimensions in Baptist Theology," 143.

7. Mohler, "Carl F. H. Henry," 291.

8. Ibid., 293.

9. Lewis and Demarest, *Integrative Theology*; Erickson, *Christian Theology*; Grudem, *Systematic Theology*.

10. Trueman, "Admiring the Sistine Chapel." Quoted in Fackre, *Ecumenical Faith*, 171.

R. Albert Mohler in his earlier *Baptist Thinkers* compared him with several other writers from that perspective,[11] and (on apologetics) discussed Henry along with several other apologists. Encyclopedias of theology, biography, and apologetics contain articles on Henry as one of the most significant contributors to twentieth-century Christian thought and action. Chuck Colson wrote a forward to a collection of quotations from his works, *Carl Henry at His Best*, in which he claimed that "When the history of the evangelical movement is finally written, Carl Henry will emerge as its dominant figure."[12]

When he died, accolades poured in from all over the globe, attesting to his greatness as a theologian, churchman, and Christian friend.

Current Neglect

On the other hand, Henry suffers today from a degree of neglect that is surprising, given his former prominence. Few read his works, especially *God, Revelation, and Authority*. Newer surveys of theology and apologetics do not always include his contributions in these fields.

For All the Saints: Evangelical Theology and Christian Spirituality, edited by Timothy George and Alistair McGrath, contains an opening chapter on a variety of subjects that Henry has discussed, but no reference to him.[13] Other earlier works by McGrath may make a passing reference to *God, Revelation, and Authority*, but only as a bibliographic entry, as if seeking completion, but not, apparently, reflecting any real knowledge of his thought. Considering McGrath's prominence and the wide sweep and expansive titles of his many surveys, this seems to be a major, but not surprising, lacuna. After all, Carl Trueman[14] admitted that Henry was "not as well-known on this side of the Atlantic [i.e., Great Britain and Europe] as many of us would like—or think that he needs to be." (More recently, as we shall see, McGrath engaged in sharp criticism of Henry's theological program.)

Even in Reformed circles, where one would expect to find immense appreciation for his basically Calvinistic point of view, the si-

11. Mohler, "Carl Ferdinand Howard Henry."

12. Halliday and Janssen, *Carl Henry at His Best*, 13.

13. George and McGrath, eds., *For All the Saints*.

14. Trueman, "Admiring the Sistine Chapel."

lence is deafening. John Frame, in two volumes on the *Knowledge of God* and the *Doctrine of God*, includes less than a handful of references to Henry, largely in footnotes. A new book on Reformed apologetics by Scott Oliphant[15] omits any mention of Henry, surely one of the leading apologists of the last century. In an extensive search of the *Westminster Theological Journal* during a day in the library of Westminster Theological Seminary, I found not a single reference to Carl Henry in the entire history of that authoritative publication. Perhaps I missed something. Douglas Kelly's learned new *Systematic Theology* entirely overlooks Carl Henry.[16]

Although dictionaries of modern theologians include articles on Carl Henry, some other major reference works do not. The *Dictionary of Major Biblical Interpreters*, for example, rightly features essays on scholars like James Barr, Karl Barth, John Bright, Rudolf Bultmann, Brevard Childs, Joachim Jeremias, George Ladd, Leon Morris, Martin Noth, and Albert Schweitzer.[17] With all of these Carl Henry engaged in ongoing dialogue, quoting them appreciatively where he agreed, and critically where he diverged, but his name is not listed in the index.

As a consequence, few evangelicals today know much about Carl Henry. I recently spoke with a graduate of Gordon-Conwell Theological Seminary, which maintains a Reformed stance similar to that of Henry. This young man had gone on to earn a ThM in systematic theology at Gordon-Conwell and could not remember even hearing of Carl Henry.

Possible Reasons for Neglect

Considering the ongoing popularity among evangelicals of Henry's main theological rivals, Karl Barth, Donald Bloesch, and Bernard Ramm, and the even greater widespread use of the works of Millard Erickson, who largely agrees with Henry, one struggles to understand why Henry suffers from such silence. Let me suggest a few possibilities, and then propose some remedies for what I consider to be a lamentable situation.

15. Oliphint, *Reasons for Faith*.
16. Kelly, *Systematic Theology*.
17. McKim, ed., *Dictionary of Major Biblical Interpreters*.

Difficulty

Many find Carl Henry's writing style hard to read. I remember how, as a seminarian, I would struggle through his articles on contemporary theology in *Christianity Today*. As I said earlier, after I heard Dr. Henry lecture from *God, Revelation, and Authority* at the China Evangelical Seminary in Taipei in 1980, I bought a copy of volume 1, but I never finished it. Only when I was asked to make an abridgement of the Chinese edition did I pick it up again, this time to discover that it is a literary masterpiece. But my initial experience probably matches that of many other potential readers.

In particular, the first volume of *God, Revelation, and Authority*, dealing with matters of prolegomena, does tend to put off those without a strong background in philosophy. Later volumes treat the usual topics of theology from a more biblical point of view, and are much easier to read, but few get to them after being intimidated by the opening salvo. Carl Henry writes for those who can handle long, compound, complex sentences and who delight in his rich vocabulary. Falling educational standards in recent decades have produced a generation that finds this sort of English very hard to digest, much less enjoy.

Nor is his thought simple. Henry deals in subtle and profound concepts, and responds to often-complicated arguments for and against the Christian faith. Like Augustine, he wields a sharp pen, alive to minute distinctions and ready to draw fine lines. Though much less verbose and dialectical than Karl Barth—whose self-contradictory statements Henry sometimes ridicules—Henry does not shy away from a fulsome style that allows him to express the richness of his own ideas.

Still, Karl Barth is not easy to read either, but that does not prevent him from being ardently followed by evangelicals like Ramm, Bloesch, and Olson. There must be something to Henry's neglect other than literary style.

Point of View

With the evangelical world turning towards Barthian dialectic, evolutionary theory, Arminian soteriology, and a commitment to the errancy of Scripture, not to mention vague impressions versus clear reasoning, we should not be surprised if Carl Henry's approach is ignored, misrepresented, or even derided. Few dare to criticize the man himself, but many simply put him into a neat theological box, wrap it up, and file it away in a museum of Christian thought.

Thus, in *20th Century Theology*, Stanley Grenz and Roger Olson give him ample space, but voice what I hope to show are inaccurate criticisms of his theology and even of his career, clearly preferring the Barthian approach of Ramm and Bloesch. Roger Olson applies this treatment also in his *Story of Theology* and *Westminster Handbook to Evangelical Theology*, as well as in other places.[18]

Harvey Conn repeats the charges of Van Til against all "neo-evangelicals." Bob Patterson reproduces various criticisms without evaluation or refutation. The authors of *Integrative Theology* refer often to *God, Revelation, and Authority*, which they clearly appreciate, but make sweeping attacks on his approach in the opening pages of their otherwise very insightful systematic theology.[19]

These highly influential authors convey various unfavorable impressions of Carl Henry, such as that he is merely a journalist and not a systematic theologian, a poor interpreter of Scripture, ignorant of modern biblical criticism, out of touch with modern theological trends, etc. (I shall detail and respond to these caricatures later.)

Perhaps Presbyterians like Conn and Van Til, as well as the faculties of prominent seminaries like Westminster Theological Seminary, Reformed Theological Seminary, and Covenant Theological Seminary, believe so strongly in covenantal theology that Henry's non-covenantal approach may in their eyes disqualify his entire program and render it of little worth for their purpose.

Nationality

In many academic circles, German theologians capture the headlines, and receive most of the attention. There are exceptions to this generalization, of course—one thinks of the two Niebuhrs, for example—but British and "mainline" American scholars seem to keep their eyes on developments in Europe, not North America. Carl Henry, despite his

---

18. We shall discuss this more in later chapters.

19. For a more detailed examination of this phenomenon, see the chapters on "Carl Henry and His Critics" later in this volume.

wide travels and frequent encounters with British and Continental theologians, seems to be locked in the "American" box, along with the much-despised fundamentalists. For example, British author Jonathan Hill's *The History of Christian Thought*, recently issued by InterVarsity Press, a leading evangelical publishing house,[20] does not even mention Carl Henry, whom even such a critic as K. R. Trembath called "the most prominent evangelical theologian of the past thirty years."[21]

Ignorance and Prejudice

In the three chapters on Carl Henry and his critics, we shall see how I believe he has been misunderstood and unfairly criticized by evangelicals from various schools of thought. Innocent readers who trust the judgment of these critics receive an impression that they have little reason to validate by actually consulting Henry's own works. After all, if authoritative scholars pronounce his theology to be outdated, rationalistic, or worse, why should they take the time or trouble to wade through *God, Revelation, and Authority* to find out the truth?

Personality and Politics?

Guessing at the motives of others carries huge dangers, and is almost always wrong. Still, an awareness of certain events and personalities may shed light on later developments.

Cornelius Van Til so abhorred the thought of Gordon Clark that he tried to have him expelled from the Orthodox Presbyterian Church. Carl Henry freely acknowledges Clark as his mentor. Since Westminster Theological Seminary seems to be wedded to the apologetic approach of Van Til, could its prestigious journal's lack of reference to Henry reflect conflicts long past? As noted in the later chapter "Carl Henry and His Critics II," one member of the faculty at Westminster, himself appreciative of Henry, told me that his neglect in Reformed circles was due to "perceived rationalism." Could this perception be based on faulty information from older teachers who had an axe to grind?[22]

20. Hill, *History of Christian Thought*.

21. Trembath, *Divine Revelation*, 30.

22. For accounts of the Clark controversy, see Hart and Muether, *Fighting the Good Fight*, 106–15.

Recovery of Carl Henry for the Twenty-first Century

As I shall try to show in the following chapters, the theology of Carl Henry, especially as contained in *God, Revelation, and Authority*, possesses great value for Christians in the twenty-first century. In graduate school, I had a Greek professor who would occasionally recommend some thick tome on an arcane subject for our "delectation and edification." Well, I continue to read and reread *God, Revelation, and Authority* not only for instruction, but also for my Christian growth and aesthetic pleasure. I covet that same enjoyment for others.

This brief introduction to Carl Henry and his magnum opus is meant as one small contribution to what I hope will be a revival of interest in the one whom many consider to be the greatest Protestant theologian of the twentieth century, even in comparison with Karl Barth.

Twentieth-Century Theologian

To appreciate the achievement of Carl F. H. Henry, we must see him in the overall context of twentieth-century theology, which sought to solve problems posed in the previous century.[1] In the following pages, we shall set the stage by glancing at the past two periods of theology, and then show how Henry tried to offer more satisfactory solutions to problems than did some of his contemporaries.

Background: Nineteenth-century Theology

Christian thinkers in the nineteenth century had to wrestle with major challenges inherited from the Enlightenment-generated ferment of the two previous centuries. A general skepticism about knowledge in general, and the knowledge of God in particular, had gained ascendancy among philosophers.

At the same time, human reason—unaided by divine revelation and untrammeled by ecclesiastical tradition or authority—reigned supreme. Humans were deemed competent to probe the nature of the universe, the history and character of mankind, and the ethical obligations that were considered to constitute the soul of religion.

Naturalism as a worldview had banished miracles from the realm of intellectual possibility. Likewise, the Creator God of the Bible had

---

1. Useful treatments of non-evangelical theology may be found in Ford, *Modern Theologians*; Grenz and Olson, *20th Century Theology*; Hill, *History of Christian Thought*; Lewis and Demarest, *Integrative Theology*; Livingston and Fiorenza, *Modern Christian Thought*; Olson, *Story of Christian Theology*; and Smith, *Handbook of Contemporary Theology*.

been replaced by a "divine watchmaker" who had set the world in motion and then withdrawn to allow natural processes to take over. We should not expect divine intervention in human affairs. Not only Jesus's miracles, then, but also the resurrection, were widely doubted.

It goes without saying that the Bible, which purports to record numerous miracles and to afford reliable knowledge of God, was increasingly considered a volume filled with superstitions which reasonable men would not consider.

Nineteenth-century Challenges to Christianity

As the nineteenth century progressed, thinkers within the church dealt with the Enlightenment, and the developing skepticism about the Bible and traditional Christian theology, in various ways.

"Higher" (as distinct from textual) biblical criticism grew into a vast corpus of works allegedly showing that the Bible was full of faults and could not be trusted as divine revelation. It seemed that the historical underpinnings of traditional Christian faith had been cut away. At the same time, the Romantic Movement had cast doubt upon the sufficiency of human reason to know all of truth, much less to satisfy the deepest longings of the human soul. Later in the century, Darwinian theory seemed to disprove the opening chapters of Genesis, and to posit an irreconcilable conflict between the Bible and modern science.

Theologians such as Schleiermacher and Ritschl responded to these massive onslaughts by shifting the locus and focus of revelation from God's Word as written in the Bible to the human soul and its consciousness of dependence upon the Ultimate. God's transcendence was played down, and his immanence in individuals and in human history emphasized. Revelation became a subjective experience, not objective truth as found in the Scriptures. Furthermore, since hell seemed a concept from pre-Enlightenment days, God's love received primary attention; his justice and wrath were replaced by universal forgiveness.

Twentieth-century Proposals

Most Continental theologians at the beginning of the twentieth century assumed that the Bible was not a reliable historical record, either of the origins of the universe or of the history of Israel, Jesus, and the early church. They also believed that science, and a generally "scientific"—that is, naturalistic—outlook on life, had made traditional doctrines untenable in modern intellectual circles.

• Since eternal punishment in hell was no longer considered the chief danger facing mankind, they turned their attention to the evils of this world. Walter Rauschenbusch and others promoted the "Social Gospel," an exposition of Christianity and of the kingdom of God that reduced the former to ethics and the latter to social progress.

Modern liberalism developed these trends into an anti-supernaturalistic religion that extolled "the fatherhood of God and the brotherhood of man," while Jesus became merely a good teacher and model citizen. The problem is society or ignorance, not original sin. Jesus's death on the cross was not an atoning sacrifice, but an example of self-giving; there are no miracles; salvation is ethical action only; and, of course, all human beings will eventually be saved. Church leaders threw themselves into various reform movements, culminating in America in the passage of the Prohibition Amendment to the Constitution.

World War I shattered the illusion of the fundamental goodness of human nature, and led to various theological reactions, notably a diffuse "movement" often called Neo-orthodoxy. Though disagreeing among themselves, leaders of this loosely defined school did share certain emphases:

God is transcendent, even, in the words of Karl Barth, "wholly other." Man is fallen, and his reason corrupted, so we can only know God if and as he chooses to reveal himself. Revelation is centered upon Jesus Christ, the divine Son of God. Barth held that there is absolutely no "natural revelation," while Brunner did believe that fallen men could discern certain truths, though not enough to know God apart from revelation. Heavily influenced by existential philosophy and the theology of Søren Kierkegaard, they believed that truth is found in personal encounter, not in propositions. God cannot be adequately described in human words, so the Bible is only a witness to revelation, not revelation itself.

Here we see the footprints of the common assumption that science and biblical criticism had disproved the veracity of the Scriptures. By asserting the essentially "existential" nature of all true knowledge, these theologians, like their nineteenth-century Romantic forebears, simply sidestepped the issue of biblical inerrancy. More than that, they declared that the Bible is *not* without error. This allowed them to avoid being charged with old-fashioned obscurantism.

On the other hand, as many have pointed out, Barth treated the Bible as if it were *functionally* the Word of God. Indeed, he endeavored to build his *Church Dogmatics* entirely upon the Scriptures, unmixed by alien thought forms. His dependence upon "pre-existentialism," and his acceptance of many of the results of critical biblical studies, left their mark on his system, but at least we know that Barth intended to be merely expounding the Scriptures. One element of Barth's theology that resembles the earlier liberalism, though based on largely different grounds, was his apparent belief in universalism, though he would never fully and explicitly say so.

Dietrich Bonhoeffer joined with Barth and Brunner in breaking with liberalism. Like them, he placed Christ at the center of God's revelation, and asserted that the knowledge of God comes from above, from God alone, as revelation. But he was not as radical as Barth in the rejection of common concepts shared by believers and non-believers alike. Bonhoeffer's distinctive influence for later theology came from his insistence that today's disillusioned seekers for truth must be able to find the presence of Christ within the church. True faith must lead to, and be expressed by, the service of God in the world.

Deeply influenced by existentialism, but abandoning traditional Christian beliefs, was Rudolph Bultmann. He engaged in radical New Testament criticism that consigned much of the scriptural world view to the realm of myth. Otherwise, he thought, modern minds simply could not accept stories that seemed to conflict with science and reason. For Bultmann, there was no truly historical Jesus accessible to us. Our problem is not alienation from God caused by sin, but anxiety and inauthenticity. The cross was not God's way of reconciling us to himself through a substitutionary sacrifice, but the greatest act of authentic living.

The "Death of God" movement of the 1960s represented a reaction to Barth's emphasis on total transcendence, and a total emptying of God into immanence. Harvey Cox, one of its main spokesmen, said, "What God is doing is politics."[2]

---

2. Grenz and Olson, *20th Century Theology*, 167.

Theologies of Hope

In the 1964, Motlmann's *Theology of Hope* appeared, and took much of the theological world by storm. Like Neo-orthodox writers, Moltmann considered the Bible to be only a witness to revelation, not revelation itself. Again, like them, he sought to affirm a God who was transcendent; but this transcendence was not "spatial"—a God "up there"—but temporal. God was the power of the future breaking into life today with transforming power.

God is present in the world, so much so that Moltmann's theology represents a form of panentheism. Like Neo-orthodox theologians, Moltmann affirms the Trinity, though not an ontological (or immanent) Trinity, but an economic one. That is, there is history in God. Like the Cappadocian Fathers, Moltmann believes that the essence of the Trinity lies in the relations among the three Persons, each of whom suffers along with the world in a distinctive way. Not development, as in process theology, but suffering and conflict, for God is love.

Unlike traditional and Neo-orthodox thinkers, Moltmann renounced any authority, power, or hierarchy in God or in the world. Instead, he emphasized the social Trinity (a concept similar to the economic Trinity, denoting relationships among the three Persons, but not an essential essence, or being common to all) and stressed the mutual love and submission of Father, Son, and Spirit.

Moltmann, like Barth, centers all revelation upon Christ. Differently from Barth however, he asserts that the basic truth about God is that, in Christ, he suffered on the cross. Even now God suffers with us.

But Christ also rose from the dead. Thus, both the cross and the resurrection form the basis of our hope; Moltmann sees revelation as basically promise, not proposition. Like Barth, but for different reasons, Moltmann believes that all of creation will be saved through the resurrection power of Christ, who will transform the universe. He is more interested in practical theory, not correct doctrine, and does not shy away from manifest contradictions and inconsistencies in his work.

"Liberation" Theologies

During the 1960s and 1970s, various forms of "liberation" theology gained a wide hearing. Though not as popular as before, they still exert profound influence. Inspired by the poverty and oppression seen especially in Latin America, the early proponents of liberation theology— mostly Roman Catholic—insisted that theology must start from the actual human situation, which they analyzed in Marxist terms. Correct doctrine, they held, is less important than correct action (orthopraxy). God cares more for the poor than for the rich. Traditional Western theology is an imposition of the powerful upon the weak. The real problems are political and economic, not "spiritual." Theologians must join in the revolution to oust tyrants.

Black theology followed, and narrowed the focus to the plight of black people in America. Soon feminists were calling for freedom from traditional "patriarchal" theology and exegesis, and for full equality in church leadership and in the home. In each case, the Bible was radically reinterpreted, but most especially by the feminists, who charged that the Scriptures were written by men and in order to maintain men in positions of power. They objected to all hierarchy, and opposed the use of titles like "King" and even "Father" to refer to God.

Wolfhart Pannenberg

Pannenberg is one of the most influential theologians in recent years, and some of his insights have been lauded as helpful by many evangelical theologians. Pannenberg believes that Christianity is the best philosophy, for it is the most reasonable. Theology is a public discipline that seeks to give a rational account of the Christian faith. Some have characterized his program as one of "thoroughgoing rationalism."[3]

He rejected Barth's stark division between revelation and natural knowledge. God's revelatory work "comes as the completion of creation." Pannenberg sought to unite the church and the public sphere. The church is the "sign of God's eschatological kingdom," and it challenges all human systems.[4]

Unlike some evangelicals, Pannenberg is not a pietist or fideist. He believes that revelation includes real knowledge and illuminates all aspects of human life. For him the starting point of all theology is the fact that humans are "naturally religious." Like Karl Rahner, he thinks

3. Ibid., 197.
4. Ibid., 188.

that we have a sense of the infinite. God is the ultimate "field" for all of life; we cannot escape his presence.

In agreement with Moltmann, and against Barth, he holds that revelation comes through history. "God is to be found *in* the world."[5] In particular, the history of religions illuminates man's quest for God and our sense of something beyond. More specifically, however, the history of Israel, including Jesus, is fundamental for our understanding of God. Supremely, the resurrection of Jesus is the central event of history, and offers promise for the future.

Another similarity with Moltmann is that his doctrine of God is grounded in the divine economy, which is Trinitarian. Our understanding of the immanent Trinity flows from the economic Trinity, the social Trinity, which is essentially a relationship of mutual self-giving. Like almost all European theologians, Pannenberg rejects the Bible as the inerrant revelation of God. The Enlightenment and its consequences mean that we can no longer just begin with the authority of the Bible to do theology. Because of his stress upon the intimate relationship between God and the world, some have asked the question whether, for Pannenberg, God is personal. Another question: Is he free over against the world?

Carl Henry's Program

A Biblical Response to Non-evangelical Proposals

Seen in this context, Henry's contribution stands out as particularly significant.

God, Revelation, and Authority meets the two major challenges to biblically-based theology head on. In the first four volumes, Henry makes a very powerful case for the trustworthiness of the Bible as God's revelation to us. The Scriptures are not just a witness to revelation; they *are* revelation. They do not only *contain* the words of God; they *are* the words/Word of God.

Whereas many others either accept the challenges of biblical criticism, or ignore them altogether, throughout *God, Revelation, and Authority* Henry engages what he terms "negative" biblical critics at every point. He gives historical, linguistic, and exegetical reasons for

5. Hill, *History of Christian Thought*, 322.

rejecting their claims that the Bible is filled with errors and not to be used as the major source of knowledge about God. He offers a carefully-nuanced argument for both infallibility and inerrancy. Those who would reject such a position out of hand would do well to read Henry before pontificating on this crucial subject.[6]

In like manner, he confronts the claims of science to have disproved the Bible. In the first volume of *God, Revelation, and Authority*, he poses incisive questions for those who accept the assertions of science to be the final arbiter of what is true about ultimate reality. On the contrary, he asserts that modern scientism, with its commitment to the empirical method as the only possible way of knowing truth, is a contemporary myth.[7]

Deploying acute observations questioning the supposed superiority of science over theology, Henry exposes the theoretical weaknesses of such a point of view, including the constant—and inherent—revisability, and therefore instability, of the so-called findings of modern science; the necessity of some form of "faith" for making scientific advance; and the limited purview of the entire scientific endeavor: it can never speak to matters of history, faith, invisible realities, or the life to come.

Referring to Thomas Kuhn's *The Structure of Scientific Revolutions*, Henry observes that "Scientists maintain the impression of progress . . . by rewriting their textbooks frequently and eliminating errors, and their newer hypotheses are not based nearly as much as scientists presume on rational or empirical supports."[8]

Volume 5 tackles the crucial question: creation. In a virtual *tour de force*, Henry pits the contradictory "findings" of eminent scientists against each other to demonstrate that science is neither a monolithic nor a steady discipline. Henry's brilliance is nowhere on clearer display than when he shows himself to be fully at home in both the philosophy and alleged findings of modern science.

Volume 1 also speaks to the epistemological assaults upon traditional Christian beliefs posed by logical positivism, Bultmann's demy-

---

6. Albert Mohler observes that in asserting the authority of the Bible, Henry "set himself against the tide of twentieth-century theology, including neoorthodoxy, narrative theologies, and the contributions of Moltmann and Pannenberg. He also set himself against any compromise within the evangelical camp and set out to refute the criticisms of revisionists such as James Barr" ("Carl F. H. Henry," 288).

7. See Henry, *GRA* vol. 1, chs. 9–10.

8. Henry, *GRA* 1:173.

thologizing campaign, Romantic intuitivism, Kantian skepticism, and a host of other failed systems. This volume, in effect, defuses most of the arguments from the eighteenth through the twentieth centuries against the authority of the Bible as God's revelation.

Other volumes respond to more recent attacks on the Bible as revelation. Karl Barth is cited, or even quoted, on almost every page, sometimes appreciatively, but often in passages that show the fundamentally confusing nature of dialectical theology. While Henry applauds Barth's *functional* use of the Scriptures as the only permissible authority for theology, he demonstrates repeatedly the internal contradictions of Barth's statements about Divine self-disclosure.[9]

He agrees with Niebuhr, the classical liberals, Bonhoeffer, secular theologians, Moltmann, and liberation theology that the Christian faith should, and does, speak to the conditions of men and women in this world at this time. As his volumes on personal and social ethics show, Henry had a lively interest in the application of biblical principles to private and public life.[10] *God, Revelation, and Authority* reflects this conviction that both theology and its implications are not just private, but very public, matters.

In particular, Henry, like Bonhoeffer and others, holds the Christian church responsible for reflecting the nature and saving grace of God in the midst of this world. Christians belong to, and are to manifest the life of, a regenerate humanity that has been freed from the shackles to sin and obligated to manifest the light of God in this dark world. Pre-Christians should be able to "find God" in the church.

But he would not follow these late-twentieth-century/early-twenty-first-century thinkers into the same error committed by the

9. Albert Mohler notes that Henry's theological mission was largely to expose the futility of mediating theologies, "especially those based on modern critical philosophy and any post-Kantian epistemology." Henry's criticism of Barth issued from his sense that Barth's theology was "grounded in a Kantian epistemology." "The fatal flaw Henry identified in Barth's system centered in the Swiss theologian's insistence on the nonpropositional character of special revelation. This, Henry lamented, led to a doctrine of revelation insufficient to provide a sturdy alternative to Bultmann's program of demythologization" ("Carl F. H. Henry," 285). For a full treatment of Carl Henry's response to the theology of Karl Barth, see Mohler, "Evangelical Theology and Karl Barth."

10. See *Christian Personal Ethics* (1957), *Aspects of Christian Social Ethics* (1964), *A Plea for Evangelical Demonstration* (1971), and *Baker's Dictionary of Christian Ethics* (1973).

Social Gospel movement that was spawned by liberal ideas. He refused to equate the kingdom of God with any political program, including the popular leftist causes that so dominate the manifestoes of mainline Protestant denominations, the World Council of Churches, the post-Vatican II Roman Catholic church, and the so-called Young Evangelicals. These all tend to locate, and confine, God's work to the reordering of political and economic structures, which Henry saw as an undertaking that is shallow, unbiblical, and futile.

Henry analyzes and responds to the different sorts of liberation theology that arose in the 1960s and 1970s, and finds them all to be based on an insufficient biblical foundation, and fatally flawed by secular, especially Marxist, presuppositions.

In agreement with Rahner, Pannenberg, and others, Henry tries in *God, Revelation, and Authority* to show that Christian theology is reasonable. It is the best of all available philosophies. Indeed, volume 1 seeks to demonstrate the superiority of biblical revelation as a way of knowing (as distinct from unaided reason, intuition, and uninterpreted experience), and biblically-informed reason as a valid, and indispensable, means of understanding God's multifaceted revelation.

One way that the biblical faith excels other worldviews is by being internally consistent. Henry will have nothing to do with Barth's glorying in paradox—what is called "dialectical theology"—nor would he countenance Moltmann's lack of concern for consistency. Henry believes that coherence and lack of internal contradiction are tests of truth, and seeks to expound an understanding of the Bible that reflects the unity of God and the internal integrity of his revelation in the Bible. Thus, clearing up some apparent contradictions in the Scriptures is part of his defense of biblical infallibility and of the truth of God's revelation in general.

Like almost all twentieth-century theologians—except for Barth—Henry believes that the image of God remains in fallen men and women, enough that "the universal disclosure of God penetrates deeply into all man's confidences and doubts. God is the Eternal with whom unrenewed man, in all his experiences, has a vagabond relationship."[11] For this reason, the Christian faith finds multiple points of contact in the moral and intellectual makeup of non-Christians.

---

11. Henry, *GRA* 1:151.

Thus, he would agree with Jonathan Hill's characterization of Rahner's basic assumption: "Everything we do involves an awareness of God."[12] Unlike Rahner, however, Henry insists that salvation requires conscious faith in the gospel as revealed in the Bible. There are no "anonymous Christians" in his theology. Nor is God infinitely mysterious; he has revealed himself clearly, as we have seen.

Though he would question the validity of their assumptions, Henry stands with Moltmann, Pannenberg, and other "theologians of hope" in affirming the meaningfulness of history as a locus and even bearer of God's revelation. He does not follow them in confining revelation to history, however, for he sees the Bible as speaking from within history, about history, but also beyond history, to the return of Christ to renew all things.

Furthermore, for Henry the biblical accounts are reliable historical records, as we have seen. In this he disagrees with those who deny the accuracy of the Scriptures and also those who, seeking to avoid the problem of history altogether, locate God's revelation outside of history. He will have nothing to do, for example, with "myth" as a valid category of divine revelation. For Henry, revelation comes primarily in the Bible, which enables us to interpret properly the ways in which God reveals himself in history, especially in the history of Israel, Jesus, and the church.

Unlike Rahner, Moltmann, and Pannenberg, Henry sees little or no "history" in God, for whose eternal continuity he argues strenuously. Though he firmly believes that God is living and active, and not at all the "unmoved Mover" of Aristotle or even Thomas, Henry will not grant the sort of change and development—much less any sort of mutual interdependence with the world—that the Germans propose. The God of the Bible is the fully transcendent Creator who stands outside, above, and beyond the world, and who directs all that happens in human history.

Nor would he identify the economic Trinity with the immanent Trinity. That is, he believes that there are real and eternal distinctions among God the Father, God the Son, and God the Holy Spirit, though they exercise different "offices" in creation, preservation, salvation, and consummation. Henry holds firmly to an ontological Trinity—one God who has always been Father, Son, and Holy Spirit.

12. Ibid., 1:303.

Furthermore, Henry believes in the full transcendence of God. He is the eternal Creator who stands above and beyond the world he has made. He is not contingent upon us or in any way dependent upon what we do for him to grow into his full potentiality. Henry's God is the Lord of the universe, exercising sovereign sway over all that was, is, and is to come.

Of course, he also believes in the immanence of God. He stands with the "theologians of hope," Barth, and others who place Christ at the center of divine revelation. In his Incarnate Word, God has disclosed his true nature and essence, and in the cross, resurrection, ascension, and outpouring of the Spirit, we see God's goodness and his greatness, his pity and his power. Unlike some, however, he refuses to collapse all revelation into Jesus Christ alone, for he shows that God has revealed himself in history, in the mind and moral sense of mankind, and especially in the Scriptures.

Relationship to Other Evangelical Theologies

As a systematic theologian, Carl Henry falls within the "evangelical" tradition.[13] More narrowly, he is Reformed—though not Presbyterian or Covenantal. That is, he agrees with Augustine of Hippo, Martin Luther, John Calvin, John Owen, Jonathan Edwards, Charles Hodge, Benjamin Warfield, Herman Bavinck, Louis Berkhof, Gordon Clark, Douglas Kelly, John Murray, Cornelius Van Til, James Packer, James Montgomery Boice, John Frame, and others like them in matters of how we know God; the sovereignty of God in creation, preservation (providence), and salvation; and the necessity of applying the Bible to all domains of life, both private and public. He would not, however, promote infant baptism, nor insist upon the Presbyterian form of government.[14]

---

13. Brief discussions of evangelical theologians may be found in Balmer, *Encyclopedia of Evangelicalism*; Ellingsen, *Evangelical Movement*; Larsen et al., eds., *Biographical Dictionary of Evangelicals*; Lewis and Demarest, *Integrative Theology*; Olson, *Westminster Handbook*; and other books cited in the note at the beginning of this chapter.

14. One of the great mysteries of contemporary Presbyterian theology is the almost total neglect of Carl Henry's writings, though these agree with their approach to a remarkable degree.

Rather, he would agree more on those "minor" matters with Baptistic theologians of the Reformed type, like John Gill, Oliver Buswell, Bruce Demarest and Gordon Lewis (in *Integrative Theology*), Millard Erickson,[15] Wayne Grudem, Albert Mohler, and the writer of popular theology John Piper.[16]

Although accepting, like all evangelicals, the common doctrines of traditional orthodoxy, he would disagree at many points with Arminian theologians like H. Orton Wiley, Thomas Oden, Stanley Grenz, and Roger Olson. Henry would have *fundamental* differences with those who have taken Arminian theology to the extreme, promoting the "openness of God," such as Clark Pinnock and Gregory Boyd.

Though sharing many of the usual traditional views held also by dispensationalist writers—such as Lewis Sperry Chafer, Henry Clarence Thiessen, and Charles Ryrie—he does not belong to that broad school of thought.

Carl Henry propounds a "presuppositional" apologetic method. Like his mentor, Gordon Clark, and in common with younger theologians such as Wayne Grudem, John Frame, Bruce Demarest and Gordon Lewis (in *Integrative Theology*), and Millard Erickson,[17] Henry begins with the *assumption* that the Bible is God's written revelation. He thus distinguishes his apologetics from Barth's fideism and the Thomistic and evidentialist views of people like Clark Pinnock, John W. Montgomery, R. C. Sproul, John Gerstner, and Josh McDowell. He does not start with either man's reason (Thomas Aquinas) or with observation of evidence (Montgomery, McDowell), but with the Bible itself.

Of course, throughout *God, Revelation, and Authority*, Henry seeks to show why belief in the Bible as the infallible revelation of God's truth is itself eminently reasonable, as we have seen. Always, however, he bases his confidence in the Scriptures upon what Calvin called "the internal testimony of the Holy Spirit." Only the Spirit of God can verify

---

15. Erickson has gratefully admitted the influence of Carl Henry upon his own theology, even as he has differed with some aspects of the New Evangelical movement (Dockery, "Millard J. Erickson," 322–23).

16. Piper is an accomplished scholar who could write—and has written—academic theology, but he has chosen to apply his considerable gifts to a wider audience, to the profit of many (including this writer).

17. David Dockery says that Erickson was early influenced by the works of Carl Henry—as well as Carnell and Ramm ("Millard J. Erickson," 18, 22).

the authority and authenticity of the Word of God, which then leads to clear observation and reasoning about both the content of the Bible and of the world around us.

Karl Barth has exercised great influence among evangelical thinkers in recent decades, largely through the writings of Bernard Ramm and Donald Bloesch. Grenz and Olson opt for the approach of Ramm and Bloesch in preference to that of Henry in their review of twentieth-century theology, and they are joined by a number of other younger theologians. All this seems to be part of an overall anti-rationalist stance, itself a feature of postmodern culture.

As I have shown in another place,[18] criticisms of Henry as a rationalist simply have no basis in his writings. On the other hand, he did vigorously oppose the sort of appeal to paradox that allowed Barth to propound fundamental contradictions as part of his dialectical theology.[19] Contrary to Bernard Ramm and Donald Bloesch, Henry held that God has spoken clearly and infallibly in the Scriptures, and that the content of what he has revealed can be stated, or restated, in meaningful propositions. Those who seek to refute this view often do so at great length, usually in sentences made up of . . . propositions![20]

Unlike Ramm, Bloesch, Henry grants far less credence to the supposed findings of either modern science or modern biblical criticism, since both lack solid evidential support. Whereas they, like Barth and the Neo-orthodox thinkers in general, would prefer not to risk ridicule in academic circles by daring to doubt the "orthodox" acceptance of nineteenth-century attacks on the Bible, Henry rises to the challenge, goes on the offensive, and shows how questionable are

18. See the three chapters in this volume on "Carl Henry and His Critics," as well as the appendix.

19. "Barth schematizes his own theology, and invokes reason and logic with great power against those whose religious views he finds objectionable, not infrequently using the exposure of contradictions to his own advantage. Nonetheless he considers the norm of logical consistency . . . to be unacceptable to theology, and does not champion a theology free of contradiction. Barth curiously both champions and disowns consistency with remarkable inconsistency" (Henry, GRA 1:206).

20. Alas, as the chapters on "Carl Henry and His Critics" and the appendix demonstrate, some evangelicals who reject Henry do so without even attempting to compose a valid argument. Like Pinnock, Grenz, and Olson, and writers whom they quote (such as Ramm and Bloesch), they rely on rhetoric and name-calling rather than on clear thinking based on solid evidence.

the almost universally-accepted assertions that the Bible is historically and scientifically unreliable.

So, Henry stands to the right of a great section of evangelical theology today. Without making inerrancy the cornerstone of his system (he spends only one chapter on it), he does insist that the Bible is without fault and forms the only source of true evangelical theology.

Again, in contrast to many recent evangelical thinkers, including Donald Bloesch, Henry was not enamored with Roman Catholicism. Conversant with Roman Catholic theology—he engages its leading twentieth-century spokesmen in ongoing dialogue in *God, Revelation, and Authority*—he rejects both its liberal (e.g., Kung and many recent biblical critics) and Barthian (e.g., Karl Rahner) wings. He would not welcome hints of universalism either in Barth or in Vatican II Roman Catholicism.[21]

Nor, as we have seen, would Henry have anything to do with contemporary "openness theology." We know this because of his extensive critique of process theology, from which openness theology derives (despite the denials of its proponents). Henry's faith in the gracious sovereignty of God (treated in volume 5) stands in stark contrast to the portrait these writers erroneously draw of a petty Oriental despot, even a horrible tyrant. The nuanced and balanced treatment of the problem of evil (volume 5) distances him from the attempts of openness theologians to solve this mystery.[22]

On the other hand, Carl Henry was, to the end, not at home in the "fundamentalist" camp either. He refused to make inerrancy a condition for being considered evangelical. In his first widely acclaimed book, he rebuked the fundamentalist movement for their lack of responsible involvement in social issues.[23] Throughout his career, he engaged modern thought more than any other major evangelical theologian, and called for involvement in culture and even politics.

21. Mohler comments, "He defines God in terms of 'incomparable love' and 'unconditioned holiness,' but he rejects universalism as an implication of this love" ("Carl F. H. Henry," 290).

22. Mohler concludes that Henry's doctrine of God is a "stalwart defense and explication of classical Christian theism based thoroughly in the biblical revelation." "Refusing to define God by means of analogy, dialectic, or empirical data, Henry bases his treatment of the divine attributes on the biblical revelation" ("Carl F. H. Henry," 290).

23. Henry, *Uneasy Conscience of Modern Fundamentalism.*

Jerry Falwell and the Moral Majority plunged into national politics in the 1980s, and fundamentalists and evangelicals have joined in many causes, such as opposition to abortion on demand and special rights for homosexuals, but fundamentalists have not been especially active in understanding and addressing major currents in either popular or intellectual culture, as Henry urged and exemplified. And, although he was open to the possibility of a literal six-day interpretation of Genesis 1, he did not excoriate those with a different interpretation.

Carl Henry's Particular Contribution

Though he is by no means the only significant twentieth-century evangelical theologian and apologist, as we have seen, there are reasons why even non-sympathetic writers like Grenz and Olson select him as the major spokesman for traditional evangelical thought.

His *voluminous writings*—including more than two dozen books, countless articles, editorials in *Christianity Today*, a variety of edited symposia and multivolume series, and his magnum opus, *God, Revelation, and Authority*—over a period of five decades kept him on the forefront of theology for the last half of the twentieth century.

As founding editor of *Christianity Today*—the first widely read evangelical periodical with serious theological content—and charter member of the National Association of Evangelicals and of the Evangelical Theological Society, Henry helped to create an entire movement that has decisively shifted the balance of power in modern theology. No longer do those who deny the veracity of the Bible and the truth of historical Christianity hold unchallenged sway in the public arena, at least in North America.[24]

His wide *travels* and extensive *lectures* on all continents exposed thousands of younger church leaders and seasoned academics alike to a first-rate mind fully submissive to the Word of God, while his *commitment to evangelism* kept him in touch with the frontiers of Christianity and saved him from entombment in an ivory tower of theoretical speculation.

His early, prophetic, and ongoing *insistence upon the application of biblical teaching to all of life* helped to launch and guide the evangelical

24. In Europe, including Britain, American biblical scholarship and theology are not well known.

movement and build what Russell Moore terms the "new evangelical consensus" on the kingdom of God. Carl Henry and others provided the necessary theological underpinnings for Christian engagement in society and politics that delivered the church from both the isolationism of the fundamentalists and the naïve idealism of the liberals' Social Gospel.[25]

•   His *powerful writing* places him with such theological literary giants as Augustine, Luther, and Calvin. The sheer eloquence and beauty of his English style at its best reflect the multifaceted wisdom of God and of his revelation. The breadth and depth of his *scholarship*, and the wide variety of the authors with whom he engages in dialogue, increase the persuasive power of his arguments.

His decision to focus in *God, Revelation, and Authority* on epistemology—the *decisive issue* for modern theology, and for modern thought in general—dealt a body blow to the assumptions with which most twentieth-century theologians worked. Henry amassed mountains of evidence and wielded incisive arguments to demonstrate that the Bible is true, trustworthy, and therefore authoritative as our main source of revelation about God.

Against "negative" biblical criticism and the arrogance of scientism, not to mention a host of philosophical and theological systems spun out of speculative air, Henry made a convincing case for the faith of the historic church, a faith founded firmly upon the written Word of God.

Finally, the thoroughgoing *biblical* nature of his theology ensures that Henry's thought will not just be another passing fad for future historians of Christian doctrine to add to their collection of theological oddities. In Carl Henry, we have a man with rare intellectual talents who humbly submitted his mind to the mind of Christ as revealed in the God-breathed Scriptures.

Without wishing to detract at all from the truly substantial achievements of other evangelical theologians named above—and I have only listed a few among many—I think we should remember this giant among them.

---

25. See the extended argument of Moore, *Kingdom of Christ*.

FOUR

The Reformed Theology of Carl Henry

The theology of Carl Henry falls clearly into that stream known as "Reformed." That is, his thinking shows affinities with that of Augustine, Martin Luther, John Calvin, John Owen, Jonathan Edwards, the Hodges, B. B. Warfield, John Murray, John Frame, Douglas Kelly, and others of similar persuasion.

Henry himself applies the term Reformed to his position throughout *God, Revelation, and Authority*. To take only one example, identifies his view of Scripture as "the Reformed view."[1]

One the other hand, his theology shares less with adherents to Roman Catholic, Arminian, Neo-orthodox, liberal, dispensational, liberation, feminist, and "hope" and "openness" theologies.

Marks of Reformed Theology

What are the characteristics of Reformed theology? A very helpful summary can be found in the introduction to volume 1 of *The Reformed Reader*, edited by William Johnson and John Leith.[2] They give the following distinctives:

Catholic

The Reformers "appealed not only to scripture but to the theologians of the ancient church and to the first four ecumenical councils. Reformed

---

1. Henry, *GRA* 4:278.
2. Johnson and Leith, eds., *Reformed Reader*, xx–xxv.

theology is catholic in its affirmation of the doctrine of the person of Christ, as formulated at Chalcedon, and the doctrine of the Triune God. It is also catholic in its acknowledgement of the authority of Augustine, as well as other ancient theologians."[3]

Protestant

In varying degrees, and with varying emphases, the Reformers and their disciples followed the great insights of Martin Luther: "the supreme authority of the Holy Spirit speaking through the words of scripture; justification by grace through faith alone; the priesthood of all believers; the sanctity of the common life; and the necessity of faith that expresses itself in a responsible deliberate decision for the reception of the sacraments."[4]

Scriptural

Reformed theology begins with the Bible and stands under the authority of the Bible. "The characteristic that dominates the theological work of the Reformed theologians is the subordination of all theology to the authority of the scriptures." Thus, Reformed theology consists in a "coherent explication of scripture."[5]

Experiential

Here we find an "emphasis on Christian experience, especially the experience of regenerating grace, and the concreteness of the situation in which theology is written. Calvin himself subjected his theology to the criticisms of common sense, human wisdom, and experience . . . Revelation . . . is believed not to contradict human experience or common sense."[6]

---

3. Ibid., xx–xxi.
4. Ibid., xxi.
5. Ibid., xxii.
6. Ibid.

Practical and Edifying

We see also a focus on "the practical and spiritually edifying rather than the theoretical and speculative. All the early Reformed theologians objected to flights of speculation. . . . The purposes of theology are to glorify God, save human souls, and transform human life and society."[7]

God-Centered

Theologians in the Reformed tradition magnify the "majesty and awesomeness of God." "Calvin's theology cannot be comprehended apart from an intense awareness of the holy." They see God as "personal and inherently communicative, overflowing in energy, power, moral purpose and intentionality. . . . [E]very doctrine of Calvin's theology presupposed the prevenient grace of God that received its classic statement in the doctrine of predestination."[8]

"Reformed theology emphasizes the all-encompassing character and 'transcendence' of God." "God is personally and immediately active in the created order."[9] "On the other hand, they insisted equally upon the integrity of human history and of human beings as moral, responsible, historical creatures."[10]

Zealous for Holiness

"The reformed have generally placed the greatest emphasis upon sanctification."[11] They never set law and gospel against each other.

Comprehensive

"Reformed theology has always been unified by a vision of the human community under the authority of God. . . . [It] never defined the Christian life in terms of personal piety alone."[12]

7. Ibid.
8. Ibid., xxiii.
9. Ibid., xxiv.
10. Ibid., xxiii.
11. Ibid., xxiv.
12. Ibid., xxv.

Notice that these editors did not list "covenantal" as an essential mark of Reformed theology. They thus implicitly acknowledge that the specifically Presbyterian and covenant theologies that have been most prominent in the Reformed wing of Protestantism do not have exclusive claim to the title "Reformed."

Carl Henry: Reformed Theologian

Taking the summary of Reformed distinctives above as essentially accurate, we find that Carl F. H. Henry was in every respect a fully Reformed theologian, as the rest of this chapter will seek to demonstrate.

To be sure, he is usually listed among Baptist theologians, and not much noticed by leading Reformed theologians of the latter part of the twentieth century.[13] I believe that this represents a misunderstanding, and leads to a great loss on the part of Reformed believers, who are largely denied access to Henry's contribution.

Let us examine Carl Henry's thought, as expressed in *God, Revelation, and Authority*, to see how he conforms to the characteristics of Reformed theology noted above.

Catholic

Without a doubt, Henry falls into the "catholic" tradition of Christianity. He fully accepts, and clearly expounds, the doctrines of the first four ecumenical councils. Unlike many prominent twentieth-century theologians, he agrees with all articles of the Apostles' Creed and the Nicene Creed. He does not qualify or in any way compromise the truths of God as Creator, Christ as fully God and fully man, or the Holy Spirit as equal to Father and Son and fully personal. Nor does he question the bodily resurrection and return of Jesus Christ, or the resurrection unto eternal life of all believers in Jesus.

Like others in the Reformed tradition, Carl Henry holds Augustine of Hippo in great esteem.[14] In epistemology, he follows Augustine's pri-

---

13. See the categories of theologians in Wayne Grudem's *Sytematic Theology*, for example, and the almost complete absence of reference to Henry's works in the *Westminster Theological Journal* and the writings of John Frame and other Reformed theologians. We shall address this issue in another chapter.

14. There are more than 150 references to Augustine in the index to *GRA*.

ority: faith accepts the revealed truth of God in the Bible, and reason seeks to understand it. In other words, as Anselm would later say, "*fides quaerens intellectum*"—faith seeking understanding. Already in volume 1, chapter 20 of *God, Revelation, and Authority*, Henry expounds what he calls "The Theological Transcendent A Priori" in contrast to the "Philosophical Transcendent A Priori" of Plato, Descartes, Spinoza, and Leibniz; the "Philosophic Transcendental (Critical) A Priori" of Kant; and "Transcendental Religious A Priori" of men like Ritschl, Schleiermacher, Anders Nygren, Ernst Troeltsch, and Rudolph Otto.

The theological transcendent a priori stresses the priority of a self-revealing God in all true religious knowledge—indeed all knowledge of any kind. Although most of the early church fathers believed that some knowledge of God was innate in all mankind, "Augustine of Hippo stands unrivalled as the brilliant exponent of the Christian thesis that the knowledge of God and of other selves and the world of nature is not merely inferential. . . . Knowledge of God is no mere induction from the finite and nondivine, but is directly and intuitively given in human experience."[15]

Arguing against both skeptics and empiricists, Augustine claimed that man's creation in the image of God enabled him to receive utterly reliable revelation directly from God. Furthermore, he insisted that such knowledge comes from God's ongoing activity each moment of our lives; the initiative lies with God. The human mind responds to the world around it with intellection that is made possible by God's prior, and continuous, enlightenment. Like Plato, Augustine believed in certain "innate ideas," but these derived from man's creation in the image of the Logos of God.

More specifically, revelation comes to us through the sacred Scriptures. "Already dependent on God alone for existence, and continually sustained as a rational creature by the activity of God, the sinner is restored to light and life only through special divine intervention."[16]

As the above quotations show, Henry follows in the footsteps of Augustine, and of Luther, Calvin, and other Reformers, in his view of knowledge. We shall see shortly that he also holds to Augustine's general concept of the sovereignty of God in providence and in salvation.

15. Henry, *GRA* 1:325.
16. Ibid., 1:329.

Protestant

Though he subscribes to the creeds of the ancient church, Carl Henry does so as a Protestant. Unlike Roman Catholic theologians, he does not recognize any authority other than the Holy Scriptures. You will find no references to papal decrees or conciliar documents to bolster his theological arguments, which are almost completely based upon biblical grounds alone.

Other typical Protestant emphases also characterize his work. Salvation comes by grace through faith alone in Christ alone, not by a combination of faith and works coupled with sacramental rites and the intermediary of a priesthood. Note the simplicity of the following statement:

> To disbelieve the salvation God provides in the Messiah of prom-ise exposes one to the condemning power of the law (Rom. 2:12; Gal. 2:16); on the other hand, faith in Christ brings justification or acquittal (Rom. 3:24–26). The final judgment will universally clarify two facts that the world disbelieves (1 John 3:2)—namely, that believers are already forgiven (John 5:24), and that unbe-lievers are already condemned (John 3:18).[17]

As his works on personal and on social ethics demonstrate, Henry believed in the Protestant principle of the sanctity of the common life. His early work, *The Uneasy Conscience of American Fundamentalism*, exposed piety that ignored the claims of the larger society, and his teachings on the nature of the church evinced a conviction that each believer has the duty and the ability to bear witness to God in both the church and in the world. He calls the church "a community of healing"[18] and nowhere speaks of a special caste of religious functionaries with special privileges to mediate grace to "ordinary" Christians.

Scriptural

Since four out of six volumes of *God, Revelation, and Authority* ex-pound the nature and content of God's revelation, with a heavy stress upon the inspiration and unique authority of the Protestant Bible, we can justly assume that Carl Henry would agree with the Reformers in

17. Ibid., 3:66.
18. Ibid., 4:507.

the principle of *sola scriptura*. We are not wrong to do so, for on almost every page he seeks to confute what evangelical Protestants consider to be the errors of both those, like the Roman Catholics, who would add to the Bible and those, like liberals of all denominations, who would detract from it.

Just a glance at the Scripture Index at the end of each volume will highlight how thoroughly *biblical* is Henry's theology. For example, volume 2 lists one thousand references from sixty-two books of the Bible; volume 3 lists more than three thousand from fifty-seven books. Furthermore, as far as I have been able to determine, these citations do not violate the original meaning of the context. Unlike some writers, Henry does not impose his own idiosyncratic interpretation upon biblical texts, but follows normal historical-grammatical principles of exegesis within the framework of generally accepted Protestant evangelical procedures for interpretation.

In contrast to a great deal of twentieth-century theology, Carl Henry refuses to allow philosophy to provide either the categories or the controlling concepts for his theology. At every point, the Bible's teaching trumps any other potential source of ideas about God, his ways, and his world. Henry's method follows this principle, for he primarily engages in coherent explication of Scripture.[19] Like many other theologians, he first surveys other points of view, and then states his own. In particular, he canvasses and responds to a wide variety of non-evangelical positions before setting forth what he believes to be the biblical doctrine under consideration. Henry never intended to be creative, and he expressed his sense of calling partly in these words:

> Evangelical theology is heretical if it is only creative and unworthy if it is only repetitious. . . . Evangelical theology . . . while preserving the Judeo-Christian verities all too often fails to project engagingly upon present-day perplexities.[20]

Like the Reformers and all who have followed them, Carl Henry insists that "The Bible is the reservoir and conduit of divine truth. The Scriptures are the authoritative written record and interpretation of God's revelatory deeds, and the ongoing source of reliable objective

19. See especially ibid., 1:232–41.
20. Ibid., 1:9–10.

knowledge concerning God's nature and ways."[21] The operative word in the sentences above is "the"—the Bible is *the only* authoritative source of "reliable objective knowledge concerning God's nature and ways." As we have said, Henry insists upon the *sola scriptura* principle.

Experiential

Returning to the marks of Reformed theology listed above, we see that Carl Henry's system is also deeply concerned with experience. He, too, holds that "you must be born again," and he defines the church as the company of the regenerate. "God proposes to etch his law upon the hearts of men and the Holy Spirit is the personal divine power who by regeneration and sanctification conforms believers to the image of Christ."[22] Here too we find an "emphasis on Christian experience, especially the experience of regenerating grace, and the concreteness of the situation in which theology is written. . . . Revelation . . . is believed not to contradict human experience or common sense," which Johnson and Leith posit as a characteristic of Reformed theology.

The second aspect of the criterion of "experiential" also applies to *God, Revelation, and Authority*: "God's revelation is rational communication conveyed in intelligible ideas and meaningful words."[23] Like Calvin, Henry believes that God himself is a rational being, whose communication to men will not be marred by inconsistency, and whose revelation will not fundamentally contradict the reality we meet each day.

Though human reason "is not a creative source of truth," yet it is still "a divinely fashioned instrument for recognizing truth."[24] That is possible because "by creation [man] bears the image of God (Gen. 1:26), and is specially lighted by the divine Logos (John 1:9), so he may intelligibly know . . . his Maker. The forms of reason and the laws of logic as a creation-endowment survive the fall; apart from them, no intelligible communication, divine or human, would be possible."[25]

21. Ibid., 1:13.
22. Ibid., 1:15.
23. Ibid., 1:12.
24. Ibid., 1:225.
25. Ibid., 1:228.

All experience must, of course, be evaluated by God's written word. However, that is not the issue here. The point is simply that the Bible will not state what is manifestly absurd. We are not told that elephants fly or that truth is false. Indeed, one element of the plausibility and power of the Scriptures is their explanatory power: biblical history and doctrine illuminate life as we know it and enable us to understand events and some of their meaning (final comprehension awaits the *eschaton*), giving believers a wisdom that the world does not possess.

Carl Henry believes that the proper use of human reason will lead to a clearer understanding of God's Word—"*fidens quaerens intellectum*" ("faith seeking understanding") again. He does not disparage critical study of the Scriptures, or the testimony of experience, including archaeology, which confirm its historical record. Eyewitnesses to the resurrection of Jesus stand at the center of his argument for its validity as a historical event. He only requires that whenever "reason" or "experience" presume to deny the truth of the Bible, our thoughts must give way to God's thoughts as revealed to and through the prophets and apostles who, under the inspiration of the Holy Spirit, penned the words written in the Scriptures.

Practical and Edifying

> All the early Reformed theologians objected to flights of speculation. . . . The purposes of theology are to glorify God, save human souls, and transform human life and society.[26]

Carl Henry consistently refuses to speculate beyond the bounds of clear biblical revelation. He begins volume 1 with this declaration:

"Theology, we shall insist, sets out not simply with God as a speculative presupposition but with God known in his revelation."[27] Surveying the history of Western thought as background to the rise of the modern mind, he faults Aquinas for stating "the case for biblical theism in a way that attracted speculative doubt. . . . Replacing [the biblical outlook] is a speculative projection of autonomous structures that are directly accessible to human reason independent of divine revelation."[28]

26. Johnson, *Reformed Reader*, xxii.
27. Henry, *GRA* 1:14.
28. Ibid., 1:36.

On the other hand, he praises the Reformers, who objected to medieval scholasticism because "its speculative metaphysics and religious superstitions . . . prompted a reactionary reformulation in modern terms."[29] This modern mind includes a reverence for science, which Henry shows is heavily dependent upon speculation when attempting to speak of the origin and nature of the universe.

He contrasts Christian theology to "speculative rivals of revealed religion [that] espouse a variety of axioms competitive with biblical revelation." [30] In confrontation with such competing belief systems, "The theology of revelation requires the apologetic confrontation of speculative theories of reality and life."[31] Christian theology today, no less than in the Middle Ages, has often fallen into the trap of speculation. Throughout *God, Revelation, and Authority*, Henry challenges all assertions of modern theologians that are not supported by Scripture. He subjects himself to the same limits when he refuses to go beyond what is written in his treatment of the problem of evil in volume 6.

God-Centered

If there is one trait of Reformed theology that sets it apart in the popular mind, and with justification from other wings of Christianity, that must surely be its insistence upon what Henry calls "The Sovereignty of the Omnipotent God."[32]

God is sovereign in *revelation*. "Revelation is a divinely initiated activity, God's free communication by which he alone turns his personal privacy into a deliberate disclosure of his reality."[33] "The God of the Bible is wholly determinative in respect to revelation. He is free either to reveal himself or not to reveal himself; he is sovereign in his self-disclosure."[34]

Because of his sovereign self-disclosure, we know also that God is sovereign in *creation* and in the *preservation* of the universe. "God's

29. Ibid., 1:37.
30. Ibid., 1:216.
31. Ibid., 1:241.
32. The title of chapter 16 in volume 5.
33. Henry, *GRA* 1:8.
34. Ibid., 1:19.

power is revealed to man by his divine creation and preservation of the cosmos (Ps. 19; Rom. 1:20). . . . God is sovereign not only as the creator and preserver of all life, but also sovereign over creaturely death and/ or afterlife."[35]

Furthermore, God is sovereign in salvation. "He displays his sovereignty in the miraculous redemption of humanity as well as its creation."[36] The pervasive theme of God's kingly rule—"the kingdom of God"—refers to this realm of his activity as well. Henry notes the Old Testament stress upon "Yahweh's universal and eternal sovereignty,"[37] and its elaboration in the New Testament, in which "the risen and ascended Jesus stands therefore at the center of apostolic preaching."[38]

God's omnipotence is not limited to his works in creation and redemption, of course. For a sample of Henry's theological writing, consider the following sentences on God's utter freedom:

> The living interrelationships of the persons of the Trinity prior to creation in the eternal nature of the Godhead already manifest divine omnipotency. . . . God freely and eternally preserves himself in triune personal distinctions. God has absolute power to be himself internally and eternally as Father, Son and Holy Spirit. . . . For this reason are not only his continuing preservation of the universe and protracted reconciliation of sinners possible, but also his coming eschatological consummation of all things. He in himself—*intra se*, as the Latin theologians put it—is the omnipotent God who freely wills to create, to preserve, to redeem, to judge.[39]

God's omnipotence, which runs from the first verse of the Bible to the last, does not include the ability to violate his own character, of course. He cannot lie or deny himself, for example. Nor can he sin. The problem of evil has evoked the most vehement denials of the total sovereignty of God, most recently by proponents of "openness" theology. Henry will deal at length with this matter when discussing God's providence in volume 6, but at this point he gets to the root of the matter:

---

35. Ibid., 5:308.
36. Ibid.
37. Ibid.
38. Ibid., 5:310.
39. Ibid., 5:314.

The living God has the creative power necessary to bring about a morally reprehensible state of affairs, for he determined and prophesied that Judas would betray Christ. But the foreordination of an evil act is not itself evil, since God need not will what he wills for the reasons others may will them.[40]

Henry agrees with Barth that the God of whom we predicate this total power is, of course, only the God of the Bible, "God the Father Almighty," and thus we must speak of his omnipotence not in general terms, but only as Scripture warrants. Likewise, Henry agrees with Barth when "he [Barth] uses God's freedom as a synonym for his power."[41]

Lest we imagine that God's omnipotence functions only as a theological construct, Carl Henry expresses one of the deepest convictions of his heart—one that drove him to strive mightily for holiness among Christians and justice in the world—when he declares that "The modern church's failure to let Jesus Christ function fully in its midst as Lord is the worst scandal of the twentieth-century ecclesiology."[42]

Even our disobedience cannot impede the plans of our sovereign Lord, however:

God's purposes and Christ's kingdom are therefore invincible. God has sovereignly so disposed the course of the universe and of history that even the severest hostility to his will instrumentally displays and promotes his sovereignly redemptive plan. . . . God himself guarantees that eternal hell will subordinate the powers of evil and subjugate the impenitent wicked, that unreconciled freedom will not forever frustrate love, and that ultimately the created universe will be totally in the service of righteousness.[43]

In *God, Revelation, and Authority*, Carl Henry intended to expound first the doctrine of the Word of God (epistemology, revelation) and the doctrine of God (theology proper). Thus, he does not treat at length

---

40. Ibid., 5:315.

41. Ibid., 5:317. Typically, however, Henry objects when Barth "translates many of these formally commendable premises into questionable and indeed highly objectionable specific positions," such as that revelation "requires sporadic nonpropositional personal encounter," etc.

42. Ibid., 5:330.

43. Ibid. I commend this entire chapter to anyone who wishes to sample the sustained eloquence of Carl Henry's theological writing.

other topics of theology, such as the doctrine of salvation (soteriology). Along the way, however, he does state clearly his essential Reformed position on this vital subject:

> The electing God and his covenant-people are central to the whole Bible. . . . He is the God who decrees and elects from eternity, who creates *ex nihilo*, who works out his purposes in nature and history. . . . He who is the God who pledges and provides redemption in Christ Jesus, the Nazarene who as King of Israel not only fulfills the divine election and calling of his people but also grafts upon them the Gentiles. He is the God who will subordinate all things to his righteous, everlasting rule.[44]

Like all good "Calvinists," Carl Henry insists also upon the necessity of faith for salvation: "The eternal election of believers is experientially effected in the personal reception and appropriation of the now openly revealed mystery."[45]

He emphasizes that God "insists upon unqualified righteousness and connects salvation with grace alone."[46] Those saved by grace must demonstrate their connection with God by the good works that his Spirit enables them to perform—a theme running from one end of Henry's long theological career to the other.[47] "Easy believism" has no place in his thought. In keeping with the Reformed tradition, Henry insists upon the highest standards of personal and corporate holiness; thus his volumes on ethics and his repeated references to the duty of Christians to reflect God's character in *God, Revelation, and Authority*. In essentials, therefore, Carl Henry is a theologian in the Reformed tradition.

44. Ibid., 2:76.
45. Ibid., 3:17.
46. Ibid., 3:65.
47. See, for example, ibid., 2:68.

FIVE

Doctrine of Revelation

Carl Henry made a huge impact on evangelical theology in a number of areas, including personal and social ethics, but his major efforts focused on the doctrine of revelation. As Albert Mohler comments, the publication of *God, Revelation, and Authority* "established Henry's stature as the primary proponent of an evangelical doctrine of revelation and scriptural authority." [1] Indeed, he avers that "Henry's exposition of the doctrine of revelation stands as an awesome evangelical achievement." [2]

Many have commented that Carl Henry's magnum opus includes discussions of virtually every other major theologian and theological program in the twentieth century. Mohler correctly pinpoints his concentration upon the doctrine of revelation in his evaluation of others' treatment of this foundational subject: "Few movements or theologians escaped Henry's critique. . . . Each system was seen . . . to be based in an inadequate epistemology and thus a faulty doctrine of revelation." [3]

Because of his firm stand for the inspiration, intelligibility, and authority of Scripture, this aspect of his teaching has become the most controversial and most criticized. At the same time, I believe that Henry's writings on revelation are the least understood. Indeed, it often seems that those who find fault with Henry at this point—including several highly respected writers—may not have taken the time to read carefully *God, Revelation, and Authority*, as I shall try to show later. [4]

1. Mohler, "Carl F. H. Henry," 284.
2. Ibid., 287.
3. Ibid., 285.
4. See the chapters on Carl Henry and his critics.

To understand (and therefore have the right to critique) Henry's complex, sophisticated, nuanced position, one should read the first four volumes of *God, Revelation, and Authority* closely. At the very least, a thorough perusal of Bob Patterson's excellent summary of the work would provide a general idea of this vital feature of Henry's theological system.[5]

Carl Henry details his understanding of divine revelation in fifteen theses, all of which much be considered in order to grasp the meaning of any one of them. A brief summary of them follows. I shall rely heavily on quotations from Henry, because he enunciates his position much more clearly and forcefully than I could.

1. *"Revelation is a divinely initiated activity, God's free communication by which he alone turns his personal privacy into a deliberate disclosure of his reality."* In other words, "Human beings know only what God has chosen to reveal concerning the spiritual world."[6] We cannot, by ourselves, know anything of God and his dealings with us apart from his revelation of these truths to us.

It is foolish and vain to try to erect the case for biblical theism or philosophical theology upon any foundation other than the self-revelation of God, known most clearly in the Scriptures. Though this revelation often, and rightly, evokes wonder, "the essential purpose of divine disclosure is not simply to beget wonder but rather to communicate truth."[7] Even the signs and wonders accompanying much of God's revelation were meant to demonstrate and point to the truths disclosed to God's appointed spokesmen, and to elicit faith in a sovereign God.

2. *"Divine revelation is given for human benefit, offering us privileged communion with our Creator in the kingdom of God."*[8] God could have avenged the sin of Adam with immediate destruction, but he graciously deals with mankind even up to the present, offering salvation by grace through faith in Jesus Christ. Those who repent and believe enter the kingdom of God, which has already come in Christ and which will come in its fullness when he returns.

---

5. Patterson, *Carl F. H. Henry*.

6. Henry, *GRA* 2:24.

7. Ibid., 2:27.

8. Ibid., 2:8.

At this point Henry briefly outlines his understanding of the kingdom of God as already and not yet:

> God's purpose in revelation is that we may know him personally
> as he is, may avail ourselves of his gracious forgiveness and offer
> of new life, may escape catastrophic judgment for our sins, and
> venture personal fellowship with him.[9]

The kingdom of God makes present demands upon us, moreover, and
not just upon individuals. Henry always insists that God's revelation
speaks to every domain, from "the vacuous simplest pursuits of life"[10]
to government and society.

Furthermore, revelation is given not only that we might have
knowledge of God and his will, but that we may repent, believe, and
obey. "Simply hearing God's revealed good news, his dramatic offer
of salvation, does not redeem us automatically."[11] Contrary to Barth,
Henry shows that revelation brings only knowledge, not salvation; the
latter depends upon "personal decision and faith."[12] "By addressing the
human mind and confronting the human will God's revelation requires
a decision that encompasses the whole self. It calls us to inner repentance, to a reversal of lifestyle, to redemptive renewal and to obedient
fellowship."[13]

3. *"Divine revelation does not completely erase God's transcendent
mystery, inasmuch as God the Revealer transcends his own revelation."*[14]
Henry opposes <u>three</u> errors: believing that God cannot be known at all;
that he can not be known as he is, in his "essence" (an Aristotelian, not
Christian, category); and that "revelation is paradoxical and cannot be
rationally formulated.[15]

> The revelation given to man is not exhaustive of God. The God
> of revelation transcends his creation, transcends his activity,
> transcends his own disclosure.[16]

9. Ibid., 2:31.
10. Ibid., 2:35.
11. Ibid., 2:38.
12. Ibid., 2:40.
13. Ibid., 2:44–45.
14. Ibid., 2:9.
15. Ibid., 2:55.
16. Ibid.

Judeo-Christian religion insists that God's revelation does not totally exhaust his being and activity; even in his revelation he is the free sovereign God. Yahweh's voluntary self-disclosure does not wholly conceal his incomprehensibility nor eliminate mystery. Scripture does not deplete all possible revelation; even on the basis of biblical revelation our knowledge of God is an incomplete knowledge. . . . Not until God's final eschatological disclosure to the redeemed in glory shall we 'know even as [we] are known.' (1 Corinthians 13:12, KJV).[17]

Humility is therefore as becoming to the Christian theologian whose affirmations are governed by prophetic-apostolic revelation, as to the secular scientist. . . . Because of their confidence in rational revelation and revealed truths, however, evangelical theologians are prone to consider their systematizations and schematizations of those truths as trustworthy as the Scripture. . . . The inspired Scriptures remain unique and normative over against even the most devout evangelical expositions of the revealed Word of God."[18]

The fact that we now know only 'in part,' however, does not destroy the validity and trustworthiness of that portion of knowledge we have through divine disclosure. That God does not reveal himself to man exhaustively does not mean that he does not reveal himself truly."[19]

4. *"The very fact of disclosure by the one living God assures the comprehensive unity of divine revelation."*[20] As God is one, so his revelation is unified. God claims supremacy over all mankind, and offers only one revelation for everyone. There is only one kind of revelation: Divine self-disclosure. Even the terms "general" and "special" revelation must be used carefully, and must not be employed to deny their essential continuity. Reason "is an instrument for knowing the truth of God, but it is not the originating source of divine truth."[21] There is no "natural theology" in the Bible, only the insistence that God "reveals himself and his ways in and through the created universe."[22]

17. Ibid.
18. Ibid., 2:52.
19. Ibid., 2:54.
20. Ibid., 2:9.
21. Ibid., 2:73.
22. Ibid. Mohler comments, "Henry acknowledges the reality of natural revelation

The unity of revelation derives not only from God's uniqueness, but also from the true content of what he reveals, which centers upon Jesus Christ, his only Son and our only Savior. The Old Testament prefigured and promised his coming, which is narrated and explained in the New Testament. These two parts of the Bible, therefore, are unified in their central theme; there is no contradiction or division between them.

5. *The "nature, content, and variety [of revelation] are exclusively God's determination."*[23]

God reveals himself in an amazing variety of ways, illustrated by the large number of different terms used to describe his self-disclosure. He has employed angels, dreams, visions, oracles, historical events, wonders, miraculous guidance; the beauty of the created order; the words and deeds of the prophets and apostles; and above all the incarnation of the Word of God in Jesus Christ. In the end, there will be one final revelation of God's justice and love when Christ returns.

As central as Scripture is, we must not reduce God's revelation to the Bible, as some fundamentalists have.

While denying that we can know God apart from his self-disclosure, either by reason or experience, Henry does affirm some sort of general revelation, based upon our creation in the image of God. The Logos in some sense enlightens every person, so that God does not leave heathen "without a witness" (Acts 17:27). Through the creation, including our mind and moral conscience, we are "never completely detached or isolated from the revelation of God."[24]

True, fallen men and women ignore, distort, disbelieve, and disobey God's revelation, but that does not negate the fact of revelation or of our (limited) capacity to perceive and understand it. Indeed, this constitutes our guilt before God. Precisely because we do know as much as we do about God and his will, we stand accused and in need of redemption. That is, of course, where special revelation comes in, to declare to us further our sinful state, and to proclaim to us the way of salvation.

---

but denies it a positive role within his dogmatic system" ("Carl F. H. Henry," 288).

23. Henry, *GRA* 2:9.

24. Ibid., 2:85.

Though Jesus Christ is the pre-existent and incarnate Word of
God, we must not follow Karl Barth and others in refusing to call the
Scriptures the word of God also, as Henry shows in later chapters. Nor
is Barth correct in rejecting all revelation of God in and through nature.
At the same time, the Thomistic "proofs" for the existence of God, rising from perceived reality, do not "work" philosophically, and do not
represent the biblical way of attesting the reality of God.

That does not mean, however, that we reject the implications of
our creation in the image of God, which include our moral and rational
capacities. "The divine image, a cohesive unity of interrelated compo-
nents that interact with and condition each other, includes rational,
moral and spiritual aspects of both a formal and material nature. . . .
But . . . it should be clear that the rational or cognitive aspect has logical
priority."[25]

> Man without rationality—or the basic forms of reason—could
> never intelligibly discriminate God from the not-God, right
> from wrong, truth from untruth. . . . All distinctively human
> experience presupposes the law of noncontradiction and the
> irreducible distinction between truth and error; man cannot
> repudiate these logical presuppositions without sacrificing the
> intelligibility of what he says and does and his own mental
> coherence."[26]

The "material" aspect of this knowledge consists in some basic
awareness of the existence and character of God, and of our moral ac-
countability before him, as Romans 1:18–25 demonstrates. This knowledge does not arise from observation, but is innate in the human soul as
created in God's image. On the other hand, Henry wants to make clear
that unaided fallen human reason has limits:

> To say that the divine image in man after the fall ongoingly in-
> cludes both formal and material elements, in no way requires a
> regard for human reason as an inherent source of truth about
> God. Rather, by dependence upon and fidelity to divine rev-
> elation, the surviving *imago* assures the human intelligibility
> of divine disclosure, preserves the universal validity of human
> knowledge, and correlates God's inner revelation to man in the
> mind and conscience with God's external revelation in nature

25. Ibid., 2:125.
26. Ibid., 2:126.

and history. It qualifies man not only as a carrier of objective metaphysical truth about God's nature and ways, but more particularly as a receiver of the special revelational truth of redemption.[27]

Lest we think that Henry imagines that the "laws" of thought and logic exist independently, or were invented by Aristotle, he states explicitly that "the forms which govern thought and the objectivity of knowledge have their basis in the transcendent God."[28] The Logos of God is his mind, his way of thinking, the original divine pattern that issued in creation by the spoken word, upholding the world even by his powerful word, and reflected in what we wrongly term the "laws of nature." Human reasoning capacity and categories merely reflect the divine mind, and even in our fallen state we retain a fundamental awareness of the distinction between right and wrong, truth and error.

At the same time, we must recognize the immense, qualitative difference between God and man. "To speak properly of 'image' requires that we respect the difference between the prefatory *omni-* appropriate only to all of God's perfections and what is reflected in created beings in a qualified way."[29] By no means does Henry believe that the mind of man and of God are coterminous; he rejects all such notions and insists that we know God not by some inherent capacity, but only by God's initiative in revelation. By stressing the image of God as rational, he only means to explicate what the Bible everywhere assumes: that God has communicated in such a way that creatures made in his likeness can comprehend his revelation.

Against Thomas Aquinas and even Vatican II Roman Catholic thought, however, Henry agrees with Calvin and the Reformers that "the fall of man was a catastrophic personality shock," and that the so-called noetic effects of sin make impossible "any knowledge of God except . . . that God exists and that he executes moral judgment."[30]

Although the fall affected every department of the human personality, it "affects the functions of the reason and of the will in different ways." Henry agrees with Gordon Clark that the will is so totally cor-

27. Ibid., 2:130.
28. Ibid., 2:133.
29. Ibid., 2:134.
30. Ibid., 2:135.

rupted that no act can be without sin; that the content of our thinking, including our philosophical premises, is likewise darkened; but that sin does not "affect the laws of valid inference. True propositions are universally true now, as they were before the fall and as they always will be."[31]

That is why the Bible can hold us responsible for our awareness of God's existence as God and his moral claim on our lives. We instinctively know that there is a difference between right and wrong, truth and falsehood, even if we fail to act correctly on such knowledge. This notional and ethical knowledge makes discussion and evaluation possible. Thus, we affirm that another is correct or incorrect, and everyone agrees that these are fundamental categories.

Indeed, the denial of this statement is self-refuting: One has to say that it is "wrong" and "false" to insist that there is in the human psyche an elemental awareness that a statement cannot be both true and false in the same way at the same time—and in saying that this is "wrong," one assumes the validity of that which he seeks to deny! That is all that Henry means when he affirms the law of noncontradiction and other laws of valid inference to be essential elements of the image of God even after the fall.

In his discussion of the varieties of revelation, Henry responds to modern theologians, and especially Karl Barth, who vigorously maintained the distinction between the Word of God and the words of the Scriptures, and who holds that Scripture is not revelation, but only a witness to it. Henry finds Barth's doctrine of revelation speculative, confusing and at odds with the statements of Scripture itself. He likewise considers Jurgen Moltmann's narrowing of revelation to eschatological promise wanting.

6. *"God's revelation is uniquely personal both in content and form."*[32]

Notwithstanding his emphasis upon the rationality of God's communication to us, Carl Henry spends more time illuminating the very personal nature of revelation.

> Revelation is personal communication. Its personal originator is
> God, and persons are its recipients; it involves personal thought

31. Ibid., 2:135–36.
32. Ibid., 2:151.

and speech . . . ; sometimes in addition to God's direct address it involves also personal agents as bearers of revelation.[33]

In stark contrast to both pagan and modern notions of ultimate reality as impersonal principle, the God of the Bible discloses his very nature and being not only in words and deeds, but also in names, which Henry expounds in detail. At the same time however, he vigorously denies popular misconceptions of the personal nature of divine revelation, such as

> that revelation is nonintellectual and nonpropositional; that God is never an object of conceptual thought; that theological assertions are nonobjectifying; that personal faith in God excludes mental assent to theological doctrines. Such assertions not only derive their inspiration from modern philosophical speculations alien to the biblical view, but they in effect also destroy divine self-disclosure in the scriptural understanding.[34]

Henry's discussion of the names of God climaxes in volume 2, chapter 16, "Jesus: The Revelation of the New Testament Name." He agrees with those who say that the distinctive feature of the New Testament is the way it places the name of Jesus either alongside the name of God, or substitutes it for God's name.

7. *"God reveals himself not only universally in the history of the cosmos and of the nations, but also redemptively within this external history in unique savings acts."*[35]

As always, each word of Henry's formulation carries weight. God reveals himself in the history of the universe and in the history of all nations: in all events he testifies to himself. He revealed himself uniquely, however, in the events recorded in the Bible, including the election

---

33. Ibid. See also Henry, ed., *Revelation and the Bible*, 9, where he notes in his preface that the contributors to this volume "discuss Biblical revelation with full reference to God's saving acts and thereby contemplate revealed ideas in association with redemptive history. They do full justice to the historical and personal elements in special revelation."

34. Ibid., 2:157. In particular, Henry shows how such Barthian emphases derive from the philosophical position of his teacher, Wilhelm Herrmann, which in turn comes from the belief of modern philosophers that the external world cannot be interpreted in anything but material and mathematical terms. That leaves only the inner self as the locus of knowledge of ultimate reality, which then makes some sort of divine encounter theory seem necessary for theologians like Barth.

35. Ibid., 2:247.

and career of Israel and of the early church. Supremely however, God showed himself in the incarnation, life, death, and resurrection of Jesus Christ. These events are historical; they happened. Though their meaning can be known only by faith, enlightened by the interpretation of the Scriptures, they must not be relegated to the realm of myth or legend. In this section, Henry both shows the limitations of historical research and gives reasons why the Bible can be regarded as a historical record of the highest value.

8. *"The climax of God's special revelation is Jesus of Nazareth, the personal incarnation of God in the flesh; in Jesus Christ the source and content of revelation converge and coincide."*[36]

In Jesus God reveals his plan for the destiny of mankind. Jesus fulfills all prophecies. He is the only divine mediator; indeed, he is the core of the meaning of the gospel. Both God and man, he is the final revelation of God; we need not look for another prophet or savior. His resurrection, which was a historical event reliably recorded in the Bible, points to the resurrection of all mankind on the last day.

Jesus' own view of the Scriptures should be our own: he affirmed that the Old Testament, as a whole and in its very words, was the Word of God. Furthermore, "Jesus in principle committed his apostles to the enlargement and completion of the Old Testament canon by their proclamation of a divinely inspired and authoritative word interpreting the salvific significance of his life and work"[37]—what we now call the New Testament.

9. *"The mediating agent in all divine revelation is the Eternal Logos—preexistent, incarnate, and now glorified."*[38]

> The overall New Testament concept of the Word, the Logos, is illuminated by Old testament backgrounds, rather than by contemporary Greco-Roman philosophy. . . . This emphasis that the eternal Logos is mediator of all divine revelation guards against two prevalent errors, namely, that of reducing all revelation to the revelation found in Jesus of Nazareth; and that of isolating general revelation by treating revelation outside Jesus of

36. Ibid., 2:11.
37. Ibid., 2:44.
38. Ibid., 2:11.

Nazareth as something independent of the Logos who became incarnate.[39]

10. *"God's revelation is rational communication conveyed in intelligible ideas and meaningful words, that is, in conceptual-verbal form."*[40]

> In the Bible 'the word of the Lord' is an intelligible divine Word, not simply a human interpretation of the deeds of God or an existential inner response to a spiritual confrontation. . . . Even Jesus of Nazareth . . . in his own teaching and practice endorses the view that revelation takes conceptual-verbal form. Not only does Jesus identify his very 'words' as revelation (John 14:10) but he also identifies the Word of God in terms of what 'stands written' (Matthew 4:4, literal).[41]

Because we are created in God's image, we have both the capacity to think and some innate categories by which to recognize God's verbal revelation. As creator, God can enable us to understand his communication, given in words that his Logos makes possible and our creation in his image makes intelligible. He is able to transcend our finiteness as well as our fallenness and to speak to us in words that convey comprehensible truth.

At this point, Carl Henry outlines a theistic view of language that is nothing less than brilliant and that would alone constitute him one of the most original and constructive thinkers of the twentieth century.

One of Henry's most controversial affirmations is that the revelation of God is "propositional." Like others, he emphasizes "the intelligible nature of divine disclosure as objectively valid truth."[42] "A proposition is a verbal statement that is either true or false; it is a rational declaration capable of being either believed, doubted or denied."[43] He agrees with Gordon Clark that, aside from exclamations and imperatives, most of the Bible consists of "historical assertions or explanations of such assertions."[44]

---

39. Ibid., 2:12.
40. Ibid., 2:10.
41. Ibid., 2:12–13.
42. Ibid., 3:455.
43. Ibid., 3:456.
44. Ibid.

By propositional revelation Henry means that "God supernaturally communicated his revelation to chosen spokesmen in the express form of cognitive truths, and that the inspired prophetic-apostolic proclamation reliably articulates these truths in sentences that are not internally contradictory."[45] In other words, in revealing himself to us, God does so by giving us information about himself and his ways. Otherwise, we would be left in the dark, each person imagining God in a different way, and incapable of either stating what or why we believe to others.

Even the personal names of God can be restated as propositions: "God is Almighty"; "God is faithful to his covenant," etc. Metaphors such as "the LORD is my Rock" can likewise be explained: "God is strong; he is steady and reliable; he will protect me." Imperatives imply propositions: "Hallelujah!" can be unpacked to mean: "There is a God. His name is Yahweh. He is worthy to be praised. We should praise him."

Henry is aware that the effect of God's revelation may—indeed, should—include wonder, awe, and reverence; and that God has left much that is not yet revealed. Here he only means to say that what God has disclosed, he has done so intelligibly and coherently, in a way that we can understand and express.

11. *"The Bible is the reservoir and conduit of divine truth."*[46]

"The Scriptures are the authoritative written record and interpretation of God's revelatory deeds, and the ongoing source of reliable objective knowledge concerning God's nature and ways."[47]

In this age of rebellion against authority, the Bible stands as the authoritative norm for all Christian thought and speech. It is "literally true" in the sense that grammatical-historical interpretation of the Bible expresses the original intent of the author, which may also have been conveyed by parable and other figures of speech.

12. *"The Holy Spirit intends the communication of divine revelation, first, by inspiring the prophetic-apostolic writings, and second, by illuminating and interpreting the scripturally given Word of God."*[48]

45. Ibid., 3:457.
46. Ibid., 2:13.
47. Ibid.
48. Ibid.

The original manuscripts penned by the prophets and apostles were inerrant, in that they were free from error of any kind. The Holy Spirit so worked upon human authors as to enable them to express God's truth in human words. Evangelicals do not believe in the "dictation theory" of inspiration, which denies the active involvement of the prophets and apostles in the writing down of what God revealed to them, but acknowledges the human element in the Bible, without, however, implying that this humanity necessarily entails error.[49] The truth of Scripture includes its statements about history—including the history of the cosmos—as well as ethics.

Current copies and translations are not inerrant, but all the copies and many translations so closely approximate the originals that they possess the quality of infallibility; that is, they "do not corrupt the original content but convey the truth of revelation in reliable verbal form, and infallibly lead the penitent reader to salvation."[50] Though not necessarily exact replicas of the autographs, they do not contain anything that would mislead an earnest seeker of the truth.

In the past two centuries biblical critics have claimed to find errors and contradictions in the Scriptures, and they have posited a variety of theories concerning the origin and composition of the various books of the Bible. These theories, often stemming from naturalistic and even evolutionary presuppositions, have been proven wrong time and again. Historical criticism may and must be used by the careful exegete, but not in such a way as to deny the authenticity of the canonical writings or the truth of their contents. Henry is aware of problem passages in the Bible, and spends an entire chapter discussing some of the more difficult ones. Though he believes that most problems can be resolved by careful study, he admits that some apparent errors and contradictions remain, awaiting further knowledge or perhaps even the return of Christ to solve. In fact, "the enormity in the range of error involved in the fallacies of higher critics in contrast to the scope of error supposedly attaching to Scriptures is striking."[51]

---

49. Albert Mohler notes that on the subject of inspiration, Henry "steers a middle course between the so-called 'dynamic' and 'dictation' theories" ("Carl F. H. Henry," 288–89).

50. Henry, *GRA* 2:14.

51. Ibid., 4:353.

Despite the small number of remaining difficulties, the doctrine of inerrancy has always been held by the church, and with good reason. Henry shows that those who assert inerrancy to be a recent aberration are historically inaccurate.[52]

13. *"As bestower of spiritual life the Holy Spirit enables individuals to appropriate God's revelation savingly, and thereby attests the redemptive power of the revealed truth of God in the personal experience of reborn sinners."*[53]

14. *"The church approximates the kingdom of God in miniature; as such she is to mirror to each successive generation the power and joy of the appropriated realities of divine revelation."*[54]

15. *"The self-manifesting God will unveil his glory in a crowning revelation of power and judgment; in this disclosure at the consummation of the ages, God will vindicate righteousness and justice, finally subdue and subordinate evil, and bring into being a new heaven and earth."*[55]

With these fifteen theses, Carl Henry has given the church as fulsome an exposition of the doctrine of revelation as can be found anywhere, and has done so with clarity and precision. A great deal of confusion about the truth of God, even in evangelical circles, would be avoided if more scholars took the time and effort to study what Carl Henry has presented.

52. Mohler notes that "Henry's defense of biblical inerrancy is one of the most thorough treatments in the evangelical literature." But Henry distanced himself from fundamentalists and some evangelicals (like Harold Lindsell) when he made inerrancy a test only of evangelical "consistency rather than authenticity" ("Carl F. H. Henry," 289).

53. Henry, *GRA* 2:15.

54. Ibid.

55. Ibid., 2:16.

SIX

Apologist for the Twenty-first Century

"When a non-Christian asks, 'What persuasive reasons have you for believing?' the basic issue at stake is, is theology credible?"[1]

With this sentence, Carl Henry exposes a major purpose for writing *God, Revelation, and Authority*: "To give a defense to everyone who asks . . . a reason for the hope that is in you."[2] "Defense" translates the Greek word *apologia*, and "reason" the word *logos*; hence the fundamentally apologetic nature of Henry's theology, and his insistence that the Christian faith is reasonable, even logical.

In this approach, Henry stands in a long line of apologetic theologians. One thinks of Athanasius, Augustine of Hippo, Thomas Aquinas, John Calvin, Charles Hodge, Cornelius Van Til, Gordon Clark, Leslie Newbigin, and even Karl Barth, who tried to expose the fallacies of non-biblical points of view.[3] As the great Chinese theologian Lit-sen Chang wrote, apologetics (formally a branch of systematic theology) is "theology at war."[4]

For Carl Henry, theology was no armchair, ivory-tower intellectual game, played with academic peers with nothing better to do than split philosophical hairs. We must not forget that he began his ministry as a pastor, spoke to the Pasadena Rose Bowl Easter Sunrise services, served as chairman of the Berlin Congress on Evangelism, and worked closely with Billy Graham for much of his career. In the final chapter of

1. Henry, *GRA* 1:213.

2. 1 Pet 3:15.

3. Helpful articles on these men as apologists can be found in Campbell-Jack and McGrath, eds., *New Dictionary of Christian Apologetics*.

4. Chang, *What Is Apologetics?*, 1.

his autobiography, he pleaded for an all-out, comprehensive effort to bring the gospel to the United States of America in the 1990s, before it was too late.[5]

On the last page, he states that "Heaven will be an unending feast for the soul that basks in his presence. And it will be brighter because some will be there whom I brought to Jesus."[6]

In the depths of his heart, Carl Henry was an evangelist, not a theorist. He desperately yearned for millions more to be saved by grace through faith in Jesus Christ. But he believed that true faith must rest upon solid convictions that the gospel is *true*. To be true, it had to command the allegiance of the whole person, including the mind. Like Paul and other biblical writers, he held that the mind was made in God's image, that it had fallen into a degenerate, darkened state, and that it had to be renewed by the light of God's Word as contained in Scripture.[7]

Thus, *God, Revelation, and Authority* qualifies both as a work of systematic theology and of apologetics.

Varieties of Apologetics

In the history of Christianity, and even today, there are varieties of apologetical approaches and methods. Some argue for the truth of Christianity on the basis of their own personal experience; others, on the power of the gospel to change lives. Still others rely on authority, and especially the authority of the church. Evidentialists appeal to the many evidences for the truth of the Christian faith.[8] Rationalists try to employ reason to refute and convince unbelievers, while fideists insist that one must simply believe the gospel in order to understand the truth. Finally, presuppositionalists emphasize the priority of one's starting assumptions.[9]

5. Henry, *Confessions of a Theologian*, 401–5.

6. Ibid., 407.

7. Rom 1:18–28; Eph 4:17–24.

8. Evidentialists believe that "Christianity's basic truth claims can be demonstrated to be true by appeals to the observed facts of nature and history" (Olson, *Westminster Handbook*, 304).

9. Rational presuppositionalists (including Nicholas Woltersorff and Alvin Plantinga) believe that everyone operates on the basis of some "unprovable assumptions or 'control beliefs'" (ibid., 305).

Actually, few really effective apologists confine themselves to only one approach.

Thus, evidentialists and rationalists are often grouped together, for they are convinced that one can make a powerful case for Christianity on the basis of the phenomena of Scripture (such as fulfilled prophecy and the internal coherence of the Bible), the evidence supporting its historical statements (like the resurrection of Jesus), and the logical arguments that have been traditionally employed to prove the existence of God (especially the "five-fold proof" employed by Aquinas and others since him). Recently, a number of prominent scientists have shown that Darwinian evolutionism runs counter to the evidence of the created order. These apologists also think they can show that other belief systems are either internally inconsistent or contrary to some forms of solid evidence.[10]

This approach sometimes goes by the name of "classical apologetics," and has been vigorously promoted by people like John Warwick Montgomery, R. C. Sproul, John Gerstner, and Josh McDowell. Their watchword might be, "I understand so that I might believe."[11]

Likewise, presuppositionalists have much in common with fideists, and in fact each is sometimes called by the other's name (some consider Henry a fideist), for they both hold that empirical evidence and human reason cannot convincingly demonstrate the reliability of God's revelation, which is self-attesting and must be accepted by faith at the beginning of one's search for truth. With Augustine and Anselm, their motto is "faith seeking understanding," or "I believe that I may understand." To complicate matters, "fideism" is often employed as a pejorative term, as an implied criticism of those who would bypass both the mind and the senses in order simply to believe. But it can also be used positively,

---

10. I am indebted to my son-in-law, Brandon Cozart, for the following comment: "The widely-read twentieth-century apologist C. S. Lewis, like G. K. Chesteron, whom he greatly admired, can be classified as a moderate evidentialist, most of the time holding to the 'cumulative case' approach, as opposed to the presuppositional or pure evidentialist approaches. This is an informal argument that looks for the general accumulation of evidence, facts, truths, and trends that over time boil down to the best argument. Given all the current data and facts, the Christian explanation of things is the best explanation we have at the time. It assumes neutrality and is basically just an argument from probability."

11. For a helpful review of Sproul, Gerstner, and Lindsley, *Classical Apologetics*, see Frame, *Cornelius Van Til*, appendix A: "Van Til and the Ligonier Apologetic," 401–22.

to emphasize the priority of faith in all human inquiry, especially the search for Christian knowledge and understanding.

Presuppositional Apologetics

Basically—though not exclusively, as we shall see—Carl Henry stands firmly in the presuppositionalist tradition. That is, he begins with an assumption that he does not seek to prove, though he thinks it is not an unreasonable one. That basic premise?

> God in his revelation is the first principle of Christian theology, from which all the truths of revealed religion are derived.[12]

Henry starts with God, whose existence he assumes, and he bases his theology, including his apologetics, on the assumption that this God has revealed himself clearly for us to know and serve him.

He specifies further that the Scripture is the "verifying principle" of theology, by which he means that no theological statement claiming to be Christian can contradict what has been revealed in the Bible. What the Bible says is true; all theological assertions must conform to the teaching in the Scriptures. In his words, "The inspired scriptures are the proximate and universally accessible form of authoritative divine revelation."[13]

To be sure, Henry believes that God has also revealed himself in the created order, including the mind and conscience of man and in human history, and he insists that "reason is the instrument" for recognizing God's truth, but, always and everywhere, he stands for the full reliability and commanding authority of the Bible as the only standard for evaluating theological statements.

Thus, he denies the priority of reason, of experience, and even of evidences (such as the resurrection of Christ, fulfilled prophecy, and miracles) as sources of "proof" for the Christian faith. Discussing each of these, he shows how they fail to withstand legitimate criticisms from nonbelievers, and how only the assumption that God has revealed him-

---

12. Henry, *GRA* 1:215.
13. Ibid., 1:229.

self (especially in the Bible) provides a firm foundation for demonstrating the truthfulness of the gospel.[14]

He shares this approach with Augustine of Hippo, Martin Luther, John Calvin, Abraham Kuyper, Cornelius Van Til, Francis Schaeffer, Lit-Sen Chang, Leslie Newbigin, John Frame, Alvin Plantinga, and others, most of them in the Reformed wing of Protestantism.[15]

On the other hand, Carl Henry, like all effective apologists, recognizes that many converging lines of evidence point towards the truth of the Christian message. Though he takes his start from the revelation of God in Jesus Christ, the Scriptures that give us our only reliable knowledge of Christ, and the created order, including the mind of man, Henry follows the Bible itself in marshalling a number of arguments to demonstrate the superiority of the gospel to every other worldview.

Thus, he employs reason to arrange and explain the doctrines found in Scripture (which he considers a beautifully coherent system of thought), as well as to expose the inconsistencies and flaws in competing religions and philosophies. Likewise, with evidentialists he fully believes in the historical reliability of the Bible, and spends hundreds of pages in *God, Revelation, and Authority* both laying out the evidence for the historicity—"facticity"—of the great works of God, such as the exodus and the resurrection of Jesus, and in refuting the charges of alleged errors and inconsistencies in the Scriptures that have arisen in the past few centuries.

Henry also exerts a great deal of effort, in several different publications including *God, Revelation and Authority*, to show that the alleged claim of science to have disproved either the existence of God or the truth of the Bible is based both on a misunderstanding of the nature of scientific investigation and of the actual solidity of its vaunted "findings." He does the same with nineteenth- and twentieth-century "negative" (Henry's term) biblical criticism by exposing the multiple

---

14. See especially ibid., 1:216–24.

15. Of course, there are differences among these thinkers. Van Til, in particular, sought to distinguish his method from everyone else's, so that even those who shared his fundamental assumptions were considered wrongheaded. John Frame's exposition in *Cornelius Van Til*, plus a bit of reading in Van Til's *A Christian Theory of Knowledge*, lead me to believe that he and Henry were in basic and wide agreement, despite Van Til's harsh criticism of Henry.

errors of assumption, methodology, and "sure results" of this constantly changing discipline.

The difference between Henry and pure fideists is that he believes the revelation of God to be reasonable and founded upon historical events, and does not presume to require a blind leap of faith. Unlike rationalists, he recognizes that the usual philosophical "proofs" for the existence of God cannot withstand careful logical attack. Finally, though he does all he can to show that the Bible contains no demonstrable historical or even scientific errors, he realizes that there is no such thing as a neutral fact; that all human experience, including science and history, is interpreted; that sensory impressions are not always reliable; and that empirical evidence for the truth of the Scriptures will not be persuasive as a starting point or foundation for proving the truth of God's revelation in the Bible.

In the twentieth century, a number of theologians questioned whether Christians had any common ground with unbelievers when discussing the revelation of God. It seems that Karl Barth denied the validity of reasoning with unbelievers on the basis of any inherent capacity in fallen men to apprehend God's truth. There are no real points of contact between unregenerate and regenerate minds, this school said. At the same time, proponents of classical apologetics have sometimes criticized presuppositionalists like Carl Henry for denying that there are any points of contact with nonbelievers.[16]

Henry replies that "It is true that belief and unbelief have no common axioms, and their entire systems of thought, if consistently developed from their differing axioms, will manifest no common propositions."[17] Nevertheless, both believers and unbelievers, being created in the image of God, possess forms of reasoning and elementary concepts of God that provide common ground and points of contact for the gospel to be heard and either accepted or rejected. That does not mean the unregenerate people can reason themselves to a correct knowledge of God by some sort of "natural theology," but that they are "wired" to receive God's revelation when it comes to them from outside.

16. They similarly criticize Van Til, though inaccurately so, according to John Frame in *Cornelius Van Til*, 415–17.

17. Henry, *GRA* 1:396.

Henry firmly rejects the idea that "man cannot comprehend God's revelation, or that he cannot do so prior to the regenerative or illuminative work of the Holy Spirit."[18] Otherwise, what meaning would evangelism have? If the unbeliever cannot understand anything, why urge him to repent and believe?

He does not thereby intend to state that without the work of the Holy Spirit anyone can savingly hear and believe the gospel, nor does he imagine that the Holy Spirit's illumination is unnecessary for our deeper comprehension of the truths in the Bible. I think that what he did mean to say was that the basic truths the gospel can be mentally understood without the work of the Spirit. In other words, he is trying to combat the idea that revelation is incomprehensible. It must be, at least to some degree, clear enough for people either to believe or reject.

Suppose you tell a man that Jesus is the Son of God who came to die for our sins. He can understand all the words and concepts in this sentence, for they make sense to anyone, without believing that they are true. "Son of God," "die for our sins," etc., can be explained in clear language, by any person. I have heard non-Christian Chinese do just that, and then tell me that the notion is ridiculous! They understood the meaning at one level, but did not receive the message with faith. Proponents of liberal theology can often explain the elements of orthodox Christian faith lucidly, but they vehemently reject traditional—we might say Nicene—Christianity. They might not say that they are regenerate, yet they "understand" the revelation of God mentally.

I think that's all Henry wants to claim at this point.

Even non-biblical religions express our universal longing for ultimate reality, however erroneously they describe that reality or how to live in the light of it. "Faith is a psychological necessity for everyone."[19] Non-Christian religions reflect, therefore, both "[u]niversal divine revelation" and "original sin and its consequences."[20] They thus provide a point of contact for the proclamation of a gospel that acknowledges their quest but challenges their errors.[21]

---

18. Ibid., 1:226.

19. Ibid., 1:404.

20. Ibid., 1:405.

21. See the helpful article Studebaker, "Common Ground."

As C. S. Evans explains, presuppositionalism and evidentialism (including both rational arguments and the historical evidence for the truth of the Bible) can and should be seen as complementary approaches to apologetics. In Carl Henry's work, we see the combination beautifully employed to build a case for the truth of God's revelation in Scripture.[22]

How does this approach work out in practice?

As a presuppositionalist, Henry begins in volume 1 of *God, Revelation, and Authority* with a sustained examination and critique of a variety of alternative worldviews and truth claims. One by one, he demonstrates their failure to construct a solid case. Along the way, he exposes the weaknesses of logical positivism, which, as an extreme form of empiricism, insisted that only empirically verifiable statements have meaning. He shows how the concept of myth, which was meant to bypass the criticisms emanating from the "assured results" of modern science and of modern biblical criticism, does justice neither to the Bible's own claim to be historically true nor to the demands of meaningful theological exposition.

Modern Western philosophical attacks on biblical revelation receive the most detailed treatment, and come up lacking. Finally, Henry tries to elucidate the superiority of divine revelation as the only valid source and conduit of reliable information about unseen realities, and even of any clarity about the significance of experience (including history and science).

In the opening volume, chapter 4, "Ways of Knowing," stands out as programmatic for the entire series, and may be one of Henry's major contributions to apologetics and the theory of knowledge in general.

In Volumes 2 though 6, Henry both expounds a comprehensive doctrine of the knowledge of God (2–4) and then of God himself (5–6). At all points, however, he enters the lists against those who would deny the Bible its full and ultimate reliability and authority. With impressive learning and powerful rhetoric, he deploys all the weapons wielded by evidentialists to defend the claims and truth content of the Bible.

As he lays out the biblical teaching about revelation and about God, Carl Henry deflects, and then breaks, the lances of both "negative" biblical criticism and of scientism. In the process, he shows himself to be a

---

22. Evans, "Approaches to Christian Apologetics," 20–21.

thorough student of both, equally aware of the ever-shifting, constantly revised "findings" of skeptical biblical scholars and scientists. Nowhere does he disparage the value of either literary-historical biblical criticism or of legitimate scientific inquiry. Always and everywhere, however, he challenges their claims to objectivity, accuracy, and finality, citing their own often-conflicting statements and the evidence presented by evangelical scholars and believing scientists.

In the process, Henry degrades—at least for this writer—the two major arguments against either the reliability of the Bible or of orthodox Christian faith. In doing so, he shows how unnecessary it was for what he termed "mediating theologians," especially Barth and others often labeled "Neo-orthodox," to concede as much ground to modern biblical criticism and scientism as they did. The same conclusion would apply, by implication, to recent evangelical spokesmen like Bernard Ramm, Donald Bloesch, Stanley Grenz, Roger Olson, and Clark Pinnock.

Apologetics for the Twenty-first Century[23]

In the introductory article to the *New Dictionary of Christian Apologetics*, William Edgar lays out a program for Christian apologists in the twenty-first century. Reading this essay, I was struck by how many of these emphases we can find in Carl Henry's works.

Henry's Place in the History of Apologetics

Edgar starts with a historical overview, and notes that early church theologians "functioned primarily as apologists." They had to respond to the external threat of persecution, and the internal danger of heresy. In addition, "the church had to define itself in relation to Judaism."[24] Carl Henry, likewise, spoke both to critics outside the organized church and to what he considered to be deviant thinkers within its boundaries. He also expended considerable energy responding to Jewish objections to Christianity.[25]

---

23. Edgar, "Christian Apologetics for a New Century," 3–14.

24. Ibid., 3.

25. See especially Henry, *GRA* 3:8 and 6:20.

Henry resembles Augustine in his ongoing polemic against both pagan detractors and mistaken notions emanating from Christian theologians. Unlike Aquinas, he does not consider the theistic proofs for the existence of God to be persuasive. He follows the Reformers' insistence upon the supreme, even sole, authority of Scripture, and affirms Calvin's awareness of the "noetic effects of sin."

As we have seen, Henry's apologetic approach falls into the category of "presuppositionalism," or what Edgar also terms "transcendental apologetics." Indeed, Henry himself uses this term in volume 1 of *God, Revelation, and Authority*, describing his position as "Religious Transcendental Apriorism." It is "religious" in that it begins with God as revealed in Scripture, as distinct from the position of Kant's "Philosophical (Critical) Transcendental Apriorism." "Apriorism" refers to the belief that we all possess certain innate ways of thinking that come from our creation in the image of God, such as a sense of the difference between right and wrong, truth and falsehood.

Not only have we received certain forms of thinking from God, but (as we saw in our treatment of Henry's doctrine of revelation) also some common content. That is, we all have a sense of God's existence, of his deity, and of his moral demands on us and our failure to meet them. These forms of thought and ideas of God are "hard-wired." They cannot be demonstrated to be true, nor do they need to be, for all our discussions and judgments assume their existence and validity.

Edgar then lists ten issues facing all Christian apologists for this century. As I have said, Carl Henry met each of them head-on in his voluminous writings. *1. "All theology should be apologetic."* In this age of globalism and pluralism, we may no longer merely restate the traditional doctrines along with Scripture proofs. Carl Henry's theology, as we have seen, mixes forceful exposition of biblical Christianity with constant reference to contrary opinions, which he patiently and fairly first presents and then shows to be wanting.

2. Heresy. As in the days of the early church, faced as it was with the twin threats of persecution and heresy, today's apologist will have to "steer believers into the clear distinctions of church and state, the need for loving one's enemies and the need for public justice."[26] Henry met this challenge from the publication of *The Uneasy Conscience of Modern*

---

26. Edgar, "Christian Apologetics for a New Century," 11.

Fundamentalism to the essays and lectures delivered in his advanced old age.

Further, since heresies abound today, the apologist must address and refute errors within the professing Christian community. Throughout his career, Carl Henry expended almost Herculean efforts to understand deviant views propounded by theologians within the church, and to show how they contradicted Scripture. Indeed, he seems to have been a prophet, for such teachings as "open theism" were not formally propounded when he was composing *God, Revelation, and Authority*, yet its pages anticipate them and expose their unbiblical nature in advance.

3. Pluralism and diversity. The issue here is how to live with people who disagree with us, and sometimes even hate us. In his own irenic demeanor, his constant interaction with thinkers of all persuasions, his careful listening to differing opinions, and his prudent prescription for the role of Christians in an increasingly hostile society, Carl Henry offers the kind of "good model" for which Edgar rightly calls.

4. Ethnicity and gender. Henry does not ignore the rise of black theology or of Christian feminism. In Volume 4, chapters 23–25, he examines Marxist theology and liberation theology, from which black theology emerged. A supplementary note in volume 5 addresses "The Feminist Challenge to God-Language." In each case, he measures these new approaches by the standard of Scripture.

5. Globalization. As the mass media, coupled with unprecedented mobility of capital, ideas, and people around the world, create a new "global hyperculture," Edgar rightly insists that "Churches, particularly in urban settings, will have a special responsibility to defend the gospel. . . . More reflection will be needed on the uses and abuses of mass communication."[27] Though Henry could not have foreseen the incredible advance of the Internet, cell phone, and e-mail, he did understand the threat to the gospel posed by mass media. Indeed, the very first chapter in *God, Revelation, and Authority* opens the entire series with the assertion that "the mass media are amazingly adroit in supplying new dimensions to the age-old crisis of word and truth."[28] Henry's perceptive analysis of this novel threat bears careful study.

27. Ibid., 12.
28. Henry, *GRA* 1:24.

6. Intelligent design. This movement did not gain its present moment until after the publication of *God, Revelation, and Authority*, but already in volume 5 Henry spends several chapters (5–9) examining the claims of evolutionism. With an impressive command of the scientific literature, he makes a powerful case for creation by an intelligent God, and marshals evolutionary proponents against each other to expose the fundamental contradictions and weaknesses of Darwinism. A spate of books unmasking the pretensions of evolutionism since the publication of *God, Revelation, and Authority* have vindicated this caution.[29]

7. Philosophical apologetics. Edgar notes the resurgence of evangelical philosophical studies, the efforts of men like John Gerstner and R. C. Sproul to revive classical apologetics, and the work of Alvin Plantinga and Nicholas Wolterstoff, and implies that their use of philosophy to demonstrate inconsistencies in non-biblical views and the rationality and coherence of the Christian faith is valuable in apologetics.

From the beginning of his career, Carl Henry's program included informed engagement with modern philosophy. Though, as we have seen, he did not assign human reason a role in discovering truth, he firmly believed that it could be used to understand God's revelation, under the illuminating guidance of the Holy Spirit. After careful study of competing philosophical positions, he sought not only to shed light on their internal contradictions and unproven assumptions, but also to develop a theology that possessed both fidelity to the Bible and logical coherence.

8. World ethics. Edgar believes that "Apologetics in the new century will interface a good deal more with ethics."[30] Particular issues of moral choice will require attention, for which Carl Henry's three major works on ethics (*Christian Personal Ethics, Aspects of Christian Social Ethics, Baker's Dictionary of Christian Ethics*) may serve as valuable resources. More fundamentally, questions about God's goodness require careful theological analysis, which Henry gives in *God, Revelation, and Authority*, volume 6, chapters 11–14, 20, and a "Supplementary Note on Auschwitz as a Suspension of Providence."

29. See, for example, Behe, *Darwin's Black Box*; Denton, *Evolution*; Johnson, *Darwin on Trial*; and Wells, *Icons of Evolution*, for devastating critiques of this now outmoded way of thinking.

30. Edgar, "Christian Apologetics for a New Century," 13.

Christians must also address a universal sense of guilt. Again, Henry provides a framework for this conversation in his belief that we are all aware of God's moral claims upon us, and in his clear delineation of the saving work of Jesus Christ.

9. *"The shape of meaning."* Edgar includes several related topics under this category: the general question of the meaning of life has now returned to the forefront. Very few descriptions of the various ways in which we try to find meaning, and the Bible's answer to our quest for meaning, can match the powerful essays on "Secular Man and Ultimate Concerns"[31]; "The Meaning or Myths Man Lives By"[32]; his theology of history in "Revelation and History in Evangelical Perspective"[33]; and his chapters on eschatology, "Prophecy and Fulfillment: The Last Days,"[34] "The Awesome Silences of Eternity,"[35] and "The God Who Stays: The Finalities".[36] Indeed, the entire series speaks to the question of meaning in all of its dimensions.

But how do we understand meaning in any text? Here Edgar rightly highlights the necessity for sound hermeneutics, and again Carl Henry comes to our assistance with half of volume 3 dedicated to the meaning of religious language, and specific principles and guidelines for proper interpretation in volume 4.[37]

10. *The gospel.* "The center of apologetics should quite naturally be the center of the Christian message," declares Edgar, and Carl Henry could not agree more. As we saw above, in his personal life—he was an ardent and tireless evangelist in public and in private—and in his writings, he sought to commend the saving message of Jesus Christ. From individual chapters like "A Place in God's Kingdom,[38] "Not by Good Tidings Alone,"[39] "The Only Divine Mediator,"[40] and "The Content of

---

31. Ibid., 8.
32. Ibid., 9.
33. Henry, *GRA* 2:22.
34. Ibid., 3:2.
35. Ibid., 4:26.
36. Ibid., 6:21.
37. Ibid., 4:12–15, 17, 19, 24.
38. Ibid., 2:2.
39. Ibid., 2:3.
40. Ibid., 3:4.

the Gospel,"[41] to the entire thrust of *God, Revelation, and Authority*, Henry "publishes" (one of his favorite words) the good news of salvation by grace through faith in Jesus Christ, in the hope that some will hear, receive, and be born again.

The above evaluation of Carl Henry as apologist should show that his works, especially *God, Revelation, and Authority*, deserve careful perusal in a day when God, revelation, and authority are all denied, doubted, or disregarded.[42]

41. Ibid., 3:5.

42. I can personally attest to his relevance for my own attempts to speak the gospel into the hearts and minds of relativistic Chinese intellectuals over the past two decades.

SEVEN

Prophet for the Twenty-first Century

Though *God, Revelation, and Authority* was written in the 1970s and 1980s, this massive work remains up to date, for Henry could read the signs of the theological times and spot a cloud the size of a man's hand before it became a thunderhead.[1]

Dominance of Mass Media

I shall never forget my surprise when, beginning the first chapter of what I thought was a work on theology, I found in "The Crisis of Truth and Word" a sustained discussion of the pervasive power of the mass media, particularly television.

> Their colossal power over modern life makes of the media an almost superhuman force. . . . Fantastic myth-making possibilities hover over this technocratic world of magic whose creative imagination and artful visualization seem able to shape a new reality almost at will.[2]

Although Henry insists that men and women have always been subject to deception and idol-making, "The mass media . . . are amazingly adroit in supplying new dimensions to the age-old crisis of word and truth."[3] His piercing critique bears quotation at length:

1. This chapter assumes a knowledge of the contents of the previous chapters on Carl Henry's theology and anticipates the detailed response to Henry's critics in Part II. Thus, I make little attempt to document my claims here, since that would be redundant.

2. Henry, *GRA* 1:20.

3. Ibid., 24.

The mass media, especially television, have become the most influential intermediary between the outer world and the modern viewer; they serve in the lives of many as a hypnotic medium possessing almost oracular power. Strategically interposed as the supreme interpretative intermediary, the media cloud the agency of divine revelation, dim the disclosure of God in nature and history, and shroud the claim of the eternal spiritual and moral order on reason and conscience. An electronic intermedium, whereby a technocratic age has shaped unprecedented possibilities of massive mis-belief and unmanageable unbelief, obscure the Mediator, the veritable Logos of God. The media are modern civilization's mightiest middlemen, through which the gods of this age charm and captivate a vagrant generation.[4]

To be sure, Carl Henry—himself a journalist—urged Christians to use the media as the Reformers had turned the printing press into a weapon of truth. Still, his analysis in this opening chapter demonstrated to me both his keen insight into the modern condition and his awareness of the potential for God's Word to recover us from blindness and error.

Thirty years later, this chapter reads like prophecy. He could not have foreseen the explosion of media—including the Internet and the iPod—but he saw the direction in which our civilization was rushing headlong, and correctly posed a return to the written revelation of God as the only antidote to neo-paganism, with its worship of visual images.

The Jesus Movement

Though we may think of the "Jesus Movement" of the 1970s as ancient history and irrelevant to our current situation, this momentous awakening among young people has had continuing impact upon evangelical Christianity. For one thing, many of today's Christian leaders and church members were brought to faith in Christ during those tumultuous and heady years.

For another, the emotionalism and anti-intellectualism that characterized the movement—part of the general revolt against the modernity of the times—have had profound effects on Christianity around

4. Ibid., 29.

the world ever since. One need only listen to some contemporary worship songs that resemble Hindu mantras, with endless repetitions of a few phrases, to see the fruits of the slogan-based piety characteristic of the Jesus Movement. Turn to the pages of almost any popular Christian magazine, or look at advertisements for youth programs, and you see the hallmarks of an essentially subjective and experience-based approach whose roots reach down into the 1960s and 1970s.

Carl Henry saw this coming. He lauded the enthusiasm, zeal, and sincerity of the massive turning to Christ among young people in the 1970s, but openly worried about the staying power of the faith they believed and proclaimed.

> At the present, while it lacks intellectual roots and is isolated from the visible church, the Jesus movement seems hardly distinguishable from many another religiously motivated ideological rebellion. . . . [The] theological sterility that pervades many congregations, except for isolated and surface intellectual concerns, characterizes much of the Jesus movement also. . . . Its doctrinal content is rather minimal. For this reason it easily falls prey to certain emphases in evangelism that hurry over problems of the mind in calling people to spiritual decision. . . . [It] tends to be intellectually shallow and doctrinally tolerant, accommodating subbiblical and even heretical concepts for the sake of "Christian love."[5]

His warnings have proven to be prophetic and relevant today.

Karl Barth's Continuing Influence

Even a cursory reading of *God, Revelation, and Authority* will reveal Henry's immense respect for Karl Barth. He quotes Barth hundreds of times, often appreciatively. He understood the power of Barth's mind and the potency of his refutation of classical liberalism. At the same time, he could not accept a number of Barth's fundamental assumptions and claims. He rejected a dialectical approach to Christian doctrine, and occasionally simply quotes a typical Barthian passage, with endless qualifications, modifiers, and contradictory statements, to show the irrationality of some of the Swiss theologian's assertions. He decried Barth's apparently passive acceptance of much German skeptical bibli-

5. Ibid., 132.

cal criticism, and also his flight into another type of history to escape confrontation with what appeared to be "the assured results" of modern criticism, not to mention the immensely prestigious claims of modern science.

Henry believed that one could build Christian faith upon a more solid foundation than the subjective encounter, revelation-as-response theory of Barth. To be sure, he praised Barth for his unflinching acceptance of traditional Christian doctrines, and his basically functional approach to biblical authority, but he thought that these rested upon shaky epistemological grounds.

Henry spent so much time refuting Barth precisely because he saw how attractive Barthianism was and would continue to be. In this he was right. Barth's influence may have diminished in some circles, but among evangelicals his fundamental approaches have gained wide and growing acceptance.[6]

Mark Ellingson has pointed to the burgeoning evangelical acceptance of neo-orthodoxy, with its stress on the personal element in revelation:

> A growing number of Evangelicals are making several pivotal modifications of earlier views: first, that Scripture is a narrative and needs to be interpreted in light of that narrative's intent and form; second, that the Word of God is primarily that which points to a Person, and only secondarily to the primary witness to that Person as recorded in Scriptures; that reason is limited and not all-encompassing; and fourth, that truth is not to be understood strictly in terms of correspondence, but that dynamic response, obedience, and effectiveness in regard to intent are just as decisive in one's conceptualization of truth.[7]

---

6. See, for example, Livingston and Fiorenza, *Modern Christian Thought*, 409: "Many Evangelicals have turned to Barth as the most viable theological alternative between what they see as a moribund rationalist theology represented by Carl Henry on the one hand and various Liberal theologies of 'correlation' on the other." Outstanding among these theologians are Donald Bloesch, Bernard Ramm, Gregory Bolich (to some degree), and Roger Olson.

7. Ellingsen, *Evangelical Movement*, 171–72.

Capitulation to Modern "Science"

Though not committed to young-earth creationism, Carl Henry refused to lie down and play dead in the face of the nearly universal acceptance of evolutionary theory as proven scientific fact. His chapters on creation in volume 5 demonstrate his clear grasp of scientific method, his understanding of the philosophy of science, his awareness of the many weaknesses of Darwinian theory, and the fundamental flaws and limitations of much of modern science.

In contrast to Bernard Ramm and others who strongly believe that evangelicals should not repeat the Scopes Trial fiasco, Henry studied evolutionary theory carefully and saw how its chief exponents often contradict each other. In this way he was truly prophetic, for the past twenty years have witnessed a flood of scientific and philosophical refutations of a theory that is increasingly being rejected on *scientific* grounds.[8] The day when Darwinists and members of the Flat Earth Society are consigned to the fringes of the academy may not be as far off as most people think.

Even deeper is Henry's fundamental critique of the dominance of "science" in modern life, and in particular its claim to be the exclusive avenue to, and arbiter of, essential truths. I put "science" in quotation marks, for no one, including Carl Henry, will deny the immense achievements of true science. What he objects to is "scientism."

As Craig Gay put it so well:

> It is important to stress that Protestant theology has continued to suffer from a crippling inability to evaluate the claims of science *theologically*. Indeed, the same displacement of theology by scientific understanding that first surfaced in the seventeenth century still plagues North American evangelicalism.[9]

Those who criticize Henry as being too negative about science love to refer to Charles Hodge, B. B. Warfield, and J. Gresham Machen, who were quite open to some aspects of Darwinian theory. But perhaps they were just swept along by the tide of their times—and ours. In multiple

8. See, for example: Behe, *Darwin's Black Box*; Dembski, *Intelligent Design*; Denton, *Evolution*; Johnson, *Darwin on Trial*; Wells, *Icons of Evolution*, and Wilder-Smith, *Man's Origin, Man's Destiny* and for devastating critiques of this now-outmoded way of thinking.

9. Gay, *Way of the (Modern) Word*, 117.

chapters of *God, Revelation, and Authority*, as well as previously published symposia, Henry shows that the claims of modern scientists to possess the key to knowledge and truth rest on superficial—and false—philosophical assumptions. He loves to point out how the "findings" of science are regularly overturned and refuted by later discoveries, and how the constantly-revised textbooks hardly ever admit previous errors of fact and interpretation.

When Bernard Ramm and others fault Henry for not taking science seriously enough, it seems that they do not fully understand either his profound analyses of scientific theories and methods or the true fragility of the latest scientific pronouncements. Evolutionary dogmatism is only one example among many, as Henry makes clear.[10]

Postmodern Attacks on "Modern" Rationality

Likewise, Carl Henry's strictures against the idolatry and "neutral" human reason throughout *God, Revelation, and Authority* anticipate the postmodern rejection of Enlightenment faith in human reason and its major manifestation, credulous acceptance of the scientific model as normative for all human thinking.[11] Long before postmodernism became popular as a movement, even within Christian circles, Henry unmasked human reason's claim to neutrality and showed that all argument proceeds from often-unacknowledged premises.

What we now call postmodernism appears already in *God, Revelation, and Authority*, as Henry observes a climate of thought in which "All that man does and achieves is shadowed by transience and relativity. Within this context of existence his station and role and all his sociohistorical institutions are conditioned by his social environment, which alone shapes and sharpens his capacities. Nothing traditional is sacrosanct."[12]

"In keeping with the modern erosion of faith in the supernatural, the decline of confidence in reason, and the nonontological orientation of contemporary science, secular scholars now routinely explain the

10. E.g., Henry, *GRA* 1:4, 10; 6:5–9, as well as the symposium he edited, *The Horizons of Science*.

11. A helpful analysis of the legitimate concerns of postmodernism can be found in Vanhoozer, "Theology and Apologetics," 36–39.

12. Henry, *GRA* 1:136.

universal phenomenon of convictional frameworks in terms of histori-cal contingency."[13]

Already in the 1970s and 80s, Carl Henry saw the coming revolt against Enlightenment rationalism that has come to be known as post-modernism. Discussing "Theology and Science," he noted that the latter has never been fully impartial and dispassionate, but that its reputation for bloodless and detached inquiry provoked a "countercultural revolt against technocratic impersonalism, in which [quoting W. J. Neidhardt] 'some of our brightest youth have adopted an extreme form of existen-tialism in which feeling alone is meaningful and rational analysis of no significance.'"[14]

Long before science was taken to task for its presumptuous claim to primacy in worldview building, Henry had demonstrated the narrow scope of even legitimate scientific investigation, its dependence upon assumptions that it could not prove by the scientific method, and the highly tentative nature of its "findings." Christians in revolt against the hegemony of rationalism and scientism would find a strong ally in Carl Henry—if they took the time to read him.

His rejection of autonomous human reason as the starting point for either theology or apologetics, and his refusal to admit non-biblical categories as norms for theological truth, highlight the prophetic nature of his theological project. Indeed, he was a major force in the demolition of modern thinking for the thousands of young evangelical scholars who read his articles and sat under his teaching, even if *God, Revelation, and Authority* remains a largely-unread *coup de grace* to the modern worldview.

Roger Olson notes that Henry saw and opposed postmodernism: He was a "'voice in the wilderness' of modern and postmodern subjec-tivism, irrationalism, and relativism."[15]

"If there is any one group of thinkers with whom Henry stands in greatest tension it is younger, progressive Evangelicals who wish to push the boundaries of traditional conservative theology by flirting with postmodernity."[16]

13. Ibid., 156.
14. Ibid., 172.
15. Olson, "Carl F. H. Henry," 490.
16. Ibid., 493.

Acceptance of "Negative" Biblical Criticism

Bernard Ramm and others discount Henry's theology because he does not give due respect to modern biblical criticism.[17] In the next chapter we shall see how unfounded is that charge. Here let us note only that Henry spends a great deal of space in *God, Revelation, and Authority* responding to the assumptions, methods, and supposed "sure results" of modern biblical criticism. Though he by no means rejects all the genuine contributions that biblical critics have made to our understanding of the Bible, Henry refuses to accept most of what he terms "negative" biblical criticism.

His dialogue with modern biblical criticism occupies hundreds of pages of *God, Revelation, and Authority*, including comments in virtually every chapter of the last four volumes, but occasionally he tackles the issue head-on, as in "Divine Authority and Scriptural Authority,"[18] where he gives examples of "spectacular critical reversals" to demonstrate the unreliability of an approach based on skeptical assumptions. See also his assessment of modern biblical criticism in "The Uses and Abuses of Historical Criticism."[19]

In all this Henry was prophetic, for some evangelical theologians and historians (such as Ramm, Bloesch, and Olson) still appear to grant far too much authority to the continually corrected "results" of non-evangelical biblical scholarship. Such concessions seem all the more unnecessary in the light of the tremendous growth of evangelical biblical studies in the past three decades, which have essentially nullified most of what passed for orthodoxy in my days at a prestigious liberal seminary.

Flight from Biblical Inerrancy

Likewise, erosion of belief in the inerrancy of the Bible, already evident in Henry's day, has increased since then. Again, the voices of Bernard Ramm, Donald Bloesch, Clark Pinnock and some commentators in the

---

17. Ramm writes that Henry's "monumental effort stumbles because he glosses biblical criticism." (*After Fundamentalism*, 26–27).

18. Henry, *GRA* 4, ch. 4.

19. Ibid., ch. 17.

otherwise evangelical Word Biblical Commentary series carry great influence in evangelical circles today.[20]

Aside from the legitimate questions of apparent errors of numbers, divergent accounts of the same incident in the Gospels and Old Testament historical books, and the relationship of our current texts to the original autographs, these people believe that modern science and biblical criticism have made any claim to inerrancy indefensible. Many polls by George Barna confirm the findings of James Hunter that "forty percent of all Evangelical theologians have now abandoned the belief in the inerrancy of Scripture."[21] As we have noted above, Henry exposes the weaknesses of the anti-inerrancy position.[22]

The Advance of Evangelical Feminism

What had only begun to appear in the 1970s and 80s has become a major, and perhaps dominant, trend among evangelicals since the 1990s. Even in formerly conservative denominations, such as the Presbyterian Church in America, women have been accorded roles previously denied them. True, the PCA has refused to ordain women as elders; the Southern Baptist Convention has issued strong statements supporting the traditional, complementarian view of the roles of men and women in the family; and the Council on Biblical Manhood and Womanhood has also launched a vigorous counterattack. But hardly anyone can fail to notice the presence of women as plenary speakers at widely publicized conferences, on seminary faculties, and in the pulpit—not to mention televangelism programs.

Carl Henry discerned the theological and biblical issues involved in this complex matter, and wrote about the "Feminist Challenge to God Language" in a supplementary note to his chapter on "Personality in the Godhead."[23] He realized that the question of the roles of women

---

20. Roger Olson seems also to favor the view that the Bible contains errors of fact concerning history and science. See, for example, Olson, "Inspiration," in *Westminster Handbook*, 215–18.

21. Hunter, *Evangelicalism*, 31.

22. He also addresses the traditional objections to inerrancy in many places, including the chapter "Perspective on Problem Passages" in vol. 4, much of which is devoted to a definition and defense of the infallibility and inerrancy of Scripture.

23. Henry, *GRA* 5:7.

in the church and in the home was aimed, ultimately, at the nature of God, and of man and woman as created in his image. Recent developments in mainline denominations, and the furious debate over "gender-neutral" versions of the New International Version of the Bible, show how prescient he was.[24]

Openness Theology

Though so-called openness theology had not emerged as an explicit challenge to traditional theology while Henry was composing *God, Revelation, and Authority*, its main source, process theology, and its first cousin, the "theologies of hope," receive sustained attention in that work.[25]

As we have seen, unlike Moltmann and Pannenberg, Henry sees little "history" in God, for whose eternal continuity he argues strenuously. Though he firmly believes that God is living and active, and not at all the "unmoved Mover" of Aristotle or even Thomas, Henry will not grant the sort of change and development—much less any sort of mutual interdependence with the world—that Whitehead, Hartshorne, • Pinnock, Boyd and others propose. The God of the Bible is the fully transcendent Creator who stands outside, above, and beyond the world and who directs all that happens in human history.

Critics have shown both the origins of openness theology in process theology, and the invalidity of its rejection of traditional theism. Indeed, much of what Pinnock, Boyd, and others assert is nothing but a caricature, bearing little resemblance to the God either of the Bible or of orthodox Christianity.[26]

Not only do they distort the picture of God's unchanging nature that classical theism has drawn from the Bible, but they portray his universal sovereignty as the attitude and actions of a horrible despot. Everything about this picture is suspect, and in no way corresponds to the evangelical theology they so heartily reject. A careful reading

24. The Council on Biblical Manhood and Womanhood (http://www.cbmw.org) carries on the work of Henry and other scholars in a journal and various scholarly and popular books that question the legitimacy of feminist hermeneutics and exegesis.

25. A very succinct but cogent critique of process theism may be found in Vanhoozer, "Theology and Apologetics," 37.

26. See, for example, Brand, "Genetic Defects or Accidental Similarities?"

of Carl Henry might have saved them and their followers from a great deal of confusion. In particular, his chapters on the timelessness, omniscience, immutability, and sovereignty of God,[27] as well as the chapters on process philosophy,[28] and numerous references to process philosophy and process theology throughout *God, Revelation, and Authority,* elucidate the case for classical theism against the extreme Arminianism of openness theology. Chapters 17–22 in volume 2 respond to various other views of revelation and history and include a statement of an evangelical perspective.

Evangelicalism's Empty Core

As Roger Olson has correctly pointed out, Carl Henry labored to warn against the hollowing out of evangelical theology and preaching.[29] Throughout *God, Revelation, and Authority* and in dozens of articles and speeches, Henry deplored the anti-intellectualism of much of modern evangelicalism, its focus on numerical growth, and its seeking emotional experiences rather than a stronger faith, hope, and love founded upon a firm trust in God's written revelation.

He was pleased, of course, to have had a part in the founding of the Evangelical Theological Society, and to see evangelical scholarship emerge from the margins to assume a position of begrudged equality in the academy. On the other hand, he deplored what he considered to be the "dumbing-down" of *Christianity Today* into a popular journal appealing to a wider audience than its earlier readership, and saw that move as symptomatic of a general drift away from rigorous thought and serious reflection among Christians. The church growth movement, with its concentration (at least at first) on numerical increase, and the rise of the megachurches in America, with their "seeker-friendly" services devoid of solid biblical teaching, greatly concerned him. He feared that they revealed an irrationalism that would leave Christians defense-

27. Henry, *GRA* 5, chs. 12–16.

28. Henry, *GRA* 4, chs. 2–4.

29. Olson, *Westminster Handbook,* 41. As we shall see in the following chapter though much of Olson's description of Henry's theology is barely adequate, he is guilty of a number of errors of fact, and seems not to understand the soul of Henry's thought. He uses terms like "rationalism" and "rationalistic" as labels that effectively simplify Henry's position without really coming to grips with it.

less against the shifting tides of cultural fads—a fear that George Barna's polls of evangelical Christians seem to have substantiated.

The Collapse of the West

Carl Henry stands in the line of Old Testament prophets, twentieth-century Jeremiahs like Aleksandr Solzhenitsyn, and the Lord Jesus Christ himself in exposing the moral declension of our "wicked and perverse generation" and warning of the apocalypse to come. Listen to his words when receiving an honorary doctorate from a Christian university in 1979:

> The stench of moral decay fouls the air as society is victimized by its own self-destructive vices. . . . The fault lines that open our land to impending disaster seems increasingly to penetrate the very heart of modern culture. The tremors that presage God's final shaking of the earth reflect ever more blatant sin and indecency. Explosive forces are rumbling at the core of modern life;
> • our civilization too may soon collapse into the same debris of human corruption that engulfed all past civilizations.[30]

Again:

> • We live in the twilight of a great civilization, amid the deepening decline of modern culture. . . . We are so steeped in the antichrist philosophy—namely, that success consists in embracing not the values of the Sermon on the Mount but an infinity of material things, of sex and status—that we little sense how much of what passes for practical Christianity is really an apostate compromise with the spirit of the age.[31]

Many similar passages can be found throughout *God, Revelation, and Authority*, as Henry detailed the intellectual bankruptcy of modern Western culture, the fatal concessions of prominent theologians, the doctrinal hollowness of much of evangelical Christianity, and the consequent moral relativism and worsening degradation of our society. In "The Christian and Political Duty," Henry continues his "Plea for Evangelical Demonstration" and concludes, "The alternatives are

---

30. Henry, "Crisis of Our Times," 147–48.
31. Henry, "Barbarians Are Coming," 15.

clear: either we return to the God of the Bible or we perish in the pit of lawlessness."[32]

He foresaw the corrosive corruption of conduct that inevitably follows compromising absolute truth, and spared no efforts to arouse evangelicals from their slumber to serve as salt and light in a decaying and darkened world. How prophetic his warnings seem now! Who would have imagined, even then, the explosion of divorce among professing Christians, the fall of so many prominent preachers and pastors, the pervasive immorality of all sorts among church-going youth, and the self-absorbed hedonism that mark evangelical Christianity in America today?

Carl Henry, with an eye to history, a mind focused on the timeless truths of God, and a heart pounding with apprehension for the imminent collapse of a culture that once widely reflected the blessings flowing from some sort of commitment to biblical revelation, cried out in warning.[33]

And yet, like the prophets of old, Carl Henry never lost hope. Not hope in America, which he feared was beyond saving, but a firm confidence in the promises of God. His final chapter, "The Finalities," rings with assurance that God's will *shall* be done, his kingdom *shall* come, and "the earth shall be filled with the knowledge of God, as the waters cover the sea."

> God who *stands* and *stoops* and *speaks* is God who *stays*: he it is who preserves and governs and consummates his cosmic purpose. But the awesome wonder of the biblical revelation is not his creation and preservation of our vastly immense and complex universe. Its wonder, rather, is that he came as God-man to planet Earth in the form of the Babe of Bethlehem; he thus reminds us that no point of the universe is too remote for his presence and no speck too small for his care and love. He came as God-man to announce to a rebellious race the offer of a costly mercy grounded in the death and resurrection of his only Son and to assure his people that he who *stays* will remain with them forever and they with him. He has come in Christ incarnate to exhibit ideal human nature and will return in Christ glorified to fully implement the Omega-realities of the dawning future.[34]

32. Henry, GRA 6:454.
33. Henry's role is mentioned also in Gasaway, "As a Matter of Fact," 61.
34. Henry, GRA 6:513.

EIGHT

Carl Henry and His Critics I

The previous chapters have delineated certain key features of Carl Henry's theology, especially as it is expressed in *God, Revelation, and Authority*. In the following three chapters, I shall attempt to respond to specific charges brought against Henry, particularly by evangelical theologians.[1]

Since we are going back over ground already covered, there will be a good deal of repetition, as I cite Henry's words to counter the criticisms of others. From one standpoint, these chapters should be unnecessary, for I think you will see that most of the criticisms seem to stem from either ignorance or misunderstanding of Carl Henry's works, including and especially *God, Revelation, and Authority*.

To substantiate that claim, however, I need to impose upon the reader's patience and quote Henry at some length. I beg your indulgence as I seek to demonstrate the inaccuracy of the standard claims made against Carl Henry's theology by prominent scholars.

To be sure, responsible critics have challenged him at different points. For example, Michael Horton argues that Henry's belief that scriptural descriptions of God are univocal rather than merely analogical makes one vulnerable to the errors of open theism.[2] I think Horton is incorrect, but acknowledge this to be a question worthy of debate,

---

1. More or less negative assessments of Carl Henry's theological project may be found in works by Harvie Conn, David Ford, James Livingston, Gabriel Fackre, Donald Bloesch, Bernard Ramm, Clark Pinnock, James White, Stanley Grenz, and especially Roger Olson in *20th Century Theology* (with Stanley Grenz), *Story of Theology*, and *Westminster Handbook*.

2. Horton, "Hellenistic or Hebrew?," 227.

and students of theology may decide for themselves whether Horton or Henry makes the better case.[3]

Other charges lack much basis, however, as I shall now proceed to try to demonstrate.

Not a Systematic Theologian

Olson and Grenz assert that Henry "published no systematic theology." Instead, he was a "type of theological journalist, describing and critiquing theological currents as they emerged."[4] They repeat that statement later: "He has never been a systematic theologian . . . he has never produced a systematic theology. Rather than a systematician, Henry is perhaps better characterized as a commentator on the fortunes of theology."[5] A theological journalist, if you will.[6] Because he "never tackled the challenge of delineating a complete systematic theology," "his writings reflect certain glaring omissions."[7]

They acknowledge the size and scope of *God, Revelation and Authority*, but complain that "even here Henry cannot but repeatedly engage in analysis of contemporary theological currents."[8]

First let me note the use of rhetoric and assertion, unsupported by solid evidence. Notice also that Grenz and Olson imply either timidity or laziness on the part of Henry, who, they say, "never tackled the challenge" of writing a complete systematic theology. Or the implication that Henry was merely a journalist who responded to others' errors, for despite the length of *God, Revelation, and Authority*, "even here" Henry cannot but comment on the views of others.

This claim—widely repeated—that Carl Henry was "not a systematic theologian" flies in the face of several hard facts: Henry's first doctorate was in systematic theology. He claims to be doing systematic theology at many points in *God, Revelation, and Authority*.[9] Throughout

---

3. Henry deals with the univocal, as opposed to analogical, nature of language about God in *GRA* 3:363–66; 5:86, 131, 148, 233, 262, 355, 369.

4. Grenz and Olson, *20th Century Theology*, 289.

5. Ibid., 291.

6. Ibid., 289.

7. Ibid., 296–97.

8. Ibid., 291.

9. E.g., Henry, *GRA* 5:334, 376.

that work, he engages in sustained systematic theology. He starts, like many before and since, with the doctrine of the Word of God in volumes 1–4. Volume 1 serves as a prolegomenon; the following three outline a doctrine of revelation. Volumes 5 and 6 treat the doctrine of God—theology proper.

Let us admit that these six volumes do not constitute a *complete* systematic theology. Fair enough. But they are nothing if they are not *at least* systematic theology. Furthermore, even the first four volumes, ostensibly treating only one doctrine (revelation), include extensive discussions of other loci of theology: Christology, anthropology, soteriology, ecclesiology, and eschatology—to name a few of the more prominent ones. In two previous volumes, Henry had dealt with personal ethics and social ethics—also traditional categories for the systematic theologian.[10]

Why emphasize this point? To give evidence for my bold claim that Henry's critics seem either not to have read his work carefully, or that they evaluate him in a way differently from their evaluation of other theologians (such as Bernard Ramm, for example). That being the case, we can expect their other charges to lack sufficient basis as well.[11]

Other Criticisms

It seems to me that almost all the criticisms of Henry's theology fall into one of two categories:

He is faulted for not having taken the Enlightenment seriously enough. That is, he is *not modern enough*, having failed to address the attacks of science, philosophy, and biblical criticism upon the inspiration and authority of the Bible and on the traditional Christian theology that now finds expression among conservative evangelicals, for whom he is the acknowledged spokesman.

---

10. Henry, *Christian Personal Ethics* and *Aspects of Christian Social Ethics.*

11. The same is true for the critique of Robert Trembath in his *Divine Revelation*, 31–58. Despite an apparently careful reading of Henry, closer examination of Trembath's argument must lead to the conclusion that he came to *GRA* with some assumptions and disagreements, and found ways to validate these. His superficial criticism appears logically tight and rigid, but rests upon such a limited knowledge of *GRA* and obvious misunderstanding that it does not deserve to be refuted in detail here.

On the other hand, Henry is also described as an unwitting product of the Enlightenment, one who relied too much on human reason, believed too firmly in propositional truth, and valued coherence and consistency too highly. These critics say that Henry is *too modern,* and represents an era that is hopelessly out of date in our new postmodern environment.

As a sort of compendium of some of the criticisms leveled against Henry, we may cite the words of Gordon Lewis and Bruce Demarest. In their otherwise very impressive and most helpful work, *Integrative Theology*, they argue for the superiority of their approach by contrasting it with systematic theology. They go on:

> Apparently unmoved by charges like those above are presuppositionalists (such as Cornelius Van Til and Rousas Rushdoony) and the deductive rationalists (such as Gordon Clark and Carl Henry). Valuable as the contribution of these writers have been in many ways, their presuppositional and axiomatic methodologies remain unchanged. Consequently, charges of *a priori* assumptions of the things to be proved, eisegesis, insufficient attention to the history of the doctrines, closed-mindedness, indoctrination, and insufficient relevance continue to limit the extent of their outreach and impact.[12]

Not "Modern" Enough

Biblical Interpretation and Criticism

Scholars who largely accept the claims of modern liberal biblical criticism charge Henry with being "less than successful in dealing with historical and critical issues relating to the biblical text and with having an unsteady hand in the area of biblical exegesis."[13] Patterson quotes Bernard Ramm to the effect that "[Henry] stumbles because he glosses biblical criticism," and adds that "Henry still has not come to terms with the Enlightenment."[14]

On the one hand, this is a matter of presuppositions. If you believe that modern biblical criticism over the past hundred years or so has

12. Henry *GRA* 1:24–25.
13. Patterson, *Carl F. H. Henry*, 162.
14. Ibid.

been largely correct, you will not find Henry's approach congenial. On the other hand, the statements above seem hard to justify in the light of *God, Revelation, and Authority*.

First, does Henry "gloss" biblical criticism? The *American Heritage Dictionary of the English Language* gives several definitions of "gloss," none of which fit Ramm's meaning, which seems to be that Henry pays little attention to, or sets aside lightly, modern biblical scholarship. The other possible meaning is "to give a false interpretation to" something.

In either case, even a cursory reading of *God, Revelation, and Authority* would disprove this allegation. For one thing, Henry engages in sustained dialogue with biblical criticism from beginning to end. Modern scholars are referred to countless times, often at considerable length. A glance at the index of any of the volumes (except volume 1, which consists of prolegomena) will show just how widely and deeply Henry had studied dozens of authors. James Barr—perhaps the most influential critic of the views that Henry holds—receives a great deal of attention, but others such as Von Rad (Old Testament) and Bultmann (New Testament) do also. If Ramm means that Henry willfully distorts the writings of biblical critics, I challenge any reader to come up with examples.

These hundreds of references aside, chapter 17 of volume 4, "The Uses and Abuses of Historical Criticism," addresses the issue head on. After a survey of different evaluations of the role of modern biblical criticism, Henry notes that "we must abandon all claims to its absolute neutrality, since a presuppositionless methodology is an absurdity and, in fact, an impossibility."[15]

Louis Igou Hodges points out that Carl Henry has no fewer than ten "guidelines for the proper use of historical criticism"—hardly possible for one who was supposed to have ignored modern biblical criticism![16]

Henry's own view is that "What is objectionable is not the historical-critical method, but rather the alien presuppositions to which neo-

---

15. Henry, *GRA* 4:388.

16. Hodges, "New Dimensions in Scripture," 228. Hodges refers to Henry's writings on Scripture frequently in this excellent evaluation of recent views of the doctrine of Scripture. He also warns against unnecessary and often acrimonious public disputes between evangelicals, a warning Clark Pinnock, writing in the same volume, seems not to have heeded. See the chapter "Carl Henry and His Critics II" in this volume.

Protestant scholars subject it."[17] "Freed from the arbitrary assumptions of critics who manipulate it in a partisan way, the method is neither destructive of biblical truth nor useless to Christian faith; even though its proper role is a limited one, it is highly serviceable as a disciplined investigative approach to past historical events."[18] Here, of course, Henry disagrees with fundamentalists, who have insisted that the methods of biblical criticism themselves are suspect.

Exegesis

Perhaps even more serious is the claim that Henry engages in poor exegesis. After all, if his understanding of the Bible is wrong, his theology does not possess much value.

Here again I would ask for evidence. As part of the process of preparing an abridgment of the Chinese edition of God, *Revelation, and Authority*, I read the entire work closely; since then, I have gone through it again. The Scripture references run into the thousands. Having studied at a liberal seminary, I am familiar with that approach. Since then, my own study, preaching, and teaching (New Testament, systematic theology, hermeneutics) have made me sensitive to the necessity of exegetical precision and accuracy. In only a very few places—no more than half a dozen—have I questioned Henry's exegesis.[19] Thus, I wonder whether Ramm and others are merely saying that they disagree with Henry, rather than that he "stumbles" in his handling of the Bible.

Backwardness

As noted earlier, Patterson observes that some have claimed that "Henry still has not come to terms with the Enlightenment."[20]

For example, Olson and Grenz, in *20th Century Theology*, although citing those who acclaim Carl Henry as "the prime interpreter of evangelical theology, one of its leading theoreticians" and "one of

17. Henry, *GRA* 4:393.

18. Ibid., 4:01.

19. I am not sure whether he is right about the meaning of YHWH (and he merely states his opinion after surveying a variety of options); his interpretation of "phōtizō" in John 1:9; his interpretations of Genesis 1 and of Romans 2:14–15.

20. Patterson, *Carl F. H. Henry*, 162.

the theological luminaries of the twentieth century," describe Henry as one of those who "turn their faces away from modern theology in any form."[21] Again: "Some have rejected him as a type of throwback to an earlier, even pre-Enlightenment, era in theological history."[22]

In contrast, Bernard Ramm, they claim, "represents those who have turned their faces toward modern thinking, in his case, toward contemporary scientific advances and the approach to modern learning advocated by neo-orthodoxy, especially by Karl Barth."[23] This approach "would allow Ramm to move beyond the tighter categories of others in the evangelical movement and at the end of his career call for his colleagues to embrace a basically Barthian paradigm for theology 'after fundamentalism.'"[24]

Grenz and Olson continue: "With his more profound understanding of the positive contributions of the Enlightenment, Ramm was able to move beyond the backward-looking approach of Carl Henry. . . . [He] provided the foundation for a generation of younger evangelical thinkers who would build on the freedom to think critically and engage in positive dialog with modern culture."[25] Note the rhetoric here: to turn the face "away from" or "toward"; "throwback," "backward." All these words are more than descriptive; they imply values and paint a portrait: old fashioned, backward, out of date. Bernard Ramm is later described as "The Irenic Evangelical"—again in implied contrast to Henry. Ramm, it is asserted, was a "thoughtful conservative, one who was able to meet the contemporary intellectual challenges with integrity."[26]

So, Henry—by implication, and to repeat these serious claims—tried to ignore, or reverse, the gains of the Enlightenment; to turn back the theological clock. He turned his face away from modern theology and science. Unlike men such as Ramm and Karl Barth, he failed to "engage in positive dialog with modern culture." He somehow lacked "the freedom to think critically." He did not "meet the contemporary intellectual challenges with integrity."

21. Grenz and Olson, *20th Century Theology*, 288.
22. Ibid., 297.
23. Ibid.
24. Ibid., 298.
25. Ibid., 309.
26. Ibid., 299.

What, we may legitimately ask, does all this mean?

Was Henry unaware of the Enlightenment, or modern biblical criticism, or modern science, or modern theology? Surely not, for his writings are filled with numberless citations of authors since the seventeenth century. He quotes, and responds to, literally hundreds of writers whose positions can be called "modern" in every sense of the word, as well as those who presage what we now call "postmodern" thought.

We have already seen that he carried on a running conversation with modern biblical criticism. He is also known as a major evangelical student of, and commentator on, modern philosophy and theology, as his many columns in *Christianity Today*, his edited volumes,[27] at least seven major monographs,[28] and virtually every page in *God, Revelation, and Authority* attest. Chapter 10 of volume 1 consists of an analysis of the respective roles and relative merits of theology and modern philosophy.

Throughout *God, Revelation, and Authority*, Henry is not afraid to challenge what used to be called the "assured results" of modern biblical criticism. As anyone who has followed the fortunes of this field of study for more than a decade knows, its "facts" and "conclusions" have been refuted hundreds of times by archaeology, history, and better exegesis. Often, what passes for biblical criticism is merely the application of yet another set of assumptions to the text, producing a novel interpretation that later research shows to be unwarranted. Already, much of what I was taught in a very good liberal seminary only forty years ago is obsolete. The Graf-Wellhausen hypothesis of the Pentateuch has been either complicated and qualified beyond recognition, or shredded by both evidence and exegesis. The reign of Bultmann's demythologizing and some of the extreme assertions of form criticism and redaction criticism in New Testament studies ended long ago. They are now considered part of the "history of interpretation." So, who is "backward" and "outdated"?

As for modern science, Henry devotes several chapters in *God, Revelation, and Authority* to the relationship of modern science to

27. Such as Henry, *Christian Faith and Modern Theology*.

28. *Reaching the Modern Mind*; *The Protestant Dilemma*; *Fifty Years of Protestant Theology*; *The Drift of Western Thought*; *Evangelical Responsibility in Contemporary Theology*; *Frontiers in Modern Theology*; *Faith at the Frontiers*.

theology, and edited a symposium on the subject.[29] Early in volume 1, in "Theology and Science," Henry explores the relative merits of each discipline. In the process, he displays an impressive awareness of then-current debates on the nature, methods, assumptions, and limits of modern science. By no means does he disparage the very real achievements of modern science—indeed, he repeatedly refers to them—but he does question the legitimacy of some of the assumptions and conclusions about ultimate reality offered by some scientists that go far beyond the evidence they have adduced.

The chapters on creation in volume 6 of *God, Revelation and Authority* demonstrate Henry's familiarity with the scientific dimensions of this question. To take only one example, his treatment of various views of the origin of the world in volume 6 demonstrates wide reading and critical assessment of dozens of works by eminent scientists. While not insisting upon a literal twenty-four-hour–day, six-day creation, he does point out the manifold difficulties in evolutionary theory, almost entirely by showing the contradictions within the evolutionary camp itself. Had he written *God, Revelation, and Authority* a few years later, he could have drawn upon a growing range of scientific studies that have appeared in recent years demonstrating the very weak case for macroevolutionary theory.[30] With more and more scientists abandoning the sinking ship of Darwinian evolutionism, those who accuse Henry of doubting its claims may end up on the wrong side of history.

Thus, it is hard to understand how anyone could assert that Henry "turned his face away from modern . . . science." So, perhaps Henry was not turning his face away from modern science, philosophy, and theology, but casting a critical eye on some projects whose wide acceptance may not be warranted. Maybe his offense was to show just how weak are the foundations of scientific theory, how subjective are its assumptions, how tentative are many of its "conclusions"—whose constant revision in textbooks goes largely unnoticed—and how little a challenge it really offers to a theology based upon the Bible.

---

29. Henry, *Horizons of Science*.

30. These include: Denton, *Evolution*; Wells, *Icons of Evolution*; Dembski, *Intelligent Design*; Behe, *Darwin's Black Box*; Johnson, *Darwin on Trial*; and Wilder-Smith, *Man's Origin, Man's Destiny*; plus multiple articles by scholars such as the mathematician Berlinski.

These, charges, then, are either meaningless, or point to something else. "Dialog" must really mean *agreement*, without questioning the assumptions, methods, or findings of much of modern science, theology, and philosophy. It seems that "to turn the face away" means to ask hard questions, point out obvious errors, note contradictions, and question anti-supernaturalistic assumptions latent in much modern scholarship.

Narrow-minded Intolerance and Rigidity

Henry has also been faulted for failing "to see in different traditions strengths which will complement his own weaknesses."[31] Specifically, "they will want to know why Henry does not also picture God as ecstasy, a personal power ever moving and become, a dynamic energy risking freedom, novelty, and tolerance." In other words, why he rejects the views of process theologians, with their challenge "to dance, to play and to invite the freedom that revolutions inevitably invite. . . . They will accuse Henry of being more afraid of embracing error than of losing truth."[32]

Roger Olson, author of a mildly evangelical history of theology, says that Henry's "star faded in the 1980s and 1990s as he retreated more and more toward a narrow, almost fundamentalistic mentality." By contrast, Donald Bloesch is described in glowing terms as one who "intended to hold the two impulses of Protestant orthodoxy and pietism together in a 'theology of Word and Spirit.'"[33]

Olson had earlier identified fundamentalists as

> those Protestant Christians who defend entire, detailed systems of very conservative doctrines against perceived modernist, liberal encroachments and dilutions, and they often call for and practice separation form Christians who are guilty of participating in or condoning modernism in theology. [They] insist on belief in the supernatural, verbal inspiration of the Bible, absolute biblical inerrancy with regard to historical and natural as well as theological matters, a literalistic biblical hermeneutic,

31. Paterson, *Carl F. H. Henry*, 165.
32. Ibid.
33. Olson, *Story of Christian Theology*, 595.

and strong opposition to any and all deviations from these principles.[34]

He later condenses that characterization to those who "consider the true essence of Christianity to be a system of detailed and precise unrevisable doctrinal propositions . . . see their primary mission as defending that true Christ faith against liberal theology and higher criticism, and that that strict biblical inerrancy is the cornerstone doctrine of evangelical Christianity."[35]

To what extent, if at all, do these criticisms apply to Carl Henry?

To begin with, let us listen to his own words, in the preface to *God, Revelation, and Authority*: "I have spent memorable hours with twentieth-century luminaries . . . [some of whom he then lists]. These scholars represent much of the wide spectrum of contemporary theology. . . . I am deeply indebted to scholars of various traditions."[36]

On the one hand, we can readily admit that he did not accept liberal theology, and spent much of his life pointing out its departures from biblical teaching. He found much of modern biblical criticism to be lacking, as we have seen, and presented a case for the essential reliability of the Bible, especially in God, *Revelation, and Authority*. Yes, he did believe in both the infallibility and the inerrancy of Scripture. And he was strongly opposed to all deviations from what he considered to be the truths found in the Bible.

So, was he therefore narrow-minded, unable to perceive the value of others' points of view, and increasingly fundamentalistic in his later years? Anyone who either met Carl Henry or has read much of his voluminous writing will find these descriptions hard to match with the man and his works. He began by criticizing the fundamentalists, continued by associating with all sorts of people whom fundamentalists would shun—including Billy Graham—and incurred the wrath of many conservative evangelicals and fundamentalists by publicly distancing himself from both the style and substance of Harold Lindsell when he began his "Battle for the Bible."

He did not make inerrancy the centerpiece of his theology, and refused to use it as a litmus test for orthodoxy. Nor would he, like most

34. Ibid., 556.
35. Ibid., 569.
36. Henry, GRA 1:9–10.

fundamentalists and many evangelicals, insist upon a detailed system of eschatology. The last chapter in *God, Revelation, and Authority*, "The Finalities," paints a sweeping panorama of the end times that would make a true fundamentalist cringe with dismay over its lack of precision—but which thrilled this reader's heart. To the end, he called for cultural engagement, while fundamentalists, and many evangelicals, were focusing on those not "Left Behind." He worked all his life for church unity, deploring the fractured state of evangelicalism and the separatist stance of fundamentalists.

By what stretch of the imagination could Carl Henry be considered "fundamentalistic"?

His reverence for God and for the revelation that he believed God had given in the Scriptures did make him afraid both to lose the truth and to embrace error—a quality, one would assume, requisite for all theologians. For good reasons, he could not join the parade with process theology, and thus did not write much about God dancing or playing—categories admittedly not prominent in the Bible, which Henry considered to be the primary source for Christian theology.[37]

His respect for Karl Barth is seen in the hundreds of quotations from the Swiss theologian's *Church Dogmatics*, which Henry had obviously studied carefully. Many are appreciative; Henry was not afraid to welcome Barth as a theological ally and to draw upon his genius. On the other hand, Henry believes that Barth's doctrine of the Word of God is hopelessly confused by its sustained dialectic, unnecessarily founded on wholesale acceptance of the assumptions and conclusions of German biblical critics, and at odds with Barth's own use of the Bible as *functionally* authoritative.[38] He could not, therefore, embrace Barthianism as Ramm and his admirers have done. Does that make him narrow-minded?

Finally, a careful reading of *God, Revelation, and Authority*, not to mention a number of other works by Henry, would show how he, too, combined both pietism and scholarship in a "theology of Word and Spirit."[39]

37. Henry addresses process theology in various places, especially *GRA* 6:3 and 5:15.

38. For a more detailed review of Henry's reasons for not embracing the theology of Karl Barth, see Patterson, *Carl F. H. Henry*, 48–50.

39. See, for example, *GRA* vol. 4, chs. 11–12 on the role of the Holy Spirit in the creation and interpretation of the Scripture.

To return to the sweeping charges of Demarest and Lewis cited towards the beginning of this chapter, which sum up much of what others have also alleged, one must simply either assume that these words are meant to apply to the other authors mentioned by Demarest and Lewis, or that they (and the others whose similar charges we have examined) have not read *God, Revelation, and Authority* very carefully. Since (unlike Bloesch) they cite it often in their own work, I am left wondering what motivated them to pen these sentences, other than a desire to set off their own method (which I personally like very much) against all others.

Lest the reader imagine that I think Carl Henry to be beyond responsible criticism, let me point out that he himself acknowledges his finitude and fallenness, and disclaims any finality to his own theological approach. Furthermore, I do not fully agree with every statement in *God, Revelation, and Authority.*

NINE

Carl Henry and His Critics II

Rationalism

Perhaps the most commonly voiced criticism against Henry is that of being a rationalist, and therefore a prisoner of the now-defunct modern project. Bob Patterson's summary of these charges provides us with a convenient outline for our consideration of what several theologians, including Donald Bloesch (followed closely by his disciple Roger Olson), Bernard Ramm, Clark Pinnock, Gabriel Fackre, and others have said of Henry:[1]

> Henry's critics have charged him with being overly concerned with reason, with being obsessed about prepositional revelation and advocating a God who reveals himself only in Euclidean terms. . . . Henry's stance has a natural affinity for modernity's highly rational mode of thought and discourse, a modern rationalism that insists that religious beliefs and moral convictions stand up to the test of logic and reason.[2]

---

1. Mohler refers to this charge and gives a partial response: "Critics have often painted him as a rationalist (or even a Thomist) and have lamented his scholastic approach to epistemological issues," citing William Abraham, *Coming Great Revival,* 37, which describes *GRA* as "turgid scholasticism." In his note, Mohler says, "This statement indicates something of the great divide between those who define evangelical faith primarily by a set of theological commitments and those who point instead to an evangelical faith experience and concern for personal holiness. To be fair, Henry has evidenced a concern for both dimensions but has given the cognitive dimension primary attention in his writings" (Mohler, "Carl F. H. Henry," 399 n. 47).

2. Patterson, *Carl F. H. Henry,* 164.

Not all evangelicals are happy with Henry's bent toward rationalism and his argument that the truth of revelation can be known prior to becoming a Christian, otherwise people would be guilty for its rejection.[3]

Grenz and Olson note that his "critics have also found him to be overly concerned with reason and prepositional revelation."[4]

Patterson cites Bloesch as representative of those who object to "Henry's giving reason a creative role prior to faith," and "for holding that revelation can be comprehended by reason alone."[5] "Bloesch and many other evangelicals prefer to say that only God can illumine the mind of the unbeliever to recognize and understand revelation, that revelation is not at the disposal of reason."[6]

Bloesch says, "The method of Gordon Clark and Carl Henry is deductive, deriving conclusions from given rational principles.... Our theology will forever fall short of the mind of God." Bloesch says, "We intend the truth in our theological statements, but we do not possess the truth, since reason is always the servant and never the master or determiner of revelation."[7]

Going further in this same direction, Patterson notes that

"Some evangelicals are uneasy with Henry's emphasis on reason because they feel that reason can be a two-edged sword cutting the one who wields it," as in the Enlightenment, when reason, "which admits the validity of that which can be perceived or

---

3. Ibid., 164–65. At least one person has charged Henry with being a Thomist. Mohler records that Thomas Reginald McNeal described Henry's "method as apologetic presuppositionalism" that is "a rationalistic theological methodology dominated by the priority of reason over faith" (McNeal, "Critical Analysis," 1; cited in Mohler, Carl F. H. Henry, 399 n. 48). Mohler replies, "Yet Henry has always stressed that revelation is *prior* to both reason and faith, even as he has championed the role of reason and rationality in human thought. . . . Henry may be *rationalistic*, if by this we indicate his reliance upon reason as an instrument of understanding; but he is not a *rationalist*, if by this he is thought to place reason prior to revelation" (ibid.). The characterization of Henry as a Thomist borders on the bizarre, given Henry's explicit repudiation of Aquinas' theological method at many points. See, for example *GRA* vol. 1, ch. 4, "The Ways of Knowing."

4. Grenz and Olson, *20th Century Theology*, 297.

5. Patterson, *Carl F. H. Henry*, 165–66.

6. Ibid., 166.

7. Ibid., 166, quoting Bloesch, *Essentials of Evangelical Theology*, 2:267, 268.

conceived," was used to overturn traditional arguments for the existence of God and the truth of the Bible.[8]

Henry, his critics say, does not make enough of the idea that the unbeliever's mind is depraved and the believer's mind is enlightened by grace, that our knowledge of God is a pure gift and not a rational or philosophical achievement. . . . Revelation, not reason, must be the final authority.[9]

Having recorded these charges, Patterson simply says, "Henry continually responds to these criticisms by saying that revelation is a disclosure of higher truth that stands in continuity with rational truth."[10]

Still, the accusations of rationalism reflected in Patterson's largely sympathetic treatment of Henry pale in comparison to the words of Harvey Conn's repetition and affirmation of Van Til's description of the approaches of "Neo-evangelicals":

These men . . . accept . . . an emphasis on "the law of non-contradiction" (Carnell) or "logic as an exercise of the reason to test for truth" (Gordon Clark) or what Van Til designates as "Greek theism" (Carl Henry) as one of their operating categories or presuppositions. And precisely here lies the basic weakness of this sort of apologetics. "It is the attempt to join higher forms of non-Christian thought in their opposition to lower forms of non-Christian thought."[11]

What Is "Rationalism"?

Rationalism has been defined as a "conviction that reason provides the best or even the only path to truth. . . . In theology the term rationalism often designates a position that subordinates revelation to human reason or rules out revelation as a source of knowledge altogether."[12] M. J. Ovey reminds us that "rationalism" carries negative overtones in

---

8. Patterson, *Carl F. H. Henry*, 166.

9. Ibid., 167.

10. Ibid.

11. Conn, *Contemporary World Theology*, 139–40, citing Van Til, "New Evangelicalism," 62.

12. Evans, "Approaches to Christian Apologetics," 98–99.

several communities, and provides a helpful discussion of some of the term's meanings.[13]

He distinguishes between rationalism and "a commitment to being rational . . . or providing reasons for actions or beliefs and a commitment to some form of classical logical process, such as accepting the law of non-contradiction." In that sense, "Christian theology has frequently been strongly rational." We'll return to that theme later. The question for theologians is, "whether and in what areas human reason is viable."[14] Protestant Christians believe that the fall impacted human reason as well as the will, and will limit the use of reason accordingly.

"Rationalism" receives criticism from Christians if it means "the supremacy and adequacy of human reason"[15] to discover truth, and even more if it sets itself against the supernatural, and rules out direct divine intervention in human affairs, including divine revelation.

"Rationalism" sometimes includes a low view of the reliability of data perceived by the senses, as well as "judgments formed for aesthetic or emotional reasons (as in Romanticism)." Thus, it is often set against empiricism, for "in its stronger forms rationalism moves primarily or purely from the a priori principles not given by sense perception."[16]

"Romantic" critics claim that rationalism rules out love and exhibits "sterility and inability to explain the richness of human experience."[17]

Postmoderns reject rationalism for the latter reason, as well as from their reaction to any assertion of ultimate, absolute truths, and the assumption that reason can decipher and describe the multiple mysteries of life.

In some circles, rationalism entails anti-supernaturalism, "because rationalism suggests that 'natural' explanations are to be sought for the resurrection, for example, rather than accepting direct divine intervention."[18] Rationalism may also be contrasted with a belief in

13. Ovey, "Rationalism" 592–94.

14. Ibid., 592.

15. Ibid.

16. Ibid., 593

17. Ibid.

18. Ibid.

revelation, "because rationalism allegedly requires one should not be under authority but exercising independent judgment."[19]

In Christian apologetics, "rationalism" may describe the conviction that "if proper evidence is produced in favor of Christian faith a listener will, as a rational being, inevitably come to faith" or that "rational" evidence for the truth claims of the Bible are sufficient to persuade an honest seeker.[20]

As Ovey rightly points out, "The current climate of postmodernism is unfavorable to rationalism in many of the above senses."
• Postmoderns reject the idea of any universal truth (except their own assertion of universal relativism!) and suspect that "reason" is only a weapon in the hands of those with an agenda. "For this reason the charge that Christian belief is 'rationalist' can be devastating in a postmodern context."[21]

When Henry's opponents brand his theological method as "rationalism,"[22] they score a rhetorical victory without really having to substantiate their charge.

Response to Criticisms of Rationalism

In the rest of this chapter and the one that follows, I shall try to show that: *1. Carl Henry's thought does not fit in any sense the standard definitions of rationalism given above.* That is, he does not believe that reason alone can ascertain ultimate truth; he does not give reason priority over God's revelation in the Bible; he does not believe that rational evidence alone will persuade anyone to believe in Christ.

In this judgment, I am joined by James White, who concludes that all evangelicals surveyed in his book

> would not fall into the classical category of "rationalists," meaning those who embrace the idea that one can autonomously begin with reason and observation and come to ultimate answers regarding reality. What can be ascribed to evangelical theology is "rationality," that which upholds the validity of thought and

19. Ibid.
20. Ibid., 594.
21. Ibid.
22. Patterson, *Carl F. H. Henry*, 164.

reason. This reason is applied to God's self-revelation, which is essential to Evangelical understandings and ultimate answers.[23]

2. *Some of the charges of a sort of "Christian rationalism" leveled against Henry by fellow Christians seem to be based either on ignorance or misunderstanding.* Even a cursory reading of *God, Revelation, and Authority* will show that they lack foundation.

3. *It seems to me that accusations that Henry is a "rationalist" sometimes proceed from premises that are false or internally contradictory.*

At the outset, let us note that Carl Henry himself repeatedly and unequivocally renounced and repudiated rationalism. Early in volume 1, for example, discussing "Four Ways of Knowing," he highlights the reliance of all reasoning upon assumptions and presuppositions. "Theology and Philosophy" in the same volume explains why the evangelical theologian cannot accept the anti-metaphysical bias of much modern philosophy:

> The speculative approach ignores the self-revelation of the living God and it propounds a rationalistic world view and life view on antithetical premises. In so doing it minimizes man's finiteness and conceals his epistemic predicament in sin.[24]

Such explicit rejection of rationalism puts the burden of proof upon those who would deny that Carl Henry understood his own theological method. To label Carl Henry a "rationalist" because he does not disavow the use of reason is akin to calling Karl Marx a capitalist because of the title of his book; one has to amass considerable evidence to support such an allegation.

The criticisms quoted above state that Henry's supposed rationalism is marked by being overly concerned with reason and prepositional revelation. We shall look in more detail at some possible meanings of "being overly concerned with reason." For now perhaps we might ask, what does "overly concerned" imply?

More concerned with human reason than with divine revelation? The first four volumes of *God, Revelation, and Authority* constitute a

23. White, *What Is Truth?*, 167.
24. Henry, *GRA* 1:195.

mammoth attempt to assert the nature, means, and priority of divine revelation, particularly written revelation in the Bible.

More concerned with reason than with emotions? Yes, if you mean emotions as a vehicle for revelation. Henry is not a Romantic. On the other hand, throughout his writings he affirms his belief in what Jonathan Edwards would call "religious affections" as essential to a normal Christina life, and in his autobiography refers several times to his own emotional responses to God's goodness and greatness. [25]

More than intuition? In the fourth chapter of the entire work, "The Ways of Knowing," Henry compares the relative role and value of intuition, experience, reason, and divine revelation, and clearly opts for the last as determinative for Christian theology. If by intuition we mean ineffable mystical intuitions, Henry counters that "mystical intuitionism is implicitly pantheistic. It obscures both the transcendence of the Creator-God and man's moral waywardness. . . . While there is a mystery side to God, revelation is mystery dispelled and conveys information about God and his purposes."[26]

Still, there is a kind of "rational intuitionism" held by Augustine, Calvin, and others, including Henry, which believes that "human beings know certain propositions immediately to be true, without resort to inference."[27] These would include the existence of God and the sense of right and wrong, the awareness of self, the laws of logic, and the truths of mathematics. "According to this view, the categories of thought are aptitudes for thought implanted by the Creator and synchronized with the whole of created reality."[28]

What about reason as distinct from experience? Henry points out that Thomistic theology builds upon sense impressions as a foundation, and that this made it vulnerable to later secular philosophical attack. He describes the weakness of modern empiricism, especially scientific empiricism and logical positivism, and asserts that it can never lead to

25. "My deepest memories are those spent waiting before God, often praying for others . . . sometimes waiting before him in tears, sometimes in joy, sometimes wrestling alternatives, sometimes just worshiping him in adoration. Heaven will be an unending feast for the soul that basks in his presence" (Henry, *Confessions of a Theologian*, 407).

26. Ibid., 73.

27. Ibid.

28. Ibid., 77.

anything but tentative conclusions. Divine revelation alone can provide certitude.

What, then, is the role of reason? In "Ways of Knowing"—placed, significantly, at the beginning of *God, Revelation, and Authority*—Henry lays bare the assumptions of what he calls "the rationalistic method of knowing," which "considers human reasoning as the only reliable and valid source of knowledge." [29] After tracing the course and fortunes of rationalism in Western philosophy, Henry declares that faith in the role of human reason has been shattered in recent years, thus acknowledging trends which later came to be called "postmodernism." From a Christian standpoint, "Human reason is not a source of infallible truth about ultimate reality," because man is both finite and fallen.[30] There is no way that any created person could know all that is necessary for "a comprehensive world-life view," and the "sinful human spirit slants its own perspectives in a manner that does violence to the truth of revelation, while its very formulations are at the same time made possible because reason is a divine gift whose legitimate and proper use man has compromised."[31]

That last clause points to the other side of Henry's view of reason: its "legitimate and proper use." Throughout *God, Revelation, and Authority* he strenuously opposes the view that "reason must in principle be antirevelational. . . . A deity related to man only in terms of contradiction and paradox can serve neither the cause of revelation, reason or experience."[32] He espouses, therefore, an "evangelical rational theism,"[33] that is, a theism based on God's revelation, and not warped by irrational, self-contradictory assertions. Its fundamental assumption—derived from the Bible—is that "the Logos of God is the coordinating reality that holds together thought, life and experience."[34] "Its basic premise is that the living God should be allowed to speak for himself and to define the abiding role of reason and the meaning of revelation. . . . The rationalistic approach subordinates the truth of revelation to its

29. Ibid., 85.
30. Ibid., 91.
31. Ibid.
32. Ibid., 93.
33. Ibid., 94.
34. Ibid., 95.

own alternatives and has speculated itself into exhaustion." Our choice now is between "human postulation or divine revelation."[35]

Now let us look a bit more closely at other aspects of the charge that Henry is a rationalist. To continue with the criticisms quoted above, he is faulted for following a fundamentally deductive method. That is, "deriving conclusions from given rational principles."[36]

If this means that Henry has fundamental presuppositions, it is true. He starts with the premise that the entire Bible is the Word of God, our only infallible guide to faith and practice. He insists that we must derive our theology from clear statements and legitimate inferences from the Scriptures, not from extra-biblical considerations or concepts. Indeed, most of *God, Revelation, and Authority* consists of a sustained defense of the Bible as the only proper starting point for theological reflection; Henry repeatedly criticizes those approaches that arise from human ideas and speculation. To quote such passages would be to repeat much of *God, Revelation, and Authority* itself.

Furthermore, he operates on the conviction that the Bible contains information about God and his ways that is clear enough to be understood. "God in his revelation is the first principle of Christian theology, from which all the truths of revealed religion are derived."[37] He knows that the Bible conveys not only information, and is intended to lead us to real wisdom—the saving knowledge of God—but he insists that the words in the Bible do reflect, and communicate, intelligible revelation from God.

He also assumes, as we have noted above, that the Holy Spirit can—and must—illumine the minds of believers who read the written form of God's revelation, enabling them to understand, believe, and share with others what they have learned.

But here we must be careful, for Henry thinks that these assumptions arise from a proper reading of the Bible itself. In other words, he did not start with these ideas and construct a theological system upon them. Rather, his preliminary encounter with the Bible as a new believer convinced him that this is the very Word of God, a Word that can be comprehended enough to communicate also with others. So,

35. Ibid.

36. Bloesch, *Essentials of Evangelical Theology* 2:268.

37. Henry, *GRA* 1:215.

even his presuppositions arose from his response to what he read in the Scriptures. "The Christian religion does not dangle midair on a postulational skyhook; it is anchored in God's self-revelation."[38]

We shall continue this examination and refutation of alleged errors in Carl Henry's theological method in the next chapter, but for now it should be evident that much of what has been said about him lacks sufficient grounding.

38. Ibid., 1:219.

TEN

Carl Henry and His Critics III

We resume our response to the various forms of the accusation that Carl Henry's theological approach suffers from captivity to modern thought forms. He has, for example, been charged with:

"Advocating a God who reveals himself only in Euclidean terms"[1]

Euclid was a Greek mathematician, famous for his textbook on geometry, the *Elements*, which argued from axioms to theorems to produce proofs, concluding with the confident, "*QED*" (*quod erat demonstrandum*, "which is what was to be demonstrated" or "proved"). Let us assume that this criticism refers to Henry's belief that theology is, in some sense, a "science," "in the deepest sense because it presumes to account in an intelligible and orderly way for whatever is legitimate in every sphere of life and learning."[2]

Of course, Christian theology differs fundamentally from much of modern science, for it does not base itself only—or even chiefly—upon empirical observation derived by the senses, and because it does not exalt human reason above divine revelation as its fundamental way of knowing. But theology, like any body of knowledge (the original sense of "science"), "is interested no less than any other science in discussing presuppositions and principles, sources and data, purposes or objec-

---

1. As in the previous two chapters, these criticisms are quoted from Paterson, *Carl F. H. Henry*.

2. Henry, *GRA* 1:203-4.

tives, methods of knowing, verifiability and falsifiability."[3] This way of speaking of theology grates upon modern Christian sensibilities, accustomed as they are to think of the faith as personal rather than propositional. Our age has lost confidence in the "assured results of science," and yearns for experience that is not simply cognitive and rational.

So, we must ask what Henry means. Does he—as the criticism quoted above implies—think that our God is a set of impersonal mathematical proofs, known by cold reasoning and ironclad logic? Of course not! That is a caricature, possible only to those who have not read his works carefully.

Henry merely means to say that God has revealed himself in such a way that he can be known, his revelation can be understood, the Bible makes sense, and we can talk about God in ways that others can understand. Indeed, those theologians who criticize Henry for being "scientific" themselves try to persuade others by the facts and the logic of their argument! Barth is unusual among serious theologians to place contradiction at the heart of his theory of God's revelation, and even he frequently departs from his own stated method. *Church Dogmatics* contains thousands of pages of doctrinal exposition that are clearly intended to be convincing. The same is true for Bloesch's massive theological works. Most Christian writers try to present their case cogently and coherently, which is all that Henry says he is assaying to do.

To be sure, Henry does speak of axioms and theorems as appropriate for theology, but does this mean that he envisions a process that is coldly mathematical and leads merely to a set of rationally deduced principles, rather than a vital knowledge of the living God? Not at all. He is simply trying to recognize that systematic theology, by definition, is *systematic*—it seeks to presents the doctrines of the Bible in an orderly, consistent, and coherent fashion. For Henry, then, "axioms" and "theorems" refer to vital truths derived from the Bible and presented in way that shows their mutual interrelatedness. Far from being a set of random observations of, and responses to, the revelation of the Scriptures, theology aims to arrange the treatment of biblical themes in a manner that makes sense and carries persuasive power.

We must admit that Henry possibly did not realize the extent to which his use of the noun "science" to describe theology would gen-

3. Ibid., 1:203.

erate massive opposition, approaching revulsion, among evangelicals. Though he did his best to define what he meant by "science" and was obviously aware of the revolt against "modern" rationalism, and science in particular, as we have seen, he did not perhaps appreciate how viscerally some evangelicals would react to his use of terms like "reason," "rational," "axiom," and "theorem."

Or did he? Much of his theological project was aimed at combating the rising anti-rationalism, even irrationalism, of twentieth-century theology, and he often lamented the emotionalism, shallowness, and fuzzy thinking of all too many evangelical leaders and thinkers. Maybe he chose his terms deliberately, in an almost desperate attempt to rescue a baby that was in danger of being thrown out with the bathwater.

Insisting that Religious Beliefs and Moral Convictions Stand Up to the Test of Logic and Reason[4]

Henry admits: "To be sure [evangelical theology] insists that reason is the test of truth. But by true knowledge it means nothing more or less than truth as God knows and reveals it."[5] In other words, Henry believes that the Bible, which is God's self-revelation of the truth, will not contradict itself. Reason does not invent truth; it discovers truth by carefully examining the scriptural witness.

> Divine revelation is the source of all truth, the truth of Christianity included; reason is the instrument for recognizing it; Scripture is its verifying principle; logical consistency is a negative test for truth and coherence a subordinate test. The task of Christian theology is to exhibit the content of biblical revelation as an orderly whole.[6]

Divine revelation is thus the "basic theological axiom" of Christian theology.[7] This fact "in no way nullifies the corollary truth that the triune God is Christianity's basic ontological axiom."[8] In other words, Henry is not unaware that theology is primarily *about* God; he is merely

4. Patterson, *Carl F. H. Henry*, 164.

5. Ibid., 1:93.

6. Ibid., 1:215.

7. Ibid., 1:216.

8. Ibid., 1:219.

saying that to know God, we must seek the truth as it is found in his revelation, especially in the Bible.

Henry then works out the nature and implications of this assumption in the rest of *God, Revelation, and Authority.* In the process, he responds to objectors from many quarters, especially Barth, whom he accuses of pervasive inconsistency. How, he asks, can the Swiss theologian insist that theology not be subjected to the law of non-contradiction and the necessity of coherence, while criticizing others for being inconsistent, and arranging his own theology in a relatively coherent manner?

Placing an Undue Emphasis on the Law of Non-Contradiction

Carl Henry certainly did insist that the law of non-contradiction plays a crucial role in all human thought and discourse:

> Distinctively human experience presupposes the law of non-contradiction and the irreducible distinction between truth and error; man cannot repudiate these logical presuppositions without sacrificing the intelligibility of what he says and does and his own mental coherence.[9]

In other words, Van Til, Conn, McGrath, and others who disparage the emphasis that Henry (and his mentor Gordon Clark) place on the law of non-contradiction can do so only by assuming that same law! With regard to this matter, either Henry is right or he is wrong; he cannot be both right and wrong at the same time. And his critics say he is wrong! What does "wrong" mean, unless there is a fundamental contradiction between "right" and "wrong," between truth and error?

To claim that Henry believes that the law of non-contradiction exists independently of God is to misunderstand his thought. After all, the Bible declares that "God is light, and in him there is no darkness at all,"[10] he cannot lie,[11] and Jesus is the Truth.[12] All such descriptions of God imply something like a law of non-contradiction within God himself. Not, of course, as an independent "law" standing outside of

9. Henry, *GRA* 2:126.

10. 1 John 1:5.

11. Heb 6:18.

12. John 14:6.

God that he must obey, but as part of the fundamental constitution of the mind of God—of the Logos—which distinguishes between truth and error, "light" and "darkness," good and evil, holy and profane, right and wrong.

It is in the context of God's sovereignty and total freedom that Henry discusses the nature of the law of non-contradiction, which "does not set limits to which God must conform; God himself wills the law of non-contradiction as integral to both divine and human meaning. . . . The laws of logic are the way God thinks; they are the organization of the divine mind."[13] God cannot speak what is both true and false at the same time; indeed, he cannot directly speak anything that is false (excluding from this discussion the record of Satan's lies in the Bible). He *cannot* lie. He has bound himself to truth, for his very mind—his Logos—is truth itself.

Thus, when Henry speaks of the "law" of non-contradiction, he is only referring to a law that underlies all human thought and communication, one that is assumed in everything we say and do. This law is implanted in us because we are created in the image of God, who distinguishes absolutely between truth and error, fact and falsehood, reality and non-reality, God and not-God.

In his own words:

> The laws of logic are the "architecture" or organization of the divine mind. They are the systematic arrangement of God's mind or the way God thinks. The laws of logic, therefore, have an ultimate ontological reality. God is the author of all meaning, the foundation of all facts; his thought is ultimately decisive for all predication.[14]

Again, to say that Henry is wrong to assert the ubiquity of this law of non-contradiction is to imply its existence. We simply cannot escape the fact that our minds distinguish between truth and error, and that all our value judgments assume and express this basic element of our mental nature.

Another point: not only Christians, but all humans, think and speak out of this fundamental reality. God addresses humans as "reasonable" (that is, capable of reason) beings. Wrong—yes; deluded—yes;

13. Henry, *GRA* 4:319.

14. Ibid., 4:334.

rebellious—yes; sunken in darkness and sin—yes; but still able to hear a word and judge whether it seems right or wrong. Their judgment may be wrong, but it comes from a mind that knows that there is a difference between right and wrong. That is what Henry means by the universal presence of the law of non-contradiction in both humans and in their Maker. As he puts it, "Those who argue that God is illogical and then presume to say anything ontologically significant about him, indulge in religious babbling."[15]

Being "obsessed with . . . propositional revelation"[16]

True, Henry does insist upon prepositional revelation throughout *God, Revelation, and Authority* and especially in volume 3, chapters 24–28.

- If revelation is a communication of sharable truth, it will consist of sentences, propositions, judgments, and not simply of isolated concepts.[17]

  Revelation in the biblical understanding involves not isolated concepts or words but units of thought. God . . . does not utter illogicalities. . . . Meaningful divine revelation involves communication in intelligible sentences.[18]

Henry confronts head-on the modern rejection of prepositional revelation in a survey of "an amazing array of specious arguments, unsupported claims, and even misrepresentations of the biblical view of revelation," such as that "God is absolute Subject and . . . cannot be an object of human knowledge." Yes, but "The fact that God as active Subject is himself Truth in the form of personal being does not at all require that we forfeit his objectivity in deference to the subjectivistic tendency of modern religious thought."[19]

Another objection is that "prepositional truth depersonalizes revelation by turning it into abstract statements that dull the call for decision and obedience. . . . But if the call for decision and obedience rests upon imperatives that cannot be logically analyzed, and are not

15. Ibid.
16. Patterson, *Carl F. H. Henry*, 164.
17. Ibid., 3:429.
18. Ibid., 3:430.
19. Ibid., 3:431.

answerable to the claims of truth, then no rational creature ought to be bound by such demands."[20]

Let us continue to listen to Carl Henry's own exposition of this key concept:

> A reading of the New Testament will quickly show . . . that the verb *believe* (*pisteuo*) does in fact have doctrinal truths or propositional statements as its object; it is therefore untrue to the Gospels and Epistles to say that the object of belief is properly only a person.[21]

"A proposition is a verbal statement that is either true or false; it is a rational declaration capable of being either believed, doubted, or denied."[22] Aside from obviously "propositional" passages like 1 Corinthians 15, "most of the sentences in Scripture are historical assertions or explanations of such assertions."[23]

> We mean by propositional revelation that God supernaturally communicates his revelation to chosen spokesmen in the express forms of cognitive truths, and that the inspired prophetic-apostolic proclamation reliably articulates these truths in sentences that are not internally contradictory.[24]

Is God "more" than what he has revealed in the Bible? Of course! But without the propositional revelation in the Bible, we would not know of this transcendence of God. "Apart from meaningful and true cognitive information, one could not know that a presence is that of Yahweh, or speak confidently of God's personality and selfhood, or even of transcendent reality."[25]

After these preliminary definitions and answers to objections, Henry backs his position with an extensive review of the Scriptures, which he finds to be composed of intelligible statements, though of course expressed in various genres, such as poetry. But "The LORD is my shepherd" is still a proposition.

20. Ibid., 3:433.
21. Ibid., 3:438.
22. Ibid., 3:456.
23. Ibid.
24. Ibid., 3:457.
25. Ibid., 3:459.

Furthermore, contrary to the claim by Roger Olson that "Henry's view of divine revelation may seem to imply that all the nonpropositional forms of revelation are unimportant compared with propositional revelation,"[26] Henry states explicitly in his chapter on "Varieties of Revelation" in volume 2 that "The Bible itself attests the considerable variety in God's revealing activity by depicting divine disclosure not by one particular term but by a vast range of descriptive concepts."[27] Against those who would restrict God's revelation to the Bible itself, he writes, "The God of the Bible is the God who revealed himself in dreams and visions, in theophany and incarnation, in words and writings. His multiform ways of revelation defy simplistic reduction."[28]

He returns later to respond to opponents of propositional revelation, such as Barth[29] and Moltmann, and evangelicals like Bloesch.[30] Henry understands that not everything in the Bible is a proposition:

> It is the case that in the Bible God not only reveals sentences, or propositional truths, but also reveals his Name, or names, and that he gives divine commands. Commands do not assert a truth and are not propositions. Such disclosures assuredly are capable of being formulated propositionally, but that is admittedly something other than expressly identifying them as propositional disclosure. Yet even the revelation of God's name requires a meaningful context for intelligibility; isolated concepts do not convey truths. . . . If it is too much to say that divine revelation must be propositionally given to be both meaningful and true, it is nonetheless wholly necessary to insist that divine disclosure does indeed take propositional form.[31]

One last point to make on this subject: Those who say that revelation is not propositional do so with an abundance of propositions, which they expect to be believed. The following quote illustrates a typical formulation of the widespread objection to Henry's insistence on revelation as being prepositional:

26. Olson, *Westminster Handbook*, 46.

27. Henry, *GRA* 2:79.

28. Ibid., 2:80.

29. Henry, *GRA* 3:466–67.

30. Ibid., 3:475–76.

31. Ibid., 3:480–81.

> From a theological perspective, this fixation with propositions
> can easily lead to the attempt to use the finite tool of language on
> an absolute Presence that transcends and embraces all finite re-
> ality . . . the truly infinite God of Christian faith is beyond all our
> linguistic grasping, as all the great theologians from Irenaeus
> to Calvin have insisted, and so the struggle to capture God in
> our finite prepositional structures is nothing short of linguistic
> idolatry.[32]

First, let us note the use of rhetoric here: "Fixation" is a highly negative word, exceeded for Christians only by "idolatry." Are we to put Henry and his kind—which includes almost all theologians from the beginning of Christian history—into the same camp as Canaanite idolaters? Second, note the straw men: Who, indeed, is guilty of a "fixation" with propositions? And who, in the history of Christian theology, has ever claimed, or thought that he could "capture God" in human language?

Finally, note the self-refuting nature of this tirade against prepositional revelation: It contains no fewer than twelve statements (i.e., propositions) about a God who is supposed to be beyond description in human language! Namely, he is (1) an absolute (2) Presence (there may be another proposition implied in the capitalization of "Presence") who (3) transcends and (4) embraces all finite reality; he is the (5) truly (6) infinite (7) God (note the capitalization, as distinct from "god") of (8) Christian (9) faith (implied is the notion of God as one in whom people believe; therefore something of him can be known and communicated) who is (10) beyond linguistic grasping/capturing; and (implied again) (11) he is unique, and deserving of unique worship, for anything else is "idolatry." Throughout, God is assumed to be a (12) "he."

Such a series of prepositional affirmations against the legitimacy of using coherent, intelligible human language to talk about God is not only inherently false, but self-contradictory.

Those who think Carl Henry too "rationalistic" naturally think he is constantly . . .

---

32. LeRon Shults, quoted in McKnight, "Five Streams," 37.

Forgetting that "our theology will forever fall short of the mind of God . . . [and that] we do not possess the truth, since reason is always the servant and never the master or determiner of revelation"

The third of his *Fifteen Theses on Divine Revelation* states clearly:

> Divine revelation does not completely erase God's transcendent mystery, inasmuch as God the Revealer transcends his own revelation. The revelation given to man is not exhaustive of God. The God of revelation transcends his creation, transcends his activity, transcends his own disclosure. We do not "see everything from God's point of view." Even the chosen apostles concede that their knowledge on the basis of divine revelation is but "in part" and not yet "face to face" (1 Cor. 13:12).[33]

Therefore, "It is sheer delusion for any contemporary theologian, however devout or gifted, to think that he or she has fully mastered God's truth as God's knows it."[34]

On the other hand:

> Although we cannot know God exhaustively, we can know him truly and adequately. Although we cannot know him apart from our finitude, we can know him as creatures divinely intended to apprehend their Creator. Although we can know him only through the forms of our understanding, these divinely created forms convey reliable knowledge about God.[35]

Holding that "the truth of revelation can be known prior to becoming a Christian," "giving reason a creative role prior to faith," and not emphasizing enough "the idea that the unbeliever's mind is depraved and the believer's mind is enlightened by grace, that our knowledge of God is a pure gift and not a rational or philosophical achievement"

Henry did believe that man was created in the image of God, and thus endowed with a rationality that makes thought and understanding of

33. Henry, *GRA* 2:9.
34. Ibid., 5:376.
35. Ibid.

some truth possible. The image of God in man concludes both a rational and a moral component. Even unregenerate men and women can distinguish between good and evil, truth and error, right and wrong, and God and not-God. They may not know the truth about God, but the concepts named above are embedded in every person's mind.[36]

On the other hand, Henry refers often to "the noetic effects of sin" and to "what Christian theologians call the epistemic predicament of finite and sinful man," that incapacitates us from knowing truth apart from revelation.[37] He repeatedly refers to "the Christian demand that the presumptions of every cultural era be tested from the standpoint of transcendent revelation."[38]

Despite the fall, which includes the mind, "the nature of truth is such that the Christian revelation is formally intelligible to all men; it convincingly overlaps ineradicable elements of everyman's experience, and offers a more consistent, more comprehensive and more satisfactory explanation of the meaning and worth of life than do other views."[39] Thus, the non-believer can understand much of what the Christian is saying, even if he disagrees and fails to submit to God's truth. As a fellow creature, he can be engaged in meaningful dialogue, even if only faith in God's revelation alone will bring him true comprehension.

Otherwise, why would Paul reason with the philosophers in Athens? Why would he and Peter use logic—as well as personal testimony and appeal to Scripture (for Jewish audiences)—to persuade their hearers to repent and trust in Christ? If the non-believer has no capacity to think reasonably, then all Christian evangelism and apologetics are useless. Henry is merely saying that non-Christians have minds that work the same way the Christian minds work, even though they are darkened and ignorant. At least they know what the categories "dark" and "ignorant" signify, and can be urged to find in Christ true light and knowledge.

36. Ibid., 2:125–26.
37. Ibid., 1:91.
38. Ibid., 1:92.
39. Ibid., 1:238.

Not understanding that "Revelation, not reason, must be the final authority"

Henry says, on the contrary, "Human reason is a divinely fashioned instrument for recognizing truth; it is not a creative source of truth."[40] "Augustine [whose epistemological approach Henry generally follows] does not hesitate at all to use reason, but he does so always—after his spiritual conversion—in the context of God as Truth and of man's dependency on divine relation."[41] Why must revelation precede and control reason? Because "human reason is not a source of infallible truth about ultimate reality."[42]

> Christianity depicts itself ... not as a supremely constructed metaphysical theory, but as a revelation, differing in kind from secular philosophies grounded in rational reflection. ... Its basic premise is that the living God should be allowed to speak for himself and to define the abiding role of reason and the meaning of revelation ... the rationalistic approach subordinates the truth of revelation to its own alternatives and has speculated itself into exhaustion.[43]

"Holding that revelation can be comprehended by reason alone"

In Volume 4 of *God, Revelation, and Authority*, Henry devotes an entire chapter to "The Spirit as Divine Illuminator" (ch. 12). Here—as in many places elsewhere—he states his views with crystal clarity:

> God intends that Scripture should function in our lives as his Spirit-illumined Word. It is the Spirit who opens man's being to a keen personal awareness of God's revelation. The Spirit empowers us to receive and appropriate Scriptures, and promotes in us a normative theological comprehension for a transformed life. The Spirit gives a vital current focus to historical revelation and makes it powerfully real.[44]

40. Ibid., 1:225.
41. Ibid., 1:87.
42. Ibid., 1:91.
43. Ibid., 1:95.
44. Ibid., 3:273.

The ministry of the Spirit of God . . . is as essential and unique in enlivening God's revelation in the lives of his people as it is in the phenomena of divine incarnation and divine inspiration.[45]

The Spirit illumines Scripture, evokes trust in God, and regenerates contrite sinners.[46]

Many more passages could be cited to show the falsity of this charge, which can only be the result of failing even to take a cursory glance at *God, Revelation, and Authority*'s table of contents, which would have directed a really serious student to at least this section of Henry's sustained explication of the meaning of revelation.

Henry's Approach Constitutes "Greek theism"[47]

For all Van Til's brilliance, this description, and Conn's (obviously approving) citation of it, reveal that Van Til and Conn either did not know what Greek theism was, or had not read Carl Henry. I assume the latter to be the case. The same charge is often leveled against proponents of traditional Christian theism by those advocating openness theology, whose own fierce attacks on Carl Henry are thus not surprising. Greek theism—as represented in Plato, Aristotle, and the Stoics, for example—is marked by confidence in virtually unaided human reason to understand ultimate truth (though Plato fudges on this at times), ignorance of divine revelation, and a concept of God as impersonal. None of these characterize the theology of Carl Henry.

Finally, to refer back to the sweeping criticism of Lewis and Demarest quoted above:[48] Leaving aside the relevance of this statement to the other theologians mentioned, I must simply object to the inaccuracy of it as a description of Carl Henry. First, he calls himself a "presuppositionalist" many times, as we have noted, for he starts with the

---

45. Ibid., 3:278.

46. Ibid.

47. Conn, *Contemporary World Theology*, 139. In his two chapters on "neo-evangelicalism," Conn makes a number of sweeping generalizations that would seem to include Henry in their broad rejection of that movement, but which do not apply to Henry. Such sloppiness is both bad scholarship and unreliable polemics, to say nothing else.

48. Lewis and Demarest, *Integrative Theology*, 1:24–25.

assumption that God has spoken, and revealed himself primary, truly, and intelligibly in the Scriptures.

Second, we have already seen how misleading the term "deductive rationalist" is when applied to Henry (or Clark, whom he acknowledges as his mentor). Henry is "deductive" only in the sense that he starts with the premise that the Bible is God's written revelation, from which all theology must be mined and by which all theology must be judged. He is "rationalist" only in the sense that he believes that God does not contradict himself, and that the Scriptures can be explained in a way that is coherent.

As for "eisegesis, insufficient attention to the history of the doctrines, close-mindedness, indoctrination, and insufficient relevance,"[49] one must simply either assume that these words are meant to apply to the other authors mentioned, or that Lewis and Demarest have not read *God, Revelation, and Authority*. Since they cite Henry's work often in their own three volumes, I am left wondering what motivated them to pen these sentences, other than a desire to set off their own method (which I personally like very much) against all others.

Conclusion

Aside from having shown how Carl Henry's actual writings bear little similarity to most of the criticisms that have been directed at his work, I hope this exercise has served to remind us all of the dangers of what I call "evangelical slander." How easy it is to say things about someone without adequate basis! How disastrous the consequences often are! And, in Henry's case, what a loss this inflicts upon the body of Christ, for, simply because people get a false impression, they are deprived of the pleasure and profit of reading his books.

At this point, allow me to quote the words of John Frame in his very fine *Cornelius Van Til: An Analysis of His Thought*, substituting only Henry's name in brackets for that of Van Til in the original:

> Mistakes like this make one wonder how seriously these authors have tried to understand [Henry]. . . . It is hard to account for this sort of blunder except as a serious lapse of scholarship stemming from ignorance and intense prejudice, a desire to make

49. Ibid.

[Henry] say something he does not actually say, in order to make him more vulnerable to criticism.[50]

Frame's words serve as a timely reminder to all who attempt careful scholarship in the pursuit of truth.

---

50. Frame, *Cornelius Van Til*, 417.

ELEVEN

Carl Henry: Twentieth-Century Augustine

Every few centuries, a Christian thinker of universal significance makes his appearance and, through force of learning and persuasiveness, puts his stamp on an entire movement or era. In the early church, we think of men like Athanasius, Ambrose, and Augustine. The Middle Ages had its Aquinas, the Reformation its Luther and Calvin. John Owen stands out among Puritan writers, Jonathan Edwards among the heirs of the Puritans.

In an article that I read somewhere a few years ago, Carl Henry was quoted as saying that he believed our age needed a new Augustine to rise to the challenge of a dying civilization and the emergence of a new Dark Ages. I believe that he is the very man for whom he called.

Since Augustine of Hippo is commonly regarded as one of the handful of theologians of world-class significance mentioned above, my comparison of Henry with him requires an explanation, which I shall try to provide.

Differences

Everyone is unique, including Augustine and Henry. Separated by more than fifteen centuries, they differ in important respects. Augustine led a life of wild self-indulgence, even debauchery, before God changed him in a garden in Italy. He wallowed in lust and fornication, early taking a mistress who bore him a son. After his conversion, he sent her to a convent. Henry, on the other hand, though mischievous and quite attracted to pretty girls as a youth, did not run into the same excesses. He married while still a student and sired several children. In other words,

Augustine was profligate before his conversion and celibate afterwards, but Henry was celibate before his conversion and then lived the rest of his life with his wife Helga.

Their lifestyles differed in other ways. Augustine stayed close to home after returning from Italy to Africa following his decision to enter the Christian ministry. Though he traveled around his diocese after he was consecrated as bishop of Hippo, he never again left North Africa. Most of his ministry concentrated upon his own church and theological college.

By contrast, few men have ranged as far and wide as Carl Henry, who flew to every inhabited continent and several dozen different countries. Though he served churches as pastor in his student years, for most of his he was connected not to a church, but to various para-church organizations, such as Fuller Seminary (where he taught for ten years as one of the founding faculty), the magazine *Christianity Today* (of which he was founding editor), and World Vision. Throughout this itinerant career, he spoke to countless churches, seminaries, university student groups, conferences, academic meetings, and press conferences.

Personalities vary widely among outstanding men. Augustine's *Confessions*—one of the most profound and eloquent books of all time—probes deeply into the author's soul, and ranges widely over complex philosophical and theological questions. Henry entitled his autobiography *Confessions of a Theologian*, in obvious imitation of Augustine, but there the similarity ends. Though engagingly written, salted with wit, and not without some self-revelation, his chronicle focuses more on his activities and crucial decisions (such as whether to become, and then remain, editor of *Christianity Today*) than either the inner workings of his mind or the grand ideas that fill the pages of *God, Revelation, and Authority*. We are blessed to have this story, with all its details of both cooperation and strife, including betrayal, among evangelicals. For one thing, it lays bare Henry's passions: evangelical engagement with the world, theological vigor, evangelistic outreach, and strategic alliances among those of like mind.

The two men hold certain opposing theological beliefs as well. To name a few examples: Augustine defended infant baptism; Henry was a Baptist who believed in the immersion of adult believers. Recalling his own boyhood baptism by an Episcopalian minister who intoned the words from the *Book of Common Prayer*, "seeing that this child is now

132 CARL HENRY—THEOLOGIAN FOR ALL SEASONS

regenerate," he remarked, "I was, in fact, no more regenerate than the Long Island telephone directory." Augustine served as a bishop in what he called the catholic (universal) church, an organization marked by clear hierarchy. Henry belonged to the Northern Baptist Convention, which holds to congregational autonomy.

Similarities

On the other hand, these theologians share so many distinctives that I see them as basically two manifestations of the same collection of ability, attitude, and activity, which allows for a close comparison.

Early Unbelief

Augustine's mother, Monica, prayed for her son for many years, and with good reason. Not only was Augustine sexually immoral; he also dabbled in all sorts of beliefs. Spurning the orthodoxy of the catholic church, he joined the chief rival to Christianity in Africa, Manichaeism. Later, he became a skeptic.

Henry was born into a family of only nominal faith. One parent was a Lutheran, the other a Roman Catholic. As a compromise, they attended the Episcopal Church, where Henry was baptized and confirmed as a teenager. As soon as he could, he abandoned any church connections and lived the life of a worldling, though never guilty of as much licentiousness as Augustine.

Perhaps these experiences of life without faith in Christ enabled both men to appreciate the transformation that conversion brings, as well as to understand the doubts and hesitations of non-believers. Significantly, each had a powerful effect on non-Christian thought and culture.

Training in "Rhetoric"

Augustine was schooled in rhetoric, the leading academic discipline of his day. He became such an outstanding rhetorician that he was invited to become a public orator in Milan, the functional capital of the Roman Empire at the time. Though freedom of speech had long disappeared from Roman life, formal addresses of all sorts still held central place on public occasions. One could not advance far in professional life without possessing eloquence. To that end, students had to master not only grammar and logic, but the literature, religion, politics, and history of both Rome and Greece.

In some ways, journalism—at least before the domination of television—holds a similar place in modern society. Not only does a good journalist have to write well, but he or she must possess a wide knowledge of a wide range of disciplines in order to know about what to write, and how to place stories in their appropriate context. Carl Henry started out as a newspaper reporter, then became editor for several small-town newspapers. No doubt, his training as a journalist sharpened Henry's natural gift for written expression, a gift that would mature into a brilliant and unique writing style.

Encyclopedic Learning

Augustine and Henry rank among the most learned of Christian theologians. You have only to skim a few pages of the former's *City of God* or the latter's *God, Revelation, and Authority* to realize that you are in the presence of a keen intellect furnished with abundant knowledge. Augustine's mastery of ancient philosophy, literature, and history is matched by Henry's grasp of the philosophy, theology, and science of the past two millennia. Each one seems to have memorized extensive portions of Scripture. Augustine had fewer books to read, but he could cite the Roman historians and poets at will. Literally hundreds of authors and titles fill the pages of the bibliography of Henry's six-volume magnum opus, and he seems to be able to quote relevant passages from them whenever necessary to illustrate a point. Each one had a sure awareness of the writings of other theologians. Of Henry, Bishop Fulton Sheen wrote that his "knowledge of theology, both of contemporary and historical theology, is positively astounding."[1]

---

1. From the dust jacket of *GRA* vol. 3.

Incessant Labors

Though Augustine did not have to work for a living as a youth, he made up for wasted years as an adult. After his conversion, he authored many volumes of ponderous theological and apologetical works. As a busy pastor, he preached almost daily, taught a school for prospective preachers, corresponded with the leading men of his age, handled the burdensome administrative duties of a big-city bishop, traveled to nearby towns and villages to oversee the churches in his diocese, and engaged in theological controversy. His literary output was enormous, and none of it can be called superficial, so he must have spent a corresponding amount of time reading and thinking.

Carl Henry was born into a life of unremitting toil. His family was not well-off, so he supplemented his father's income with his earnings from several jobs in addition to helping with household chores. With his siblings he pushed a cart loaded with produce to a nearby village, where they "peddled fresh vegetables and flowers house to house" until dark. Later, he worked as a caddy in a country club, cut down pine trees for a local realtor, served in a hospital as assistant attendant. Finally, as a result of phenomenal typing speed (eighty-five words per minute on an old-fashioned machine) he earned a position with a local newspaper, thus beginning his career as a journalist.

Never a person to do only one thing at a time, Henry typically carried multiple responsibilities simultaneously—reporting and writing for three or four newspapers; working as a journalist while earning various academic degrees; pursuing two Master's degrees at one time, then two doctoral degrees; speaking; teaching in seminaries; lecturing around the world; writing books and articles; editing a major magazine. His biography abounds with references to long days and nights; weekends at his desk; vacations spent on some urgent project.

The result, as with Augustine, was an amazing productivity well into his mid-eighties. *God, Revelation, and Authority* is only the longest of his publications. He edited many volumes on vital subjects such as science and theology and the nature of the inspiration of the Bible; wrote countless editorials, columns, and articles; and authored standalone volumes on ethics, both personal and social, that still command attention for their balance and challenge.

Henry traveled to every continent, giving lectures to dozens of seminaries, conferences, churches, student groups, and seminars. His speaking schedule alone would daunt most men; coupled with the constant travel, Henry's public teaching ministry seems almost apostolic. The preface to volume 3 of *God, Revelation, and Authority*, for example, lists Manila, Singapore, London, Hong Kong, Zagred (Yugoslavia), Toronto, Vancouver, and Taipei alongside almost a dozen cities in the United States as places where parts of various chapters were delivered in lecture form. Without secretarial help for the last two decades of his ministry, Henry nevertheless carried on a voluminous correspondence with professors, students, denominational executives, and church leaders all over the world.

Commitment to Theological Education

Like St. Augustine, who founded a theological college, Henry always cherished a burden for advanced Christian education. As one of the founding faculty of Fuller Seminary, he helped to shape an institution that soon rose to preeminence. We have already noted that he lectured and taught courses at seminaries all over the world in pursuit of a more theologically-informed pastoral ministry among evangelicals. Henry had a flair for mobilizing others to cooperate in new ventures of strategic value. To strengthen theological education among evangelicals, he helped to start the Evangelical Theological Society, which has convened leading scholars from universities and seminaries in North America to discuss both burning issues and long-term perspectives for theologians. Almost all his books were aimed at theologically-trained readers. Even *Christianity Today* began as a magazine for clergy, seminarians, and theologians, not for laymen. Henry perceived that the pulpit led the church; to influence preachers and teachers was always his first priority.

Eloquent Writing

Another reason for linking Augustine and Henry is their common possession of a rare gift, that of powerful writing. Interestingly, each employs a style that features a rich vocabulary, plays on words, scathing humor, long paragraphs, complex sentences, and tight construction.

Somehow, both men achieve fullness of exposition without excess verbiage. Unlike his great antagonist, Karl Barth, Henry does not wear the reader out with endless qualifications and nice but unnecessary distinctions, nor does he weave a fabric of mutually contradictory statements. Always clear and consistent, Henry, like Augustine, seems to have at his disposal a limitless supply of pointed words and phrases that express exactly what he wants to say.

To be sure, he sometimes does seem to go on too long when explaining the views of contemporary thinkers, which is why this writer has made an abridgment of the Chinese edition of *God, Revelation, and Authority*. Nevertheless, Henry's prose is always excellent, and at times his style rises to the sublime. Some chapters in *God, Revelation, and Authority* were so beautiful that I had to force myself to omit anything when making the abridgment.

Controversies

Like their primary theological model, Paul, Augustine and Henry penned most of their works in the midst of controversy. The bishop of Hippo refuted the Manichaeans, Donatists, and Pelagians, asserting that God has no equal but that evil is a force with whom or which to contend, that the church contains sinners, and that salvation comes through God's sovereign grace alone.

Henry will always be known for his definitive defense of the inspiration, infallibility, and inerrancy of Scripture, which he rightly saw to be the primary point at issue in the twentieth century and beyond. Along the way, he expounded the knowability and sovereign freedom of God, the serviceability of language for revelation, the unique deity and humanity of Jesus, the meaning of history, the nature and purpose of the church, and the certainty of the Christian hope—among other key doctrines.

Like Augustine in his early *Against the Academics*, and later in *City of God*, Henry in *God, Revelation, and Authority* dealt a body blow to intellectual relativism and skepticism. If, as the relativist asserts, there is no absolute truth, or at least none that can be known, how can this "absolute" claim be made by skeptics? His analyses of the four ways of knowing, the rise and fall of logical positivism, the questionable use of science to challenge the Bible, and the inconsistencies of Neo-orthodoxy and its offspring will remain essential weapons of evangelicals for decades to come.

The Key to History

Augustine heard the news of the sack of Rome from his home in North Africa. Not many years later, the Vandals were banging on the gates of Carthage as he lay dying. Truly, Rome's days of glory had long passed. From his perspective, Augustine could analyze both the rise and the fall of that great empire. Much of the relevance of his *City of God* stems from its analysis of the causes both of Rome's rise and of her descent into chaos. He turned current events, seen in the light of history, into a platform for propounding the deepest doctrines of God's justice, love, and sovereignty, as well as the meaning of the flow of history. Indeed, Christian historiography began with *City of God*, just as his *Confessions* paved the way for Western writers to share their deepest secrets and strongest longings (though Europe had to wait until Rousseau penned his own *Confessions*).

Just as Augustine enjoyed citizenship in a dying Rome, so Henry carried an American passport throughout many decades of America's rise to world preeminence. *God, Revelation, and Authority* laid bare for all to see the seeds of internal rot that would eviscerate the mind and then cripple the will of a once great nation. With a prophet's perspective, Henry spied the coming intellectual and moral collapse of a civilization that had jettisoned its precious Christian heritage and taken on the scraps and refuse of Europe, itself a victim of its own mental suicide. For decades, Henry pleaded with both private individuals and public leaders in the church and the academy to stand firm against the encroaching plague of relativism. Towards the end, he seems to have understood that, lacking a sustained and reasoned cooperation among evangelicals, American society would follow down the same path that had turned the Old World into a hollow shell.

At the same time, few seem to have a clearer sense of the purpose and goal of history than he. Despite the almost inevitable ruin of his beloved nation, Henry could remain positive about the future. His travels had merely strengthened the conclusions reached in his study that the gospel would penetrate to, and influence, the far corners of the globe. One day, no matter which nation temporarily sits on the throne of world power, Jesus Christ will return to take his rightful place as visible and unchallenged ruler of nations and of individuals.

Indeed, one of the clearest links between Augustine and Henry can be found in their unwavering confidence that God's plan to build his city on earth would prevail. In contrast to competing views of the progress of human events, Henry's analysis stands strong and bright, like a lighthouse in a raging hurricane, while the lights in little houses below flicker and fail one by one. To read his exposition of the revelation of God in history (found in the last section of volume 2 and the last two sections of volume 4) is to stand on a very high mountain surveying a seemingly wild and convoluted terrain below. "The Awful Silences of Eternity" (vol. 4, ch. 26) and "God Who Stays: The Finalities" (vol. 6, ch. 21) contain passages that seem to cast a heaven-sent beam illuminating the entire course of mankind's arduous pilgrimage to the New Creation.

Theological Breadth

Although he never intended *God, Revelation, and Authority* to be a complete systematic theology, by restating key doctrines in dialogue with their chief detractors, Henry covered almost all the fundamental truths of the Bible and of historic theology. He thus achieved more than topical and temporary relevance in his ceaseless critique of spokesmen of the Hydra of modern gnosticism. He never lived in some ivory tower, unaware of the currents of controversy swirling around the church and even sending torrents of false teaching down the aisle and into the pulpit (or perhaps we should say, from the pulpit to the pew!).

Even a cursory glance at the contents of *God, Revelation, and Authority* will show how widely Henry ranges in this six-volume set. Like Athanasius, Augustine, Martin Luther, John Owen, Jonathan Edwards, and a host of lesser theologians, Henry did not set out to write a complete systematic theology. Instead, like them, he concentrated upon the issues needing the most attention at the time, or those that he felt most burdened and equipped to address.

Henry's first well-known book, actually a very short work, was *The Uneasy Conscience of American Fundamentalism*, which called the church to more active engagement with the world. It was followed by volumes on personal ethics and on social ethics.

God, Revelation, and Authority, on the other hand, goes to the root of the matter: the truth and how we know it—or, more properly, Him. Perceiving that the fundamental challenge facing the church is a crisis in authority, he spent four volumes on what may be called the doctrine of the Word of God, or the doctrine of revelation. After an initial survey of different ways of knowing and the strengths and weaknesses of each, concluding with a presentation of what might be called Augustinian or Calvinistic (as distinct from Thomist) epistemology, Henry moved on to treat God's different forms of divine revelation from a variety of viewpoints.

In the process, he included chapters on the nature of Scripture, its inspiration, infallibility and inerrancy, along with a theistic view of language and of human logic. We would expect all of that in a work on revelation and authority. As he expounds the doctrine of the Word of God, he treats us to a buffet of chapters on the image of God in man; the Logos of God; the incarnation, death, resurrection, and return of Christ; the work of the Holy Spirit in revelation and in the church; the names and nature of God, including his being, becoming man, and attributes; the Trinity; the knowability of God; God as creator (with a brilliant *expose* of the mutual inconsistencies of various theories about evolution); angels, Satan, and the fall of man; the goodness of God and the problem of evil; the fatherhood, holiness, and love of God; the doctrine of providence; the nature of the church and its role in society; and the last things—and this is only a partial list.

Along the way, he discusses matters commonly associated with biblical—as distinct from systematic—theology, demonstrating a mastery of modern scholarship dealing with both the Old and New Testaments. It was not for nothing that Henry earned a bachelor of divinity, two masters of theology, and two doctorates (one in theology, one in philosophy). His skill in Hebrew and Greek allows him to interact with other scholars in matters of exegetical detail, while his grasp of both ancient and modern philosophy and theology enables him to see the big picture.

Thus, I was disappointed when I read in *20th Century Theology*, by Stanley Grenz and Roger Olson, that "Henry has never been a systematic theologian. . . . Henry is perhaps better characterized as a commentator on the fortunes of theology in the twentieth century."[2] The authors admit that *God, Revelation, and Authority* is systematic in nature, but chide Henry for constantly referring extensively to other writers even in this work.

True, Henry does not deal with all the topics of systematic theology, and in that sense is not a "systematic theologian," but neither have most of the theologians they discuss in their overview of twentieth-century theology, nor have many of the greatest thinkers of the Christian church, as we saw above. One may as well criticize Augustine for citing so many non-biblical writers in his *City of God!* This fact highlights the thesis of this chapter: that Henry is a twentieth-century Augustine, and no less important an author for our time than Augustine was for his.

Apologetics

Like Augustine in *The City of God*, *Against the Academics*, and several other works, Henry shows himself to be a skillful apologist. Realizing that the church was swamped with anti-Christian theories from without and intellectual confusion from within, Henry sought to equip evangelicals to answer objections to biblical truth, as well as to restate the fundamental points of Christian doctrine for believers. Non-Christians reading *God, Revelation, and Authority*—or any of his several important compendia of essays assessing modern theology and expounding an evangelical position—would be challenged to rethink their assumptions and conclusions and to admit that, at the very least, biblical Christianity is a reasonable faith, and perhaps even the most credible of all worldviews.

He shows that skepticism about God flows more from prejudice than sound reasoning or solid knowledge of the Bible. He demolishes the various twentieth-century objections to biblical faith, including logical positivism. He demonstrates why a belief both in God and in the Bible stands on very solid ground.

Augustine, after a long attachment to Platonism (or at least the form in which he found it), later wrote against speculative philosophy in *City of God*. Likewise, Henry, armed with a PhD in modern philosophy and a sound knowledge of ancient philosophical systems, shows in

---

2. Grenz and Olson, *20th Century Theology*, 291.

many places why philosophers who ignore God's revelation cannot ever arrive at a solid, clear knowledge of God.

In *City of God*, Augustine replied to those who blamed the fall of Rome on the failings of Christians. Henry's earlier ethical writings refuted the charge that Christians are "so heavenly minded that they are no earthly good." The sections in *God, Revelation, and Authority* on the role of Christians, and of the church, as the new society of God state more briefly the case for engagement with the world by individual believers and the church as a whole.

As we have seen, Henry's apologetic approach stands squarely in the Augustinian tradition. Unlike Aquinas in the Middle Ages and such modern Protestant apologists as C. S. Lewis, Norman Geisler, and R. C. Sproul, he does not try to reason from the visible world to the invisible God. He rejects as insufficient the so-called "arguments" or "proofs" for the existence of God, which Aquinas popularized in his *Summa Theologica*. Noting the question of whether the traditional five arguments are really one, he merely shows why they are logically inconclusive. Instead, he believes that they demonstrate that belief in God is reasonable. Thus, like Augustine, Henry employs all the tools of reason, not to prove the Christian faith, but to understand it and manifest its superior internal consistency and logical power.[3]

Nor does he adopt the evidentialist approach of J. W. Montgomery and the popular Josh McDowell. Though he fills the first four volumes of *God, Revelation, and Authority* with sufficient evidence to support his conviction that the Bible is true in every respect (see, for example, his chapter on the evidence for the resurrection of Christ) he knows that mountains of evidence will never persuade the determined skeptic.

Both the rationalist and the evidential approaches fail, Henry explains, because of what he calls "the noetic effects of sin" or of the fall. In other words, the doctrine of original sin—which he believes is fully biblical—teaches that the mind, as well as the will, has been corrupted by the rebellion of Adam and our willful resistance to God (as outlined in the first chapter of Romans). Thus, neither our reason nor our senses can grasp eternal verities unless they have been liberated and enlightened by the revelation of God.

---

3. See, for example, Henry's extended discussion of Augustine's view of innate ideas in *GRA* 1:325–31.

On the other hand, he does not fully subscribe to the view of Cornelius Van Til and his disciples. Indeed, he shows their similarity to Karl Barth, who argued that there is absolutely no common ground between faith and unbelief, no contact point between biblical and non-biblical worldviews. Like Gordon Clark, whom he freely acknowledges as his mentor, Henry affirms that, though the mind is corrupted by sin, we are still bearers of the image of God. Just as our wills are capable of some virtuous acts (though not good enough to satisfy God's absolute standards), so our minds are capable of receiving words from God and of reasoning out the implications of His divine revelation.

Few have defended the universal validity of the laws of logic more fiercely than Carl Henry. Against the confusing and self-contradictory dialectical ramblings of the other great "Karl" of the twentieth century, Henry argues for the clarity and consistency of biblical revelation. Turning to those who would propose the existence of many kinds of logic, he insists that all humans think in basically the same ways, though their manners of expression may vary.In other words, he has imitated Paul in Athens when he reasoned with the pagan philosophers. Henry dignifies the unbeliever by treating him like a fellow person created in the image of God. He assumes that an honest pagan will recognize certain arguments and lines of evidence as either true or at least valid. Throughout his long career, Henry eagerly engaged in debate and dialogue with those who rejected outright the Christian position, and always with the gentility and courtesy for which he was justly famous.[4]

Theology

Like Luther, Calvin, Owen, and Edwards before him, Henry shares Augustine's basic theological framework: God has revealed himself through the Scriptures as a sovereign and gracious Creator, Sustainer, and Redeemer of men and women created in his own image. Henry's theology is first, last, and always biblical, though he uses reason, intuition, and experiential evidence to elucidate and support the words of the Bible.

4. Although this chapter compares Henry to Augustine of Hippo, we should not ignore the resemblance at many points to the great "Angelic Doctor," Thomas Aquinas, who was also known for his affability during controversies as well as for his willingness to interact with the viewpoints of his most brilliant opponents.

He holds to the doctrine of the Trinity, though he does not accept all of Augustine's formulations of it in *De Trinitate* (*On the Trinity*). For him, as for Augustine, God's grace is free, unmerited, and totally independent of man's choice. He too believes in election and predestination, based, as these doctrines are, on both the nature of God and the pervasive corruption of human sin, which makes "free" choice of God impossible for the unregenerate.

He shares Augustine's intense passion for personal holiness and for the purity of the church, which he also sees as a bastion and foretaste of the kingdom of God on earth. Though we await the full manifestation of God's total rule over a renewed heaven and earth, we are not without responsibility. Indeed, the lives of Christians individually and corporately reflect the character of the God whom they profess to worship, and make the gospel credible or incredible to a watching world. As we saw above, both men believed that the Bible applies to the state and to humanity as a whole, including all the arts and sciences.

Despite their different church affiliations, neither Augustine nor Henry was a "puritan." They recognized that sin will remain in the fellowship of the converted, and that even ministers of the gospel will be infected by its corrosion. Allowing for the necessary changes in situation, I assume that Henry would also have disagreed with the Donatists, who believed that they could build a pure church.

Throughout his career, Henry sought to strengthen the hands of those who chose to remain in denominations that were repudiating the apostolic faith. He kept his own membership in the American Baptist Convention, and gladly lectured at seminaries where, because of his convictions, he would not have been allowed to join the faculty. Some evangelicals might fault him for an excessive desire to influence "liberal" church leaders, but at least we can say that he, like Augustine, eschewed the notion that any Christian organization could be free from sin and error.

Worldwide Influence

Though confined to his own diocese, Augustine exercised international influence through his writings, including his extensive correspondence with Christian leaders around the Mediterranean world. Henry, too, has made an impact on the church in every continent. We have already noted his globe-circling travels. His many books added to the reach of *Christianity Today*, and not just only during his twelve-year term as editor of that journal. Given the opportunity, former students of his at Fuller Seminary and eager listeners to his lectures would join grateful readers of his substantial works in giving thanks to God for the insight and encouragement Henry has conveyed to countless believers and seekers.

Humility

If others did express appreciation, from my experience I think both theologians would both deflect all praise towards God. As he lay on his deathbed, Augustine ordered that the penitential psalms be put up on the walls and ceiling of his room, that he might bewail his manifold offenses and call upon the mercy of the God in whose grace he had trusted. As I wrote these lines some years ago, Henry lay in bed, unable to walk. A back injury in his youth caused pain, but did not stop him from going wherever duty called until the very end of his life, when it finally gave out. I can only guess, but it would not surprise me if he, like his illustrious predecessor, spent his days in confession and humble contrition.

Passion for the Salvation of Souls and for God Himself

Despite its marked dissimilarity to the *Confessions* of Augustine, Henry's autobiography leaves no doubt about the driving passions of his life. Through profound theological writing, incisive commentary, sharp debate; through evangelistic sermons and articles; and through the steady determination that pushes through pain and does not complain; Carl Henry always pursued the salvation of souls through faith in Jesus Christ.

At the end of his story, Henry recounts a dreamlike experience he had while waiting in yet another airport for yet another flight. It seemed that someone like his son was prodding him with pointed questions about his life.

"What do you treasure most?" this person asked. "What is your greatest treasure?"

Let Henry's last words in his autobiography conclude this chapter:

> I'd begin with the Scripture . . . the most read book of my life. And communion with God . . . waiting before God. I have done less waiting than working, and my works would have been better had I waited more. But I have enjoyed God's incomparable companionship. . . . My deepest memories are those spent waiting before God, often praying for others . . . sometimes waiting before him in tears, sometimes in joy, sometimes wrestling alternatives, sometimes just worshipping him in adoration. Heaven will be an unending feast for the soul that basks in his presence. And it will be brighter because some will be there who I brought to Jesus. . . . It is Christ alone who will give unending meaning to a future that will become and remain ever present.[5]

5. Henry, *Confessions of a Theologian*, 407.

PART II

Theological Index to *God, Revelation, and Authority*

The following index shows where the traditional topics (or loci) of systematic theology are treated in the six volumes of *God, Revelation, and Authority*. This list indicates the work's extensive scope of the work, though it also reveals its focus on revelation and on God.

The doctrines are listed in the order in which they are usually discussed in theology texts (though there is some variation among them). Number references indicate volume and, where applicable, chapter, separated by a period (e.g., 5.12, 17–21 refers to volume 5, chapters 12 and 17–21).

Revelation, 1–4
  Preliminary considerations
    (*prolegomena*), 1
  Revelation, 2–4
    Natural revelation, 2.7–11
    Christ, 2.16; 3.4–13, 18
    History, 2.17–22
    The Bible (bibliology), 3.3,
      14–15, 18, 25–28;
      4.2–19
    Revelation as cognitive,
      3.16–17
    Wisdom, 3.18
    Language, 3.19–24
    Propositional
      revelation,
      3.25–27
    Authority, 4.1–5
    Inspiration, 4.6
    Inerrancy, 4.7–8, 16
    Infallibility, 4.9–10

    Illumination, 4.11–14
    Criticism, 4.17
    Canon, 4.18
    Unity of the Bible, 4.19
God (theology proper), 2.1, 4, 10,
    13–15; 3.24; 5–6
  Names of God, 2.12–16
  Reality and objectivity, 5.1
  Being, coming, becoming, 5.2
  Life, 5.3
  Attributes, 5.4–7, 10–17
    Personality, 5.7
    Spirituality, 5.10
    Infinity, 5.11–16
      Omniscience, 5.14
      Eternity, 5.14–15
      Omnipotence, 5.16
    Intellectual attributes,
      5.17–21
    Knowability, 5.19
  Trinity, 5.8–9

God (theology proper)—*continued*
Transcendence and immanence,
6.1–3
Election, 6.4
Creation, 6.5–9
Goodness, 6.11–13
Fatherhood, 6.14
Holiness, 6.15
Love, 6.16
Justice, 6.18–19
Providence, 5.12–13; 6.20
Christ (Christology), 2.16; 3.3, 4,
6–13, 18
The Holy Spirit (pneumatology),
4.11–12; 5.10; 6.17
Man (anthropology), 1.8, 9,16; 2.5,
10, 17–22; 3.14, 19–23, 26;
5.2; 6.9
Angels and demons (angelology,
demonology), 6.10
Sin (hamartology), 1.8, 9; 16; 4.1;
5.18, 20; 6.10
Salvation (soteriology), 3.5; 4.21–2;
6.15–19
The church (ecclesiology), 4.20–23.
Ethics, 4.22–25; 6.15, 18, 19
Last things (eschatology), 3.2; 4.26;
6.21

Macro Index to *God, Revelation, and Authority*

Number references indicate volume and chapter, separated by a period (e.g., 2.19 refers to volume 2, chapter 19). Asterisks indicate that the topic is covered in a sub-section of the given chapter.

a priori views of religion, 1.16, 17

Adam and Christ, 6.9*

angels, 6.10

apriorism

   criticism of, 1.21

   philosophical transcendent, 1.18, 19

   theological transcendent, 1.0

   transcendental religious, 1.22

Aquinas, Thomas, 1.11*

   "proof" of the existence of God, 2.9*

   separation of God's being and activity, 5.6*

atheism

   explanation of nature of man's mind, 5.20*

Augustine of Hippo, 1.11*

   apriorism, 1.20*

authority, revolt against, 6.1

authority, biblical, 4.2*

   reductions of, 4.3

      divine inspiration, 4.4

      inerrancy, 4.7*

Barth, Karl, 1.12* (What follows here is only a very selective list of passages where Henry interacts with Karl Barth;

quotations from Barth in *GRA* run into the hundreds, if not more.)

"common ground" controversy, 1.24*

criticism of natural theology, 2.9*

denial of rational revelation, 3.17*

dialectical theology, 5.18*

doctrine of the Trinity, 5.8*

intelligibility of revelation of God, 3.10*

knowability of essence of God, 5.6*

propositional revelation, 3.14*

rejection of objective interpretation, 4.13*

role of Holy Spirit in revelation, 4.11*

transcendence and immanence of God, 6.2*

biblical narrative, historicity of, 2.19

biblical theology movement, failure of, 4.19*

Big Bang theory and creation, 6.6*

Calvin, John, and apriorism, 1.20*

canon of Scripture
  criteria for canonicity, 4.18*
  debate over, 4.18
  unity of, 4.19
capitalism and evangelicals, 4.25
catastrophism, 6.9*
Christianity, medieval, 1.2*
classical idealism, 1.2*
"common ground" controversy, 1.24
counter-culture, 1.6
creation
  and sexual differentiation, 6.10*
  ex nihilo, doctrine of, 6.6
  goodness of, 6.11*
  in six days, doctrine of, 6.7
    process of, 6.5*
death, 4.26*
Descartes, René
  apriorism, 1.19*
dialectical-existential theology,
    critique of, 5.1*
doctrinal belief and the Word
    (Logos) of God, 3.28
election, doctrine of, 6.4
empiricism, 1.4*
  in Christianity, 1.15
epistemology, 1.4; but all of vol. 1,
    and most of vols. 1–4
eschatology, 3.2, 6.21
evangelicals and capitalism, 4.25*
evil, problem of
  free will, 6.12*
  humanistic views, 6.11*
  philosophical aspects, 6.12
  religious aspects, 6.13
evolutionary theory
  critique of, 6.8
  human rights, 6.7*
exegete, fallibility of, 4.14
fall, 6.10
Feuerbach, Ludwig, 3.14*
God
  as lover, 6.14*

as source of guidance, 6.11*
as sovereign Creator, 6.5
as Spirit, 5.10
attributes of
  methods of determining, 5.4
  personality, 5.7
  relationship to essence, 5.5,6
being, coming, becoming, 5.2
fatherhood of, 6.14
freedom of in election, 6.4
future manifestations of
  character, 6.21
goodness of, 6.11
holiness of, 6.15
immanence of, 6.1*, 2
infinite nature of, 5.11
intellectual attributes of,
    5.17justice of, 6.18, 19
kingdom of, 6.19*
knowability of, 5.19
living, 5.3
love of, 6.16
  and righteousness, 6.16*
mind of, and man's mind, 5.20
omnipotence of, 6.12*
problem of evil, philosophical
    aspects, 6.12
problem of evil, religious aspects,
    6.13
providence of, 6.20
  and Holocaust, 6.20*
    (supplementary note)
reality and objectivity of, 5.1
transcendence and immanence
    of, 6.2
gospel
  as hope for the oppressed, 4.23
  content of, 3.5
Hegel, G.W.F., 1.11*
  apriorism, 1.19*
  dialectical thought, 3.15*
hermeneutical nihilism, 6.13
historical-critical method, 4.17

holiness, 6.15
Holocaust, 6.20* (supplementary
    note)
Holy Spirit
    ministry of, 6.17
    role in church proclamation, 4.20
    role in inspiration of Scripture,
        4.11
image of God
    and Charismatic Movement,
        4.21*
    and suffering/health, 4.21*
    in man, 2.10
    in redeemed man, 4.21
incarnation, 5.10*
    and problem of suffering, 6.13*
inerrancy
    historic perspective, 4.16
    modern struggle over, 4.16*
    teachings of Protestant
        theologians on, 4.16*
    teachings of Reformers on, 4.16*
infinity of Spirit of God, 5.11
inspiration, meaning of, 6.6
intuition, 1.4*
irrationalism, 5.18
Israel, religion and history,
        uniqueness of, 2.18
Jesus
    God's gift of love, 6.16*
    holiness of, 6.15*
    mediator, 3.4
    Messiah, 3.7
        Jewish response, critique of,
            3.8
    suffering of, 6.13*
    the Word of God, 3.6
    view of Scripture, 3.3
Jesus Movement, 1.7
Judaism, response to Messiah, 3.8
Justification, 6.18
    and justice, 6.18*
Kant, Immanuel

philosophic transcendental
    (critical) a priori, 1.21*
    skepticism, 3.17*
    theory of knowledge, 5.1*
Kierkegaard, Søren, and
    irrationalism, 5.18*
kingdom of God
    and justice, 6.19*
language
    origin of, 3.19
        naturalistic explanations,
            3.19*
        theistic explanation, 3.23*
        theistic view of, 3.23
last days, 3.2
Leibnitz, Gottfried, and apriorism,
        1.19*
liberation theology, critique of, 4.24
linguistic philosophy: logical
        positivism, 3.26
literary style, critical views, 4.14*
Locke, John, and apriorism, 1.19*
logic, 3.14
    similarities of Hebrew and Greek,
        3.15*
logical positivism, 1.5, 3.20*
Logos, 3.11
    and Greek philosophy, 3.12
    and logic, 3.14
    and modern world, 3.12*
    and New Testament, 3.11*
    and Old Testament, 3.11*
    counterfeits, 3.12
    as mediator of revelation of God,
        3.13
love, 6.16
Luther, Martin, and apriorism, 1.20*
man
    origin and nature of, 6.9
    priority in creation of, 6.10*
Marxism, 4.25
    and Christians, 4.25*
    and transcendence of God, 6.2*

Marxism—*continued*
    explanation of nature of man's
        mind, 5.20*
    view of societal problems,
        Christian critique of, 4.25
Moltmann, Jürgen, 2.21*
monotheism
    biblical, 5.8*
    of non-Christian philosophies
        and religions, 5.8*
mystery and revelation, 3.1
myth, 1.3, 9
names of God, 2.13
names of Jesus as revelation of God,
    2.16
natural theology, rejection of, 2.9
naturalism, failure of in explaining
    man's reason, 5.20*
Neo-protestantism
    objections to prepositional
        revelation, 3.25
Pannenberg, Wolfhart, 2.21*
Paul of Tarsus, conversion of, 3.9*
Pentateuch, authorship of, 4.14*
philosophy, relationship to theology,
    1.11
Plato
    apriorism, 1.18*
prayer
    and providence of God, role of,
        6.20*
problem passages of the Bible,
    perspective on, 4.15
process philosophy, rise of, 6.3
proper names of God
    Elohim, 2.14
    El-Shaddai, 2.14
    Yahweh, 2.15
propositional revelation
    and the Bible, 3.27*
    objections to, 3.25
providence, 6.20
    and Holocaust 6. 20*
        (supplementary note)

reason, 1.4*
religious language
    and logic, 3.15
    distinctiveness of, 3.22
    meaning of, views, 3.21
    meaningfulness of, 3.20
resurrection of Jesus, 3.9
revelation of God, 2.1
    and cultural conditioning, 5.21
    and infinite nature of God, 5.11
    and mental action, 3.16
    and mystery, 3.1
    and nature, 2.8
    and wisdom, 3.18
    as personal, 2.12
    as prepositional, 3.27
    cognitive aspects, 3.17
    comprehensibility, 2.4; 3.10
    did God *speak*?, 3.24
        instances of, 4.26*
        silences of God, 4.26*
    evangelical view, 3.16*
    forms of, views, 2.11
    general, value of, 1.9*
    in history, 2.17
        critique of recent theories of,
            2.21
        evangelical perspective, 2.22
        views of, 2.20
    in names of Jesus, 2.16
    modern errors of, 3.16*
    purposes, 2.2
    responses, 2.3
    turn of modern theology from,
        3.17*
    unity of, 2.6
    varieties, 2.7
salvation, 3.5
    goodness of, 6.11*
Satan and demons, 6.10
science and epistemology, 1.10
Scripture
    inerrancy, 4.7
        and infallibility of copies, 4.9
    infallibility of, meaning, 4.10

secular worldview, 1.8
  secular science, failure of, 5.20*
self-transcendence, 2.5
sexual differentiation and creation,
      6.10*
silence of God, 4.26
soteriology, 3.5
Spinoza, Baruch, 1.11*
  apriorism, 1.19*
suffering
  and goodness of God, 6.13*
supernatural, concept of,
      meaningfulness of, 6.1
Tertullian, 1.11*
theology
  as science, 1.12
  method and criteria, 1.13, 14
theophanies, 5.10*
Trinity
  doctrine of, 5.9
      inadequate formulations
            of, 5.8
Western culture, 1.2
wisdom and the revelation of God,
      3.18
women, creation of, 6.10*

Outline of *God, Revelation, and Authority*

Number references indicate the page and paragraph number, separated by a period, where the treatment of a topic begins (e.g., 121.2 refers to page 121, paragraph 2, of the pertaining volume). Paragraphs are numbered beginning with the first full, indented paragraph on a page; a 0 indicates a paragraph continued from the preceding page. References correspond to the edition published by Word Books, Waco, TX, 1976–83. Note that Henry used "man" generically throughout *GDA*; this outline follows his usage.

Volume I

Introduction: Introduction to Theology

    I.   Theology not a popular subject (13.3)
    II.   Theology not considered reasonable today (13.4)
    III. Christian theology must deal with truth (14.2)

Chapter 1: The Crisis of Truth and Word

    I.   Distrust of final truth (17.1)
    II.   Two competing forces (17.2)
        a. The Christian gospel (17.3)
        b. The mass media (18.1)
            i.   False claim to objectivity (18.2)
            ii.   Skepticism (19.2)
            iii. False claim to immediacy (20.1)
            iv. An ancient conflict (21.1)
            v.   The challenge of science (21.3)
            vi. Media power (22.2)
            vii. Truth in doubt (24.2)

        viii.   Non-verbal communication (26.2)
         ix.   Restoring speech to the Word of God (28.2)

Chapter 2: The Clash of Cultural Perspectives

   I.   Classical Idealism (31.2)
         a.   Naturalism (31.2)
         b.   Challenge to naturalism (32.1)
         c.   Idealism (32.2)
   II.   Medieval Christianity (32.4)Failure of classical idealism
         (32.4)
         a.   Divine revelation (33.1)
         b.   Contrast with classical philosophy (34.1)
         c.   Medieval synthesis of reason and revelation (36.1)
   III. Modern Western philosophy (36.2)
         a.   Connection with Aquinas' error (36.2)
         b.   Problem of terminology (37.1)
         c.   Similarity to classical mind (37.2)
         d.   Early modern naturalism (37.3)
         e.   Later modern naturalism (39.1)
         f.   The current view of man (39.2)
         g.   The choice: Christianity or nihilism? (41.3)

Chapter 3: Revelation and Myth

   I.   The universality of "myths" (44.1)
   II.   The nature of myth (45.3)
   III. Ancient views of myth (46.3)
         a.   Greek philosophers (46.3)
         b.   Old Testament (47.2)
         c.   New Testament (48.2)
   IV.   Modern critical ["critical" means non-evangelical] views of
         myth (51.3)
         a.   Application to Bible stories (51.3)
         b.   Myth is necessary: Bultmann (52.3)
         c.   Different types of "myth" in the New Testament? (55.1)
         d.   Basic assumption of critical views (56.1)
         e.   Meaning of "myth" unclear (59.2)
   V.   Criticism of the use of myth in Christian theology (63.2)
         a.   Could any myth be true? (63.2)

       b.   Logical problems with modern views of myth (65.2)

       c.   The importance of objective truth for Christian theology (68.1)

Chapter 4: The Ways of Knowing

Introduction (70.1)

    I.   Intuition

       a.   Religious mysticism (70.4)

          i. Basic idea of mysticism (70.4)

          ii. Weaknesses of mysticism (71.2)

              1.   The mystic cannot speak clearly about God (71.2)

              2.   The mystic cannot have any personal knowledge of God (71.3)

              3.   The mystic cannot talk about God (71.4)

              4.   The mystic cannot talk about ultimate reality (71.5)

              5.   The mystic cannot explain why others should believe him (72.1)

          iii. The Bible contradicts mysticism (73.1)

              1.   God is different from the world; mysticism is pantheistic (73.1)

              2.   God is not "beyond good and evil" (73.2)

              3.   God reveals himself in space and time (73.3)

              4.   The biblical view of our relationship to God (73.3)

       b.   Rational intuition (74.1)

       c.   Empiricism (74.6)

          i. Modern empiricism (74.6)

          ii. Kant's critique (75.3)

          iii. Hegel (76.1)

       d.   Summary: difficulties of all these views (76.2)

       e.   Christian rational intuition (76.3)

    II.   Experience (78.1)

       a.   Introduction

       b.   Empiricism of Aristotle and Thomas Aquinas (78.3)

       c.   Modern philosophical and theological empiricism (78.4)

      d. Influence of evolutionary thought (79.1)
      e. Hume attacks Thomism (79.2)
      f. Schleiermacher: religious consciousness (80.1)
      g. Humanism (82.3)
      h. Scientism: limitations (83.3)
      i. Logical Positivism's total reliance on science (84.3)
      j. Limitations of empiricism (85.1)

III. Reason (85)
      a. Introduction (85.1)
      b. Philosophical rationalism: strengths and weaknesses (90.1)
      c. The eclipse of reason (90.3)
      d. Modern prejudice against revelation (91.3)
      e. The only reasonable alternative: evangelical Christian revelation (93.3)

Chapter 5: The Rise and Fall of Logical Positivism

I. The challenge of logical positivism (96.1)
II. Positivism criticized (98.2; 102.2, middle; 110.3)

Chapter 6: The Countercultural Revolt

I. Causes of the countercultural revolt (112.1)
II. Significance of the countercultural revolt (113.3)
III. Growing concern over technological society (113.4)
IV. Similarity between youth quest and evangelical faith (114.1)
V. Mythology of the youth culture (117.2)
VI. Scientism and youth revolt's existentialism compared (118.1)
VII. The need for reason (119.1)
VIII. Is the new Marxism "rational"? (119.2)
IX. Weakness of the technocratic world view (120.1)
X. The need for the biblical view (121.2)

Chapter 7: The Jesus Movement and Its Future

I. Introduction (122.1)
II. Similarities to youth counterculture (123.3)
III. Differences from youth counterculture (123.4)
IV. Similarity to contemporary culture (126.2)
V. Relationship to evangelicals' increasing concern for social justice (128.2)

VI.   Relationship to Charismatic Movement (131.2)

VII.   Theological weakness of the Jesus Movement (131.4)

VIII.   General weakness of American evangelical movement (133.1)

Chapter 8: Secular Man and Ultimate Concerns

I.   Introduction (135.1)

II.   Outline (135.3)

III.   The secular world view (135.4)

    a.   Theory of reality and knowledge: secular empiricism (136.1)

    b.   View of man: autonomous (136.3)

    c.   Implications (137.2)

        i.   Comprehensive contingency (137.3)

        ii.   Total transience (138.3)

        iii.   Radical relativity (139.1)

        iv.   Absolute autonomy of man (139.2)

IV.   Inconsistency of the secular view (140.4)

    a.   Search for meaning (141.1)

    b.   Lack of control (143.2)

V.   Dilemmas of secularism (144.1)

    a.   Unwarranted moralism (144.2)

    b.   Secularism and revelation (148.1)

Chapter 9: The Meaning or Myths Man Lives By

I.   Introduction: the debate (152.1)

II.   Modern myths (153.1)

III.   Presence of myth in philosophy (154.0)

IV.   Biblical explanation of origin of myths (155.2)

V.   Secular and Christian views of the origin of myths (156.2)

VI.   Scientism vs. Christianity (156.4)

VII.   Myth is the response to revelation (158.2)

VIII.   Value of "general revelation" (160.1)

IX.   Conclusion (163.1)

Chapter 10: Theology and Science

I.   Introduction: science looks down on Christianity (165.1)

II.   Some Christians also worship science (166.2)

III.   Loss of confidence in science to benefit man (167.1)

IV.   Loss of confidence in science to discover the truth (167.2)

V.   The necessity of faith (169.1)

VI.   Lack of agreement among scientists (171.2)

VII. Science is not objective (172.1)

VIII. Science also deals with metaphysics (172.2)

IX.   Is science knowledge or opinion? (174.2)

X.   Is science rational? (174.3)

Chapter 11: Theology and Philosophy

I.   Introduction (181.1)

II.   Christian views of the relationship between theology and philosophy

    a.   Paul (181.2)

    b.   "Three ways" (182.2)

        i.   Tertullian (182.3)

        ii.   Augustine (183.1)

        iii. Aquinas (184.1)

III. Philosophers' views (185.1)

    a.   Exaltation of reason: Spinoza and Hegel (185.3)

    b.   Limitation of reason (187.1)

        i.   Hume and Kant (187.2)

        ii.   Schleiermacher and dialectical-existential theology (187.4)

        iii. Barth (188.1)

IV.   Evangelical theology and philosophy (192.2)

    a.   The need for revelation (193.2)

    b.   Intelligibility of revelation (193.3)

    c.   Relationship of philosophy and theology: some statements (194.1)

    d.   Revelation demands a certain metaphysical view (198.2)

    e.   The decisive question: relationship of revealed theology and secular philosophy? (199.2)

    f.   A tense partnership (200.2)

    g.   Primacy of revelation (201.1)

Chapter 12: Is Theology a Science?

I.   Introduction (202.1)

II.   Theology as science (202.2)

III.   New definitions of science exclude theology (202.3)

IV.   Aquinas' error (203.1)

V.   Barth's rejection of scientific nature of theology (203.2)

VI.   Christianity is not "pre-scientific" (203.3)

VII.   The priority and uniqueness of theology (204.4)

VIII. The Christian's freedom from "science" (206.4)

IX.   Theology must be rational and "scientific" (207.4)

X.   A partnership between science and theology (209.3)

Chapter 13: The Method and Criteria of Theology (I)

Revelation: The basic epistemological axiom

I.   The necessity of identifying method and criteria (213.2)

II.   A transcultural method (214.4)

III.   The first principle: God in his revelation (215.3)

    a.   Challenges to this principle (216.1)

        i.   Universal relativity (216.2)

        ii. Rival religions that deny revelation (217.3)

        iii. Liberal subjectivity (218.2)

        iv. Evangelical denials of this principle (218.3)

    b.   Re-affirmation: God's revelation in Scripture is primary (223.2)

Chapter 14: The Method and Criteria of Theology (II)

The role of reason, scripture, consistency and coherence

I.   Introduction (225.1)

II.   Reason (225.2)

    a.   The effects of the fall (226.2)

    b.   Man's ability to reason (227.1)

    c.   The importance of truth (278.2)

    d.   Summary (228.3)

III.   Scripture (229.1)

    a.   The universal truth claim of Christianity (229.3)

    b.   Christian theology can be investigated by anyone (229.4)

    c.   Objections refuted (230.1)

    i.   Karl Barth (230.1)
    ii. Clark Pinnock (230.2)
    iii. John Montgomery (230.3)
  d.   Summary: the Bible verifies theology (232.1)
IV.   Logical consistency (232.2)
  a.   The role of logical tests of truth (232.3)
  b.   The necessity of logical consistency (232.5)
  c.   Objections to logical consistency as a test of truth (234.1)
  d.   The value and limits of appealing to the logical consistency of Christian truth (238.2)
V.   Coherence
  a.   The nature and origin of systematic theology (238.3)
  b.   The limits of all attempts at coherence in theology (240.1)
  c.   The value of systematic theology (240.3)
VI.   The apologetic nature of Christian theology (241.2)
  a.   Using the laws of logic (241.2)
    i.   Barth's objections answered (241.3)
  b.   The apologetic task of Christian theology (244.1)
  c.   Summary (244.3)

Chapter 15: Empirical Verification and Christian Theism

I.   Truth claims should be open to verification by an appropriate method (245.4)
II.   The demand for empirical verification (246.1)
III.   Different presuppositions lead to different interpretations of sense experiences (248.1)
IV.   True faith is not unreasonable (248.3)
V.   The value and limits of scientific thought (250.2–3)
VI.   Beware of making experience the test of Christian truth (250.4)
VII.   Errors of some evangelical theologians (251.1)
VIII.   Example # 1: Genco (251.2; 253.4)

Chapter 16: Man's Primal Religious Experience

I.   The return to *a priori* views of religion (273.1)
II.   Introduction to the *a priori* view (273.3)

III.   Varieties of *a priori* thought (275.1)
IV.   Brief review of several types of non-rational *a priori* thought among theologians (275–79)
V.   Evangelical *a priori* thought emphasizes rationality

Chapter 17: *A Priori* Explanation of Religion

I.   Introduction to the *a priori* view (280.1)
II.   Three types of *a priori* thought (281.1)
III. The importance of the *a priori* view (282.2)
IV.   The distinctive nature of modern *a priori* thought

Chapter 18: The Philosophical Transcendent *a Priori* (I)

I.   Plato's apriorism (285.1)
    a.   Plato's theory (286.2)
    b.   Plato and Christian theology (286.3)
II.   Medieval apriorism (287.4)

Chapter 19: The Philosophical Transcendent *a Priori* (II)

I.   Cartesian apriorism (301.3)
II.   Separation of innate ideas from supernatural revelation (301.1)
III. Emphasis upon the soul and sensation (303.2)
IV.   Explanation of Descartes' abandonment of the ancient and medieval view of the reality of innate ideas (He also shows how Descartes' rejection of the supernatural source of innate ideas, and his separation of mind and matter, influenced later Western philosophy.) (303–7)
V.   Summary: Descartes' influence on Western philosophy (308.0)
VI.   Spinoza and the *a priori* (308.1)
VII. Spinoza embraces pantheism (308.2)
VIII. Locke's rejection of modern innatism (310.1)
IX.   Ideas come from sensation and reflection (310.3)
X.   Leibnitz's apriorism (314.3)
XI.   Leibnitz rejects both Locke and Augustine (314.4–5)
XII. Leibnitz's influence upon Hume (and modern philosophy) (318.1)
XIII. Hegelian apriorism (320.1)

XIV. Hegel's pantheism (320.2)

XV. Conclusion (321.4)

XVI. Philosophical transcendent apriorism (321.5)

XVII. Theological transcendent apriorism (322.4)

Chapter 20: The Theological Transcendent *a Priori*

I. Introduction

II. Augustine's apriorism (325.1)

    a. Augustine differs from Plato (325.3)

    b. The need for special revelation (329.1)

    c. General revelation: from Creator to creature (330.2)

    d. The importance of faith (331.1)

III. Luther's apriorism (331.2)

    a. Sin distorts man's reason (331.3)

    b. Nevertheless, innate knowledge of God is possible (332.3)

IV. Calvin's apriorism (334.5)

    a. All knowledge comes from divine revelation (334.7)

    b. Knowledge of God and of self are related (335.2)

    c. What men know about God (336.2)

    d. The purpose of our knowledge of God (336.3)

    e. The role of the will and the affections (336.2)

    f. All men have some knowledge of God (337.3)

    g. The clarity of general revelation (337.4)

    h. Two distinctives of Calvin's view (339.2)

        i. What the sinner can know about God (340.2)

        ii. The effects of innate knowledge of God (340.4)

            1. Rational: idolatry (340.1)

            2. Moral: conscience (341.2)

    i. Knowledge of man and nature also comes from God (342.1)

    j. Necessity for special revelation (343.2)

Chapter 21: The Philosophic Transcendental (Critical) *a Priori*

I. Introduction (344.1)

II. Kant's philosophic transcendental (critical) *a priori* (344.2)

III. The transcendental *a priori* (345.1)

IV. The Christian answer to Kant (360.4)

V. The failure of the post-Kantian empirical movement (361.1)

Chapter 22: Transcendental Religious Apriorism

I. Introduction

II. All humans have religious experience (364.1)

III. Rejection of innate ideas about God (365.0)

IV. Validity of religious experience shown by its universality (365.2)

V. Subjective rather than objective knowledge (366.3)

VI. Critiques of the views of thinkers such as Anders Nygren, Ernst Troeltsch, Rudolph Otto, and Carl Stange, who deny the possibility of objective knowledge of God (367–76)

VII. Difficulties of transcendental religious Apriorism (376.1)

VIII. A new definition of "validity" (378.1)

IX. Triumph of modern pragmatism and naturalism (378.2)

Chapter 23: Reflections on Religious Apriorism

I. The necessity of religion for civilization (380.1)

II. Failure of the critical approach (381.3)

III. Connecting innate ideas with ultimate reality (382.2)

IV. Explaining the existence of religion (385.2)

V. Human knowledge based upon the divine Logos (386.4)

VI. Critique of Kant's response to empiricism (387.4)

VII. An alternative to both Hume and Kant (392.2)

VIII. Christian religious *a priori* (394.1)

Chapter 24: The "Common Ground" Controversy

I. Introduction (395.1)

II. The gulf between Christian and non-Christian views (396.1)

III. Debate between Barth and Reformed views

    a. Traditional Reformed view "common ground" (396.2)

    b. Barth's view of God's image in man (396.3)

    c. Reformed view (397.3)

IV. Biblical view of "general revelation" (399.5)

    a. Man's reason can receive divine revelation (399.5)

    b. Sinful man suppresses truth (400.1)

V. The role of logic in man's reasoning (400.2)

VI. Underlying knowledge of God comes from God's image (401.2)

VII. The effects of the fall (403.1)
- a. Creation of different world views
- b. Everyone has some kind of faith (404.2)
- c. Biblical view of world religions (405.1)
- d. No common axioms between Christianity and other religions (405.2)
- e. The need for special revelation (405.3)

VIII. Conclusion (409.3)

Volume II

Introduction

Chapter 1: The Awesome Disclosure of God

I. If we are to know God, he must decide to reveal himself (18.1)

II. God reveals previously hidden truth about himself (20.3)

III. The duty of the church to proclaim God's revealed Word (22.1)

IV. The exclusiveness of God's revealed truth (25.2)

V. The certain triumph of God's revelation (26.1)

VI. Signs and wonders (27.1)

Chapter 2: A Place in God's Kingdom

I. God reveals himself for his own glory (30.1)

II. God's revelation is given for human benefit
- a. Man's special distinction: his personal relationship with God (30.2)
- b. God could have withheld his revelation from man (30.4)
- c. God could have ceased his saving revelation (31.1)
- d. God speaks to us now (31.2)
- e. God's purpose in revelation is that we might know him (31.3)

III. God's revelation offers us privileged communion with our Creator in his kingdom
- a. God has sovereign authority (32.1)

         b.   God has a special interest in men (32.2)
            i.   Creation (32.2)
           ii.   Redemption promised to Jews (32.3)
          iii.   Redemption in the New Testament (33.1)
          iv.   Christ's ministry for us now (33.2)
         c.   God is King (33.3)
            i.   Many reject his kingship (34.1)
           ii.   Jesus fulfills Old Testament promises concerning the kingdom (34.2)
          iii.   Jesus promised entrance to the kingdom (34.3)
          iv.   Jesus manifested the presence of the kingdom (35.1)
           v.   The Apostles preached the present reality of the kingdom (35.2)
          vi.   Christians experience God's kingdom even now (36.1)

IV.   God's revelation is for our benefit (36.2)
V.   Christ's present kingly rule must be proclaimed and obeyed (37.1)

Chapter 3: Not By Good Tidings Alone

I.   To reject or accept God's revelation brings great consequences (38.2)
II.   God's revelation must be received by faith to benefit us (40.2)
III.   Eternal punishment awaits the unbelieving and unrepentant sinner (41.3)
IV.   Knowledge alone is not enough to save us (42.1)
V.   Summary (45.2)

Chapter 4: The Hidden and Revealed God

I.   Introduction (47.1)
II.   God's revelation does not exhaust his mystery
         a.   Biblical prophets different from pagan prophets (48.1)
         b.   Biblical prophets often resisted God's revelation (50.1)
         c.   No man can understand God without God's revelation (50.2)
         d.   Biblical revelation differs from modern pantheism and mysticism (51.2)

e. All theologians are fallible; only the Bible is infallible (52.1)
III. But God has revealed himself
a. God's revelation is reliable, rational, and clear (54.1)
b. Summary (56.2)

Chapter 5: Self-transcendence and the Image of God

I. Introduction: the problem with the idea of self-transcendence (58.2)
II. The difference between biblical and non-biblical religion (62.2)
III. God's revelation requires intelligent meditation (64.1)
IV. The nature and results of pagan mysticism (64.3)
V. The origins of Western ideas of self-transcendence (66.1)
VI. The "new man" (66.4)
VII. Challenges to modern ideas of self-sufficiency (67.2)

Chapter 6: The Unity of Divine Revelation

I. Unlike pagan "gods," Yahweh is one (69.1)
II. From the beginning, God revealed himself as the only God (70.1)
III. Beware of dividing God's revelation (71.3)
IV. Revelation can have different forms (73.2)
V. The unity and interdependence of the Old and New Testament (74)
VI. Conclusion (76.2)

Chapter 7: Varieties of Divine Revelation

I. God decides in what forms he will reveal himself (77.1)
II. God reveals himself in many ways (79)
III. We should not neglect any of the forms of revelation (82.1)
IV. God's revelation through creation: "general revelation" (83.1)
V. General and special revelation (86.3)
VI. Problems of Neo-orthodox theology (87.3)
VII. Summary (90.1)

Chapter 8: Divine Revelation in Nature

I. Modern denials of revelation through nature (91.1)

II.   The unity of nature and history in the Bible (92.1)

III.   The contrast between Hebrew and pagan views (93.2)

IV.   Modern naturalism (95.3)

V.   The contrast between the Bible and modern naturalism (96.2)

VI.   The biblical view of nature (98.1)

VII.   God's purpose for nature (99.1)

VIII.   The cause of the ecological crisis (100.1)

IX.   The salvation of nature (101)

Chapter 9: The Rejection of Natural Theology

I.   Introduction (104.1)

    a.   Roman Catholic natural theology

    b.   Aquinas' "proof" of the existence of God (104.3)

    c.   Weakness of Aquinas' view (113)

    d.   The unintended result of Thomism (115.1)

II.   Protestant natural theology

    a.   James Orr's natural theology (115.2)

    b.   Criticism of Protestant natural theology (117.2)

    c.   Modernism (120.1)

III.   The rejection of natural theology

    a.   Barth's criticism of natural theology (120.2)

    b.   Conclusion: the proper reason for rejecting natural theology (122.2)

Chapter 10: The Image of God in Man

I.   Introduction: the image of God in man has many aspects (124.1)

II.   "Formal" aspects of the image of God (125.4)

    a.   The rational aspect (125.4)

    b.   The moral aspect (126.2)

    c.   The faith aspect (126.3)

    d.   Importance of "formal" aspects (126.4)

III.   "Material" aspects of the image of God in man (128.2)

    a.   The Bible says man knows something about God (128.2)

    b.   God is the source of all true thought and knowledge about God and the world (133.2)

   c. Man is not God (134.2)

   d. But man knows a great deal because of God's image (134.3)

 IV. The effects of the fall of man: before (134.4)

   a. The effects are greater than Roman Catholics say (135.1)

   b. The fall did not obliterate the ability to think or to know something about God (135.4)

 V. Recent interpretations of the image of God (Here Henry critiques the views of Barth, Brunner, and other scholars.) (137.3)

Chapter 11: Recent Conjectural Views of Revelational Forms

 I. Introduction (143.1)

 II. Karl Barth (143.2)

 III. Moltmann (147.4)

 IV. Ogden (148.2)

Chapter 12: Divine Revelation as Personal

 I. Introduction (151.1)

 II. God's Name (151.2)

 III. Prohibition of images (152.1)

 IV. God's incomparability (152.3)

 V. Theophanies (155.1)

 VI. God takes initiative in revelation (156.3)

 VII. Modern distortions of God's self-presentation (157.2)

 VIII. Philosophical roots and consequences of modern views (162.3)

 IX. Conclusion (166.1)

Chapter 13: The Names of God

 I. God's name reveals God's nature (172.4)

 II. God uses human language to reveal himself (175.3)

 III. God's names accurately reflect God's essence (177.1)

   a. Several names for one God (177.1)

   b. God's names reveal rational truths about God (178.4)

 IV. God's names are connected with history (180.3)

 V. Cumulative revelation (181.4)

 VI. The relationship between different names of God (182.1)

Chapter 14: God's Proper Names: Elohim, El Shaddai

- I.   Introduction (184.1)
- II.   Elohim (184)
  - a.   Elohim and related names (187.1)
    - i.   Elohim (187.2)
    - ii.   Eloah (191.1)
    - iii.   El and its compound names (191.3)
- III.   El Shaddai (193)
  - a.   The patriarchal name (193.1)
  - b.   Derivation and meaning (193.2)
  - c.   Distinction from Elohim (194.1)
  - d.   Elohim and Yahweh (195)
- IV.   The Significance of Exodus 3:14 (6:2–3)
  - a.   The debate (195.2)
  - b.   Evangelical views (202.3)
  - c.   Weaknesses of critical view (206.2)
  - d.   Conclusion (208.1)

Chapter 15: God's Proper Names: Yahweh

- I.   Yahweh: Introduction (210.1)
  - a.   The uncertain derivation and original meaning of Yahweh (210.2)
  - b.   Different interpretations of the meaning of Yahweh in Exodus 3:14 (212.2)
    - i.   "I am the One who is" (213.1)
    - ii.   "I am who I am" (215.3)
    - iii.   "I will be what I will be" (218.1)
    - iv.   "I cause to be what I cause to be" (218.3)
    - v.   "I am present is what I am" (219.2)
  - c.   Yahweh: the God who is present with his people (221.3)
  - d.   Yahweh: the highest revelation of God in the Old Testament (223.1)
- II.   Adonai and other names (223.2)
  - a.   Adonai (223.2)
  - b.   Other names (223.5)
  - c.   Yahweh=Lord=Jesus (224.3)

III.   Conclusion: God's names show his sovereign power and redemptive presence (224.4)

Chapter 16: Jesus: The Revelation of the New Testament Name

I.   Introduction: God's name given to Jesus (226.1)
II.   Jesus: God with us (227.4)
III.   Jesus: "I am" (228.3)
IV.   Correct names for Jesus are important (229.2)
V.   The meaning of "Jesus" (230.1)
VI.   Christ
VII.   "Son of Man" as a name for Jesus (232.2)
VIII. Lord (Kurios) (235.2)
IX.   Son of God (239.2)
     a.   Origin of the term Son of God (239.2)
     b.   The Son of the Father (241.2)
X.   Jesus, the manifested presence of Yahweh (243.1)
     a.   The revelation of the Triune name of God (243.2)
     b.   Jesus and the Spirit (244.1)
     c.   Jesus is "I Am" (244.3)
XI.   Conclusion (245.2)

Chapter 17: Divine Revelation in History

I.   Modern rejection of the biblical view of history (247.1)
II.   Old Testament view of nature, history, and God (247.2)
III.   God rules history from beginning to end (250.2)
IV.   God judges not only Israel, but all the nations (251.2)
     a.   In this present age (251.2)
     b.   At the end of time (252.4)
V.   The Gentiles are accountable for their rejection of God's revelation in nature and history (253.1)
VI.   Salvation also available to Gentiles (253.2)
VII.   The uniqueness of Israel's view of history (253.3)
VIII. Nothing falls outside of God's sovereign rule of history (254.1)
IX.   The unity and purpose of history (255.2)
X.   The historical nature of Christian revelation (255.3)
XI.   Conclusion (256.1)

Chapter 18: The Leveling of Biblical History

    I.   Introduction: The denial of the uniqueness of Israel's religion (257.1)
    II.   Response: the Bible claims that God acts in history (258.3)
    III.   The idea of the covenant (260.3)
    IV.   Israel's relationship to her neighbors (265.2)

Chapter 19: Faith, Tradition, and History

    I.   Introduction (267.1)
    II.   The Old Testament is rooted in history (272.1)
    III.   Secular theology (275.3)
    IV.   Theology of revolution: a critique (278.2)

Chapter 20: Revelation and History: Bart, Bultmann and Cullmann

    I.   Introduction (281.1)
    II.   The skepticism of secular philosophers and historians (282.3)
    III.   Dialectical-existential theology: "revelation" occurs only within the human mind (284.1)
        a.   Bultmann (284.3)
        b.   Barth (287.1)
        c.   Salvation-history school: Cullmann (289.2)

Chapter 21: Revelation and History: Moltmann and Pannenberg

    I.   Introduction (294.1)
    II.   Moltmann's theology of revelation and history; critique (294.1)
    III.   Pannenberg's theology of revelation and history (296.2)
        a.   Rejection of Word theology (296.3)
        b.   Critique of Pennenberg's view (297.4)
    IV.   Further critique of Moltmann (305.2)
    V.   Evangelical critique of some recent theologies of historical revelation (30.1)

Chapter 22: Revelation and History in Evangelical Perspective

    I.   Introduction: the importance of history to the Christian religion (311.1)
    II.   The Bible's unique idea of history (312.2)
    III.   The historical reliability of the Bible (314.2)

IV. Historical evidence is valid, though it is not conclusive (315.1)

V. All writing of history is influenced by philosophy and theology (318)

VI. The limits of historical evidence (319.3)

VII. The Bible sheds light upon history (320.3)

VIII. Is the New Testament a trustworthy historical document? (323.2)

IX. The historical method and miracles (325.3)

X. Fact and meaning in history (330.2)

XI. Two pivotal events in history (331.1)

XII. Secular and Christian history compared (332.3)

Volume III

Chapter 1: The Disclosure of God's Eternal Secret

I. The biblical idea of "mystery" is unique (9.1)

II. Revelation unveils the mystery (11.1)

III. The mystery centers upon Christ (11.2)

IV. The mystery fulfills the prophets (12.1)

V. The mystery is not accessible to human reason (12.3)

VI. The mystery points to a future fulfillment (13.3)

VII. The mystery declares Jesus to be the center of the universe (14.1)

VIII. Our security comes from God's choice of us in Christ, as revealed by the mystery (15.2)

Chapter 2: Prophecy and Fulfillment: The Last Days

I. Introduction (20.1)

II. The Last Days are here (20.2)

    a. The Old Testament is being fulfilled (20.2)

    b. The in-between era (21.2)

    c. The new era comes in Jesus (22.4)

    d. The age of the Spirit (23.3)

III. The last hour is coming soon (24.1)

    a. The end has not yet come (24.1)

    b. Jesus taught the distinction between this age and the next (24.3)

  c. Our response in this age is crucial (25.2)

  d. Signs of the coming end of time (26.1)

  e. The end will come only with the return of Jesus (26.4)

  f. Jesus will come soon (27)

Chapter 3: Jesus' View of Scripture

 I. Jesus considered the Old Testament to be God's Word (28.1)

 II. The Old Testament cannot be invalidated (29.1)

 III. Jesus modified some current views of Scripture (30.1)

  a. Scripture is superior to tradition (30.2)

  b. Scripture points to fulfillment in Christ (31.3)

   i. But Jesus nevertheless considered Old Testament history to be reliable (33.3)

   ii. The contrast of "letter" and "spirit" (35.3)

  c. Jesus claimed authority for his own words (38.1)

   i. But Jesus did not criticize the Old Testament (38.3)

  d. Jesus inaugurated the "new covenant" (41.2)

   i. "New heart" predicted by Old Testament (42.4)

   ii. Jesus promises the coming of the Spirit (43.2)

  e. Jesus pointed toward the writing of the New Testament (44.1)

 IV. Summary

Chapter 4: The Only Divine Mediator

 I. The fundamental distinction between biblical faith and other religions (48.1)

 II. The Old Testament contains the concept of mediator (50.1)

 III. Judaism rejects the idea of a substitutionary mediator (52.2)

 IV. Human mediators in the Old Testament (53.2)

 V. The Angel of the LORD (54.3)

 VI. The Spirit (55.2)

 VII. The Word of God (56.1)

 VIII. How can God forgive sins? (57.2)

 IX. The New Testament portrays the final Mediator (59.2)

Chapter 5: The Content of the Gospel

 I. Jesus: the center of the gospel

a. The heart of the gospel (63.1)

b. The prophets announced the coming savior (65.1)

c. Jesus announced the fulfillment of Old Testament prophecy (65.2)

d. Jesus himself manifests the coming of the kingdom (65.3)

e. Men are judged by how they respond to Jesus Christ (65.4)

f. Jesus has already begun to rule (66.4)

II. Crucial points of the gospel (67.1)

a. God, the holy Creator and Judge (67.2)

b. God's promise of a Messiah (67.3)

c. Jesus fulfills God's promise (67.4)

d. Jesus brings true liberation (68.1)

e. Jesus brings personal renewal (68.2)

f. Jesus brings corporate renewal through the church (68.3)

g. Jesus rules over, and through, civil government (69.3)

h. Jesus will establish perfect righteousness when he returns (73.2)

Chapter 6: Jesus and the Word

I.   Introduction: the modern debate (75.1)

II.   The place of Christianity in the history of religions (75.2)

III. Jesus Christ combines both the act of revelation and the word of revelation (76.1)

IV. God's word calls for decision (78.1)

V.   The "amen" of Jesus (82.3)

VI. The very words ("*ipsissima verba*") of Jesus (85)

a. Introduction (85)

b. Redaction criticism (87.3)

c. Differences among Gospel accounts (89.2)

d. The role of the Holy Spirit in the composition of the Gospel accounts (91.2)

e. The relationship of Jesus' words to the Apostles' teaching (94.1)

VII. Conclusion (98.1)

Chapter 7: Jesus Christ: God-Man or Man-God?

I. Jesus Christ: the essential unity of the Old and New Testaments (101.3)
II. The importance of proper exegesis of the Old Testament (103.1)
III. The limitations of Old Testament revelation (105)
IV. The controversy about Jesus' person (105.2)
V. The importance of special revelation (106.1)
VI. The New Testament claims that Jesus fulfilled messianic prophecies (108.3)
VII. The New Testament also claims that Jesus is God (109.1)
VIII. Jesus is God's unique Son (112.2)
IX. Jesus is David's "Son" and Lord (113.1)

Chapter 8: Shall We Look for Another?

I. Introduction: objections based upon the work of Christ (118.1)
II. The role of the Jews in God's plan (120.1)
III. Christianity and social concern
   a. The role of the church in God's plan (121.3)
   b. The limits of social action (122.2)

Chapter 9: The Resurrection of the Crucified Jesus

I. Introduction: the importance of Jesus' resurrection (147.1)
II. The evidence from Jesus' enemies (147.2)
   a. The empty tomb (148.1)
   b. The conversion of Saul of Tarsus (150.1)
   c. Summary of evidence from enemies (154.2)
III. Evidence from Jesus' friends (154.3)
   a. Jesus' rebukes (154.3)
   b. The reasons for the disciples' initial unbelief (159.1)
IV. Summary (162.1)

Chapter 10: The Intelligibility of the Logos of God

I. Introduction (164.1)
II. Barth's inconsistency (164.2)
III. The rational nature of the Word (Logos) of God (165.2)

IV.   The Logos of God is also a person: Jesus (166.2)

V.   The deity of the Logos (167.1)

VI.   Loss of rational revelation from God in Western thought (167)

VII.   The true function of human reason (168.2)

VIII.   The renewed search for logical meaning (169.3)

IX.   The centrality of the Logos of God for human existence and knowledge (171.1)

Chapter 11: The Biblically Attested Logos

I.   Introduction: the centrality of the Logos (Word) of God in Christ (173.1)

II.   The Logos in the Old Testament (173.4)

    a.   Logos as *dabar* (173.4)

    b.   Logos as wisdom (175.1)

III.   Christ and the Old Testament Yahweh (175.2)

    a.   Identity of Christ and Yahweh (175.2)

    b.   Christ is superior to the Law (176.1)

IV.   Logos in the New Testament (176.3)

    a.   Various meanings of logos (176.3)

    b.   The connection of Logos with Jesus (177.1)

    c.   The creative word of Jesus (178.1)

    d.   The Logos is the message about Jesus, his person, his word, and his works (180.2)

    e.   The incarnate Logos is the eternal Logos, the Son of God (181.3)

    f.   The New Testament doctrine of the Logos is independent of Greek philosophy (184.3)

V.   Conclusion (190.2)

Chapter 12: The Living Logos and Defunct Counterfeits

I.   Introduction: Western philosophy's many competing logoi (192)

II.   Logos in the ancient world (193)

III.   Logos in Greek philosophy (193)

IV.   The contrast between the biblical Logos and that of the Greeks (193.5)

V.   The Church's recognition and proclamation of the Logos
        (Word) of God (194.3)
VI.   The Logos in the modern world (195.1)
        a.   The modern Western rejection of God's Logos (195.1)
        b.   Attempts to posit a rational universe (195.4)
        c.   The loss of confidence in a rational, ordered universe
             (196.2)
        d.   Neo-orthodoxy's subjective Logos (197.1)
VII.   Consequences of rejecting an objective, revealed Logos
        (199.2)
VIII.   The necessity of the Logos of God (201.2)

Chapter 13: The Logos as Mediating Agent of Divine Revelation

I.   Introduction (203.1)
II.   The role of the Logos in creation (204.1)
III.   The role of the Logos in all revelation (205.3)
IV.   The revelation of God is both personal and propositional
        (206.2)
V.   The present ministry of the Risen Logos (207.1)
VI.   The relationship of Jesus Christ to all of God's revelation
        (207.3)
VII.   Erroneous views of revelation in Western thought (209.2)
VIII.   Jesus: the supreme, but not the only, form of God's revelation
        (211.2)
IX.   Jesus: the answer to the modern search for meaning (212.1)
X.   Summary: the correlation of divine revelation with the Logos
        (214.4)

Chapter 14: The Logos and Human Logic

I.   Feuerbach's challenge: "All religion is psychological illusion"
        (216.2)
II.   Torrance's inadequate reply (217.2)
III.   Karl Barth: propositional statements only "point to" God's
        revelation (224.3)
IV.   The evangelical counterview: the laws of logic belong to the
        image of God in man (229.2)

Chapter 15: The Logic of Religious Language

I.   Introduction: is religious language unique? (230.1)
II.   Dialectical thought: Hegel and Buddhism compared (231.4)
III.   The role of logic in language and thought (234.2)
IV.   Ancient Christian and non-Christian views of language (237.2)
V.   Hebrew and Greek logic are not different (238.2)
VI.   There is only one human logic (239.1)
      a.   Hebrew and Greek logic are the same (241.3)
      b.   Does modern man have a different logic? (243.1)

Chapter 16: Revelation as a Mental Act

I.   Introduction: God's revelation is a mental conception (248.1)
II.   Modern errors concerning revelation (248.2)
      a.   Basic assumption: not "God says" but "God does" (248.2)
      b.   Revelation as internal divine confrontation (249.1)
      c.   Revelation as external event (251.3)
         i.   The influence of logical positivism (252.3)
      d.   Rejection of history in favor of "myth" (253.4)
         i.   The idea of myth makes Christianity incredible (256.2)
         ii. The idea of myth contradicted by historical research (256.3)
      e.   Revelation as interpreted events (260.3)
III.   The evangelical view (265.1)
      a.   Some questions about Ladd's views (269.3)
IV.   Conclusion: The importance of divinely communicated truths (271.1)

Chapter 17: Cognitive Aspects of Divine Disclosure

I.   Introduction: the error that faith is only subjective (272.2)
II.   Secular thought (273.2)
III.   Nineteenth-century optimism (273.2)
IV.   Twentieth-century denial of divine revelation (274.1)
V.   Objective revelation from God (274.3)

VI.   The necessity of objective revelation (274.4)
    a.   God's revelation is voluntary self-giving (275.1)
    b.   God's revelation is prior to our knowing him (275.2)
VII.   Modern theology turns from divine revelation (276.1)
    a.   Some turn away from rational theology (e.g., liberalism; Kierkegaard; Neo-orthodox thinkers like Barth, Bultmann, etc.) (276.2)
    b.   The influence of Kant's skepticism (278.1)
    c.   The unity of biblical faith and true knowledge (279.1)
        i.   Christian faith does not fear honest debate (279.2)
    d.   Some claim that divine truth is irrational (280.3)
        i.   The result: no way to say the Bible is uniquely true (281.2)
        ii.   Barth's error: denial of rational revelation (282.1)
        iii.   The weakness of neo-Protestant theories of revelation (283.3)
        iv.   The modern idea that language is not trustworthy (290.1)
VIII.   Conclusion: the evangelical assertion of the cognitive aspect of revelation (302.2)

Chapter 18: Wisdom as a Carrier of Revelation
I.   Wisdom writings in the Old Testament (305.3)
II.   Modern rejection of "wisdom" (306.1)
III.   Wisdom is God-centered (309.3)
IV.   Wisdom as a channel of revelation (315.1)
V.   Biblical wisdom and other ancient views (315.2)
VI.   Royal wisdom and the coming Messiah (316.1)
VII.   Unity of moral law and natural law found in the wisdom of the Creator (316.2)
VIII.   God's revelation the only source of wisdom (317.1)
IX.   Wisdom and the Torah (319.1)
X.   Wisdom and Christology (319.2)
    a.   Old Testament (319.2)
    b.   New Testament (321.2)

Chapter 19: The Origin of Language

    I.   Introduction: human language is unique (325.1)

    II.   The origin of human language: naturalistic explanations (325.3)

         a.   Early modern philosophy (325.3)

         b.   Evolutionary views (326.1)

             i.   Rationalist naturalist critique of evolutionist theory (326.2)

             ii.   Evolutionist response (327.2)

             iii. Lack of evidence for the evolutionist view (328.1)

             iv. The difference between sound and speech (330.5)

             v.   Summary: the weaknesses of the evolutionary view (333.1)

         c.   The theory that language is instinctive (333.2)

         d.   The theory that language ability is innate (334.2)

             i.   Non-theistic views (334.2)

             ii.   Theistic views (344.1)

    III.   Conclusion: language comes from the image of God in man, and thus from God himself

Chapter 20: Is Religious Language Meaningful?

    I.   The challenge: does Christian language convey literal truth? (347.1)

    II.   Logical positivism (347)

    III.   Analytical philosophy (language philosophy) (351.2)

    IV.   The necessity of clarity in religious language (354.3)

    V.   Secularism's rejection of theological statements (356.1)

    VI.   The distrust of all words (357.1)

    VII.   Debasing of language by religious leaders (358.1)

    VIII. The abiding meaningfulness of theological language (359.0)

Chapter 21: The Meaning of Religious Language

    I.   Introduction: many writers affirm that religious language has no literal meaning (362.1)

    II.   The analogical view (363.3)

    III.   The pragmatic view (366.2)

IV.   The motivational view (367.1)

V.   The pictorial view (368.1)

VI.   The "language of hope" (368.4)

VII.   The language of praise (369.3)

VIII.   The language of politics (370.2)

IX.   The language of experience (371.1)

X.   The language of inner response (376.2)

Chapter 22: Religious Language and Other Language

I.   Introduction: is religious language unique? (380.1)

II.   Theological language is a part of ordinary language (381.1)

III.   Christian language includes logic and information (382.2)

IV.   Revelation is not "paradoxic encounter" (383.2)

V.   Theological language is distinctive but not unique (384.2)

Chapter 23: A Theistic View of Language

I.   Introduction: biblical language is part of human language (386.1)

II.   The origin of language (386.1)

    a.   A gift from God (387.1)

    b.   The result of experience and evolution? (388.4)

III.   A biblical view of language (390.4)

    a.   The living God speaks (390.5)

    b.   God's word is intelligible and orderly (390.6)

    c.   God used words as symbols (391.1)

    d.   The use of words to express value (391.2)

    e.   The unity of God's speech (391.3)

    f.   Special revelation began before the fall (391.4)

    g.   The early use of names (391.5)

    h.   Sin involves the distortion of language (391.6)

    i.   Listening to the wrong words brings a word of judgment (392.1)

    j.   The role of written revelation (392.2)

    k.   Revelation includes both history and interpretation (392.3)

    l.   God's word revealed to the prophets (392.4)

    m.   The prophetic call: a new literary form (393.1)

       n. The living God speaks in many ways (393.2)

       o. The Bible: God's authoritative written revelation (393.3)

       p. The role of Hebrew and Greek in revelation (395.3)

       q. The Bible can and must be translated (396.2)

       r. Jesus Christ: judge of all language (397.3)

       s. No conflict between Hebrew and Greek (398.1)

       t. New Testament Greek: a new language? (399.3)

       u. The importance of choosing words carefully (400.2)

IV. Summary: implications and presuppositions of a biblical view of language (401.2)

Chapter 24: The Living God Who Speaks

I.   Introduction: the eternal God has spoken (403.2)

II.   The personal God speaks to persons about himself (403.3)

III.   God's speech is voluntary (405.1)

IV.   God spoke to certain chosen men, who wrote the Bible (405.3)

V.   The manner in which God spoke to biblical writers (406.1)

       a. "God spoke" is not just a metaphor (406.2)

       b. But God did not speak as man speaks (409.1)

       c. God's speech was clear, direct, and verbal (409.3)

       d. God's speech was sometimes audible (410.3)

       e. The prophets and apostles (including Jesus) spoke the words which God gave them (412.1)

       f. God used human language to communicate his words without error (418.1)

VI.   "God says" and "Scripture says" (420.1)

VII. God revealed his thoughts through specific human words (421.3)

VIII. The theologian's responsibility (426.2)

IX.   Conclusion: the choice facing us (428.1)

Chapter 25: Neo-Protestant Objections to Propositional Revelation

I.   Introduction: do God's names reveal propositional as well as personal truth? (429.1)

II.   Does truth consist of units of thought? (429.3)

III.   Answering neo-Protestant objections to propositional revelation (430.3)
    a.   "God is absolute Subject" (430.4)
    b.   "Propositional truth depersonalizes revelation" (433.3)
    c.   "Divine revelation conveys no cognitive information" (433.7)
    d.   "Propositional truth is culturally conditioned" (436.1)
    e.   "Faith in Christ is different from belief in doctrines" (436.3)

Chapter 26: Linguistic Analysis and Propositional Truth
I.   Introduction: the attack on religious language (439.1)
II.   Unnatural allies: "Kerygmatic" theology and logical positivism (439.3)
III.   The essence of meaningful communication (446.2)
IV.   The importance of propositions (452.3)

Chapter 27: The Bible as Propositional Revelation
I.   Introduction: is God's revelation propositional or non-propositional? (455.1)
II.   The importance of propositional revelation (455.3)
III.   The nature of propositional revelation (456.1)
IV.   Is there non-propositional revelation? (457.2)
V.   The limits of general revelation (460.2)
VI.   Special revelation: introduction (460.3)
    a.   Old Testament revelation (460.5)
    b.   New Testament confirms the Old Testament (461.2)
    c.   The propositional teaching of Jesus (462.2)
    d.   The Apostles' use of propositions (462.3)
    e.   The propositional nature of all genres in the Bible (463.3)
VII.   The modern rejection of propositional revelation (463.4)
    a.   Neo-Protestant theologians (463.4)
    b.   Evangelical scholars (472.2)
VIII.   Conclusion (480.1)

Chapter 28: Doctrinal Belief and the Word of God

I.   Introduction: is the Logos of God restricted to Jesus Christ? (482.1)

II.   God's Word (Logos) in the Fourth Gospel (482.4)

III.   Conclusion: the connection between God's Word (Logos) and propositions (486.8)

Volume IV

Chapter 1: The Modern Revolt against Authority

I.   The modern revolt against all types of authority (7.1)

    a.   Political authority is questioned (7.2)

    b.   God's authority rejected (8.3)

    c.   Human autonomy affirmed (9.2)

II.   The authoritarian nature of biblical faith (15.2)

III.   Western civilization once accepted biblical authority (16.2)

IV.   The modern turn from biblical authority (16.3)

V.   The persistent power of the Bible (22.2)

VI.   The importance of the Bible for philosophy (23.1)

VII.   The amazing turn of many people towards the Bible (23.3)

Chapter Two: Divine Authority and the Prophetic-Apostolic Word

I.   Intnroduction: biblical emphasis upon authority (24.1)

II.   All authority resides in God and flows from God (24.2)

III.   Authority given to Christ and his disciples (26.2)

IV.   Authority and Scripture (27.1)

    a.   Apostolic authority (27.3)

    b.   God is known trough the revealed Word (31.1)

    c.   Authority of Apostles' oral and written communication (31.2)

    d.   Authority of Old Testament scriptures (33.1)

    e.   Christ and Scripture are inseparable (35.2)

    f.   Unique authority of apostolic writings (38.3)

    g.   God spoke through human messengers (39.3)

Chapter 3: Modern Reductions of Biblical Authority

I.   The unique challenge of modern theology (41.1)

II.   The necessity of defending scriptural authority (41.2)

III. The scope of biblical authority (42.2)

IV.   The need for an authoritative revelation (Henry criticizes modern attempts to affirm biblical authority in theory while denying it in practice. He cites C. H. Dodd as an example, and then mentions Richardson, Tillich, Brunner, Knox, Ogden, and other modern thinkers.) (43.1)

V.   The connection between words and truth (46.1)

VI.   The relationship between the authority of the Bible and the authority of Christ (50.2)

VII. The folly of modern relativism (52.3)

VIII. The relationship between culture and the interpretation of the Bible (55.2)

IX.   The missionary role in relationship to culture (56.3)

X.   Distinguishing the cultural from the supercultural in the Bible (57.5)

    a.   Relativistic pluralism (58.2)

    b.   Greek thought forms? (58.3)

    c.   Marxist exegesis (59.2)

    d.   Revelation is historically orientated (60.3)

    e.   The biblical revelation is eternally true (61.1)

    f.   Are some parts of the Bible not applicable to us? (63.1)

        i.   Paul's teaching about women (63.3)

        ii. Paul's exegetical method (64.3)

XI.   Conclusion: the critics of biblical authority are inconsistent (66.2)

Chapter 4: Divine Authority and Scriptural Authority

I.   Introduction: the connection between biblical authority and inspiration (68.1)

II.   The credibility of the Bible: a fundamental truth (68.4)

III. The source of biblical authority: the Holy Spirit (75.2)

IV.   Doubts about the inspiration of the Bible (75.3)

V.   Weakness of modern biblical criticism (76.1)

Chapter 5: Is the Bible Literally True?

I.   The need for clear definition (103.1)

II.   Allegorical interpretation not acceptable (103.3)

III.   Definition of "literal interpretation" (104.2)

IV.   Literal and symbolic language

    a.   Legitimate understanding of symbols (105.4)

    b.   Does symbolism rule out literal truth? (106.1)

    c.   Literary genres differ (109.1)

    d.   Can religious language communicate literal truth about God? (109.3)

        i.   Anthropomorphisms (110.2)

        ii.   Is all language culturally conditioned and therefore relative? (113.4)

        iii. Can finite language depict the infinite? (115.2)

        iv.   Is only analogical knowledge about God possible? (117.1)

        v.   Is all religious language inherently metaphorical or figurative? (119.5)

            1.   The Bible and science (122.3)

            2.   Dubious uses of literal interpretation (126.2)

V.   Conclusion: only one kind of truth (128.3)

Chapter 6: The Meaning of Inspiration

I.   Introduction: definition of inspiration (129.1)

II.   The Bible claims inspiration for itself (129.2)

III.   Three decisive texts (131.1)

    A.   2 Timothy 3:14–16 (131.2)

    B.   2 Peter 1:19–21 (132.1)

    c.   John 10:34–36 (133.1)

    d.   Summary (133.5)

IV.   The entire Bible witnesses to itself as inspired (134.1)

V.   An evangelical view of inspiration: what it does not mean (137.4)

    a.   That the Bible was dictated (138.1)

    b.   That inspiration was only a heightening of human powers (142.2)

VI.   The evangelical view: what it affirms (144.1)
  a.   That the text is divinely inspired as an objective deposit of language (144.2)
  b.   That inspiration does not violate the humanity of the authors (148.3)
  c.   That the human authors remained fallible (151.3)
  d.   That inspiration was limited to a few chosen prophets and apostles (152.4)
  e.   That inspiration from God communicated information beyond the natural resources of the writers (155.1)
  f.   That God is the ultimate author of the Bible (159.1)
  g.   That all of the Bible is inspired (160.3)
  h.   That this view of inspiration is the historic teaching of the Christian church (160.4)

Chapter 7: The Inerrancy of Scripture

I.   The Scriptures were "breathed out" by God (162.1)
II.   The Bible teaches its own inerrancy (162.3)
III. The evangelical definition of inerrancy (166.5)
IV.   Inerrancy is the teaching of the church throughout history (167.1)
V.   The scope of inerrancy (168.3)
VI.   The major issues of the debate about inerrancy (169.2)
VII. The relationship between the Bible's reliability and inerrancy (170.1)
VIII. The role of biblical data in the doctrine of inerrancy (171.2)
IX.   Dealing with apparent contradictions in Scripture (174.2)
X.   Authorial intent and inerrancy (Henry here critiques views of Pinnock, Carnell, Orr, Harrison, Fuller, Rogers, Coleman, Beegle, Bloesch, Marty, Ridderbos, Berkouwer, Ramm, and others who would claim that the Bible has authority but is not inerrant.) (175.2)
XI.   The weakness of separating authority from inerrancy (192.1)

Chapter 8: The Meaning of Inerrancy

I.   Negatively, scriptural inerrancy does not imply that: (201.2)
  a.   Modern technological precision, historiographical standards, or scientific terminology should be expected in the Scriptures (201.3)

       b.   Metaphorical or symbolic language cannot communicate literal religious truth (202.1)

       c.   Verbal exactitude is used in New Testament quotation and use of Old Testament passages (202.3)

       d.   Personal faith in Christ is unnecessary (203.2)

       e.   Evangelical orthodoxy will necessarily follow from accepting this doctrine (204.1)

II.   Positively, verbal inerrancy does imply that: (205.2)

       a.   Truth attaches not only to the theological and ethical teaching of the Bible, but also to historical and scientific matters insofar as they are part of the express message of the inspired writings (205.3)

       b.   God's truth inheres in the very words of Scripture, that is, in the propositions or sentences of the Bible, and not merely in the concepts and thoughts of the writers (205.6), but divine dictation is not implied (206.3)

       c.   The original writings or prophetic-apostolic autographs alone are error free (207.2)

       d.   Evangelicals must not attach finality to contemporary versions or translations (209.3)

Supplementary Note: The Chicago Statement on Biblical Inerrancy

I.   Preface (211.1)

II.   A short statement (212.2)

III.   Articles of affirmation and denial (212.7)

IV.   Exposition (215.2)

       a.   Creation, revelation, and inspiration (215.3)

       b.   Authority: Christ and the Bible (216.1)

       c.   Infallibility, inerrancy, interpretation (217.2)

       d.   Skepticism and criticism (218.3)

       e.   Transmission and translation (218.4)

       f.   Inerrancy and authority (219.1)

Chapter 9: The Infallibility of the Copies

I.   Introduction: vopies and translations are not inerrant (220.1)

II.   Are the copies infallible?

III.   Claims for the infallibility of the Roman Catholic pope (220.2)

IV.   The danger of promoting biblical errancy (234.1)
V.   The origin of errors in the copies (235.2)
VI.   The essential reliability of the copies (235.4)
VII.   The importance of having inerrant originals and infallible copies (240.2)
VIII. Why did the autographs disappear? (240.2)

Chapter 10: The Meaning of Infallibility

I.   Inerrancy and infallibility (243.1)
II.   What infallibility does not mean (244.2)
    a. That copyists, translators, or church teachers are inspired (2434.2)
    b. That copies of the original manuscripts were without error (244.4)
    c. That the men who copied the Scriptures were infallible (244.5)
    d. That all types of texts and translations are equally reliable (245.6)
III.   What infallibility does mean (246.3)
    a. The copies reliably communicate God's truth (246.4)

Chapter 11: The Spirit and the Scriptures

I.   Barth re-emphasizes the role of the Spirit in revelation (256.1)
II.   Barth: inspiration includes the current activity of the Spirit (256.3)
III.   The evangelical view (257.3)
    a. The Spirit works in interpretation as well as inspiration (257.3)
    b. Inspiration is not limited to the Scriptures (258.4)
IV.   Barth's "dynamic" view of revelation (259.2)
V.   The evangelical view of illumination (266.3)
VI.   The objective nature of biblical revelation (267)
VII.   Summary: the error of separating the authority of the Word of God from the biblical text (269.1)

Chapter 12: The Spirit as Divine Illuminator

I.   The need for a full delineation of the Spirit's ministry (272.1)

II.   The Holy Spirit reveals truth (272.3)

III. The Spirit enables believers to understand God's revealed Word (273.2)

    a.   Twentieth-century biblical critics emphasize cultural factors (273.4)

    b.   But God's truth was revealed to the prophets and apostles (275.1)

    c.   The Spirit now illumines believers to comprehend written revelation (276.1)

    d.   Without the Spirit's work, unbelievers cannot fully accept God's revelation (277.12)

    e.   Barth detaches revelation from the objective Word of God (278.3)

    f.   By the Spirit, ordinary believers may understand biblical revelation (279.1)

    g.   Church tradition and Scripture (280.4)

    h.   Authorial intent (281.1)

    i.   How much can the reader comprehend by reason? (281.2)

    j.   The Spirit enables us to recognize and accept God's truth (282.2)

IV.   Critique of claims made by members of the Charismatic Movement (283.3)

    a.   Prophetic utterances (284.1)

    b.   Glossolalia (285.2)

    c.   Disdain for the use of reason (287.3)

V.   Conclusion (289.1)

Chapter 13: Are We Doomed to Hermeneutical Nihilism?

I.   The "hermeneutical problem" (296.1)

    a.   The meaning of "hermeneutics" (296.2)

    b.   The grammatical-historical method (296.4)

    c.   Anti-supernatural prejudices (296.5)

    d.   Barth rejects objective interpretation (297.3)

II.   Barth rejects revelation in objective history 298.4

III. Barth and Bultmann compared (300.2)

IV.   Can the past be known? (304.1)

V.   The importance of the author's intent (308.2)

VI.   The errors of modern exegesis: a summary (311.3)

VII.   How to understand the Bible (314.1)

Chapter 14: The Fallibility of the Exegete

I.   Exegetes can make mistakes in their interpretation of infallible Scriptures (316.1)

II.   The debate over authorship and dating (316.2)

III.   A critique of Barr's attack on evangelical scholars (317.2)

    a.   Did Moses write the Pentateuch? (317.2)

        i.   Problems of the critical view of the Pentateuch (317.3)

    b.   The importance of assumptions about inspiration and predictive prophecy (322.3)

        i.   Problems with the critical view of the date of Daniel (323.1)

    c.   The importance of the issue of authorship (316.3; 324.1)

        i.   Problems with the critical views of literary style (325.3)

    d.   The role of source criticism (326.2)

        i.   The synoptic problem (327.1)

    e.   The importance of presuppositions in biblical interpretation (335.1)

        i.   Historical criticism of the Bible (336.1)

    f.   Diversity of interpretations (343.1)

    g.   Acceptance of miracles in Scripture (345.2)

IV.   The fallibility of the exegete and the infallibility of Scripture (350.2)

    a.   Unfortunate example: the views of some evangelical scholars on the historicity of the Gospels (351.1)

Chapter 15: Perspective on Problem Passages

I.   Several important considerations (353.1)

    a.   Critics of the Bible have made many mistakes (353.2)

    b.   The list of alleged problems in Scriptures keeps getting shorter (354.1)

    c.   Critics hide their mistakes (355.1)

d. The critical attack has widened in scope in this century (356.2)
e. The Bible contains some real problems of numbers and chronology (358.2)
f. There are some apparent contradictions or "errors" in Scripture (262.1)
g. We must retain a balanced view of the importance of inerrancy (365.1)

Chapter 16: The Historic Church and Inerrancy

I. Introduction: has the historic church affirmed inerrancy? (368.1)
II. Recent use of the word "inerrancy" (368.1)
III. The concept of inerrancy is ancient (Henry lists evidence from the church fathers.) (370.1)
IV. The modern flight from inerrancy (374. 3)
V. The Reformers' teaching about inerrancy (375.1)
VI. Seventeenth- and eighteenth-century Protestant theologians' teaching about inerrancy (378.1)
VII. The modern struggle over inerrancy (380.1)

Chapter 17: Uses and Abuses of Historical Criticism

I. Introduction: should the historical-critical method be used? (385.1)
II. Describing and defining the historical-critical method (386.1)
  a. Every methodology has presuppositions (388.2)
  b. Critique: the modern historical-critical method's false assumptions (389.2)
III. The search for an evangelical alternative (393.2)
IV. The evangelical view of the historical-critical method of biblical interpretation (403.2)

Chapter 18: The Debate over the Canon

I. Introduction: the unity of "Holy Book" and Holy Spirit (405.2)
II. The biblical view of "Scripture" (406.1)

III.   The early church's view (406.3)
IV.   Books excluded from "Scripture" (407.3)
V.   The Old Testament canon (409.5)
VI.   The New Testament canon (415.3)
   a.   The Bible created the church (415.3)
   b.   Criteria for canonicity (417.2)
   c.   Neo-orthodoxy's claim that the Bible is superior (417.2)
   d.   Liberalism's rejection of the canon (417.3)
   e.   Internal witness of the Spirit (419.2)
   f.   Authority of apostolic writings (426.2)
   g.   Neo-orthodoxy's mistaken view (427.2)
   h.   Is the canon closed? (431.3)
   i.   The earliest evidence for the canon (434.2)
   j.   The formation of the canon (436.2)
   k.   The importance of apostolicity (436.4)
   l.   An "increasing" canon (438.1)
   m.   The growing consensus of the early church (440.1)
   n.   An explanation for different lists of canonical books (441.3)
   o.   The role of divine providence (443.2)
   p.   Reasons for determining canonicity (446.2)

Chapter 19: The Lost Unity of the Bible

I.   Introduction: the chaos of modern biblical criticism (450.1)
II.   The search for a "canon within the canon" (450.4)
III.   Alien presuppositions lead to confusion about the canon (452.1)
IV.   The failure of the "biblical theology" movement (454.2)
V.   Criticism of the critics (457.4)
VI.   We must focus on the meaning of the biblical authors (463.1)
VII.   Consequences of ignoring biblical meaning (465.3)
VIII.   Renewed search for the unity of the Bible (466.3)
IX.   The unity of the Bible (467.2)

Chapter 20: The Spirit and Church Proclamation

I.   Introduction (476.1)

II.   The necessity of personal evangelism (477.1)

III.   The impersonal nature of modern science (478.2)

IV.   Challenges facing churches today (478.3)

V.   The role of the sermon (484.2)

VI.   The relationship between systematic theology and preaching (488.3)

VII.   The priority of proclamation (488.4)

VIII. The creative and re-creative word of God (491.1)

Chapter 21: God's Graven Image: Redeemed Mankind

I.   God writes his will upon human hearts (494.1)

II.   The image of God in man (497.1)

III.   The age of the Spirit and the Charismatic Movement (499.2)

IV.   Between justification and glorification (501.2)

    a.   The message of Hebrews (501.2)

    b.   Privileges of the new covenant: Paul (503.1)

    c.   Our present suffering (503.3)

    d.   Good health for all believers? (506.1)

V.   The community of healing (507.2)

VI.   Rival concepts of the "new man" (508.1)

    a.   Created by science? (508.1)

    b.   Homosexual love? (511.1)

    c.   Feminism? (514.2)

    d.   Self-actualization? (516.2)

VII.   The only hope for modern man (520.1)

Chapter 22: The New Man and the New Society

I.   The New Man is Jesus; the new society is the regenerate church (522.1)

II.   Inadequacies of Marxist exegesis

    a.   Marxist theory and practice are unclear about the new man and society (522.2)

    b.   Marxist-oriented theologians (523.2)

III.   Biblical teaching: The New Covenant

    a.   Basic principles (524.1)

    b.   Old Testament (524.2)

    c.   The centrality of Jesus

        i.   Misconceptions (525.1)

        ii. Sociopolitical relevance (526. 2)

IV.   A new, visible social order: the church (527.3)
    a.   A non-violent challenge to rival powers (528.2)
    b.   Mission
        i.   To be "salt" and "light" in the world (529.3)
        ii.   Not to impose its will politically (530.1)
        iii. To be the new society (530.2)
        iv.   Political implications of gospel truth (530.3)
        v.   Mutual subordination (531.1)
        vi.   Pacifism? (532.1)
        vii. An alternative to radical political pacifism:
            1.   Basic principles (537.1)
            2.   Dangers of both organizational unity and independence (537.3)
            3.   Dangers of both pietism and revolution (538.2)
            4.   The appeal of the Charismatic/Pentecostal movement (539.1)
V.   Conclusion: the church must be renewed! (540.2)

Chapter 23: Good News for the Oppressed

I.   Good news for the needy (542.1)
II.   The worldwide call for liberation (543.1)
III.   The church must reflect justice (343.3)
IV.   All men are responsible (346.1)
V.   Answering Marxist propaganda (546.2)
VI.   The value of personal compassion (548.1)
VII.   The value of a new view of life (549.1)
VIII. Moral and spiritual poverty (549.4)
IX.   The church's obligation (550.1)
    a.   Use of resources (550.1)
    b.   Word and deed (551.2)
    c.   A new view of work (551.4)
    d.   Volunteer work (552.3)
    e.   Political involvement (553.1)
X.   Complete liberation is coming (553.3)

Chapter 24: Marxist Exegesis of the Bible

I.   Introduction: politically oriented theology (555.1)
II.   Theology of revolution (555.2)
III. Theology of liberation (555.3)
    a.   The priority of action (556.1)
    b.   Commitment to Marxism (556.3)
    c.   Focus on Latin America (559.3)
    d.   Departure from biblical truth (560.1)
    e.   Salvation by man's effort (561)
    f.   Weaknesses (562.4)
    g.   "Evangelical" liberation theology (566.4)
    h.   Needed: a biblical view of society (570.1)
    i.   The failure of Marxist theory and practice (570.3)
IV.   An evangelical response (573.1)

Chapter 25: The Marxist Reconstruction of Man

I.   Introduction: the new man (578.1)
II.   Marx envisions a "new man" (578.2)
III. Removing the fear of God (579.2)
IV.   The "new man" fails to emerge (579.4)
V.   The reason for the failure (581.1)
VI.   Failure to eradicate religious faith (582.2)
VII. Modern socialists fail to learn the lessons of communism (584.1)
VIII. The danger of focusing only on the poor (586.3)
IX.   Christians in a socialist state (587.2)
X.   Christianity superior to Marxism (588.4)
XI.   Evangelicals in capitalist America (589.1)
XII. The example of the early church (590.3)

Chapter 26: The Awesome Silences of Eternity

I.   Only God speaks (593.1)
II.   God speaks to man (594.2)
III. God spoke uniquely in the Old Testament (594.4)
IV.   God sometime says nothing (595.1)
    a.   Jesus' silence (595.1)
    b.   God's listening silence (596.1)
    c.   God's eternal silence toward the lost (596.3)

V.   God continues to speak (598.1)

VI.   Modern man's aversion to silence (599.1)

VII.   The proper balance of sound and silence (600.1)

VIII.   The silence of God and of man (601.4)

IX.   Death (602.3)

    a.   Is it the end of existence? (602.3)

    b.   Euthanasia (604.2)

    c.   The Christian view of death (605.3)

    d.   Death and sin (606.3)

    e.   Sleep and death (611.3)

    f.   Death and life (612.4)

X.   Endless joy in the presence of God (614.1)

Volume V

Chapter 1: The Reality and Objectivity of God

I.   God *is* (21.1)

II.   God's objective existence challenged (21.3)

III.   A critique of dialectical-existential theology (22.2)

    a.   Relationship to existentialism (22.3)

        i.   Denial of the subject-object distinction (24.2)

        ii.   Objections to the existentialist position (26.1)

    b.   Relationship to logical positivism (28.2)

        i.   Introduction (28.2)

        ii.   Influence of Kant's theory of knowledge (30.3; see vol. I, ch. 21)

        iii.   Critique of logical positivism (32.1; see vol. I, ch. 5)

        iv.   The verifiability principle (32.2)

        v.   Testing theological statements (33.4)

            1.   The limits of scientific knowledge (33.5)

        vi.   Modern theology's debt to secular philosophy (35.1)

    c.   Loss of the reality of God (36.3)

        i.   Loss of reality of both God and man (36.3)

        ii.   Radical secular theology affirms the reality of only the world (37.3)

        iii.   Barth's attempt to re-affirm God's reality (39.1)

      d.   God's objective existence (40.2)
          i.   God *is* (40.2)
          ii.   What—or who—is God? (41.1)

Chapter 2: The Being and Coming and Becoming of God

    I.   Introduction (43.1)
    II.   Christian view differs from that of secular philosophy (43.2)
    III.   The being of God
        a.   The Greeks (43.3)
        b.   Medieval theologians (45.3)
        c.   Early modern philosophy (45.4)
        d.   The modern era (46.1)
        e.   Tillich's idea of "being-itself" (46.2)
        f.   Process theology (48.1)
        g.   God's being known only through revelation (48.3)
        h.   God's being *can* be known (51.2)
    IV.   The coming of God (52.3)
        a.   The biblical idea of God's coming (52.3)
        b.   Twentieth-century views (55.1)
    V.   The becoming of God (56.2)
        a.   God is not the world (57.1)
        b.   God became a Man—Jesus (57.3)
        c.   The Word became flesh (58.2)
        d.   Can a man be God? (60.3)
        e.   The contrast between the Bible and process theology (62.1)
        f.   Modern man's worship of "becoming" (65.1)
        g.   The unchanging God changes us (65.2)

Chapter 3: The Living God of the Bible

    I.   God lives (66.1)
    II.   The living God (66.2)
    III.   The only living God (67.3)
    IV.   The independent God (69.2)
    V.   False "gods" (69.3)
    VI.   The God of the Bible and the "gods" of ancient pagans (72.3)
    VII. Idolatry, past and present (75.2)
    VIII. Serving the true God (79.3)

IX.   God's gift of life to man (79.4)

X.   Knowing the living God (81.1)

Chapter 4: Methods of Determining the Diving Attributes

I.   Two fundamental questions (83.1)

II.   Christian theology and secular philosophy (83.2)

III.   Six methods of identifying God's attributes (84.1)

  a.   The way of negation (from Plato) (84.2)

  b.   The way of eminence (analogy, from Aristotle) (86.1)

  c.   The way of causality (88.2)

  d.   The way of intuition (90.5)

  e.   The way of encounter (Neo-orthodoxy) (93.1)

  f.   The way of biblical revelation (99.1)

IV.   Identification (99.1)

V.   Classification (101.2)

Chapter 5: Relationship of Essence and Attributes

This chapter mostly deals with Western philosophical and theological speculation about the fundamental reality of the universe and of God.

I.   Introduction (104.1)

II.   "Realism" (104.3)

III.   Modern attack on "realism" by "idealism" (Note: Both "realists" and "idealists" believe that mind is the fundamental reality of the universe. The difference between them is that "realists" believe in the fundamental reality of both mind and matter; they are thus metaphysical dualists, whereas "idealists" believe that only mind is truly "real," and are thus metaphysical monists. Henry sometimes also calls "idealists" either "personalists" or "spiritualists.") (105.2)

IV.   Christians insist upon the priority of mind in the universe (105.4)

V.   The importance of this question (105.5)

VI.   The debate between Thomists and Neo-orthodox theologians (105.6)

VII.   The Bible does not clearly support either view (106.3)

VIII.   The core of the debate (107.1)

IX.   Modern philosophy is divided (Henry briefly discusses the views of Descartes, Spinoza, Leibniz, Locke, Berkeley, Hume, and Kant.) (107.2)

X.   The medieval theological debate (109.0)

XI.   Pantheism: Hegel and his followers (109.3)

XII.   Personalism (111.3)

XIII.   Modern Christian views (113.2)

Chapter 6: God's Divine Simplicity and Attributes

After rejecting the idea of an underlying essence of God, separate from his attributes, Henry continues the discussion of the relationship of God's essence and attributes.

I.   The relationship of attributes and essence (127.1)
    a.   Two contrasting views (128.3)
    b.   Aquinas: Separation of God's essence and attributes, his being and activity (128.4)
    c.   Barth: God's essence cannot be known (129.1)
    d.   God: a unity of essence and attributes (130.1)
    e.   God's simplicity (131.1)
    f.   The relationship of God's attributes to each other (132.3)
    g.   The danger of discussing the "being" of God (133.1)
    h.   The position of the Reformers (134.1)

II.   Equality of all attributes (135.4)
    a.   Some ideas about God's "basic" attributes (136.3)
    b.   Modern philosophical views (136.4)
    c.   Neo-orthodox emphasis upon God's love (137.1)

III.   The number of God's attributes (138.3)
    a.   The reality of separate attributes (139.1)
    b.   Exegesis: the deciding factor (139.2)

IV.   Summary (139.3)

Chapter 7: Personality in the Godhead

I.   Religion includes the concept of personality (142.4)

II.   Christianity implies a personal God (145.1)

III.   Asian and Greek views (145.3)

IV.   Christianity's new contribution (146.3)

V.   Ancient origin of the Christian view (146.4)

VI.   Modern views of impersonality (146.5)

VII.   Implications of the denial of personality (150.2)

VIII. The Christian view is based on revelation (150.3)

IX.   Influence of existential view of personality (152.3)

X.   The Triune God is personal (152.5)

Chapter 8: Muddling the Trinitarian Dispute

I.   Is the doctrine of the Trinity reasonable? (165.1)

II.   Its mathematical simplicity (165.2)

III.   Logic and the Trinity (166.2)

IV.   Human personality and the Trinity (166.4)

V.   Solving the problem of the One and the Many (168.1)

VI.   Biblical monotheism (168.3)

VII.   Defective "monotheism" of non-Christian philosophies and religions (170.1)

    a.   Greek (170.1)

    b.   Oriental (171.1)

    c.   Christian heresies (171.4)

    d.   Monism and modalism (172.2)

    e.   Process theology (177.2)

VIII. Objections to the doctrine of the Trinity (182.3)

    a.   It is self-contradictory (182.4)

    b.   It depends upon Greek philosophy (183.1)

    c.   It comes from church history, not from the Bible (183.2)

       i.   Barth's doctrine of the Trinity (184.3)

       ii. The proper order of discussing God's names (185.3)

       iii. New Testament evidence for the doctrine of the Trinity (186.1)

Chapter 9: The Doctrine of the Trinity

I.   Introduction (191.1)

    a.   The challenge of the life of Jesus (191.4)

    b.   Choices to be made concerning Jesus (193.1)

       i.   To reject Jesus is to reject the sending God (193.3)

       ii.   Jesus affirmed monotheism (194.1)

      iii.   Rejection of bare monotheism (194.2)

    c.   Rejection of modalism and of tri-theism (195.1)

II.   The progressive self-revelation of God (195.4)

    a.   The Old Testament (196)

    b.   The New Testament (197.2)

III.   The Trinity in church theology (199.1)

    a.   The need for clear teaching (199.1)

    b.   Gnostic and Platonic influences in the early church (199.3)

    c.   Modalism (Sabellianism) (200.2)

    d.   Arianism (201.1)

    e.   The ecumenical councils (202.1)

       i.   Nicene Council (202.3)

      ii.   Terminology (202.4)

         1.   Refutation of errors (203.5)

         2.   Theology (204.1)

      iii.   Later councils and creeds (204.3)

      iv.   The Reformers (206.1)

    f.   The eternal subordination of the Son (207.1)

    g.   One essence, three persons (208.3)

    h.   Modern theology (212.1)

    i.   The practical importance of the doctrine of the Trinity (212.2)

Chapter 10: God the Ultimate Spirit

I.   God is Spirit (214.1)

II.   Self-consciousness (214.3)

III.   Self-determination (214.5)

IV.   The Trinity's self-consciousness (215.1)

V.   Non-Christian views of spirit (215.2)

VI.   God is immaterial and invisible (216.3)

    a.   "Theophanies" (217.3)

    b.   The incarnation (217.4)

Chapter 11: The Self-Revealed Infinite

I.   Introduction (Henry first surveys ancient Greek philosophy, which hesitated to apply the term "infinite" to God.) (219.1)

II.   Christian theology includes the idea of God as infinite (220.4)

III.   Infinity is not an extension of finiteness (221.3)

IV.   The universe is not infinite (222.4)

V.   "Proving" infinity from the finite creation (222.5)

VI.   Views of different philosophers (Henry briefly surveys the ideas of Spinoza, Lock, Hume, Voltaire, and Kant.) (224.3)

    a.   Hegel (226.2)

    b.   Feuerbach and Marx (226.4)

    c.   Is God finite? (227.3)

    d.   Existentialism (229.3)

    e.   Modern theology: Barth (230.4)

VII.   Evangelical theology (232.1)

VIII. The Bible reveals God as infinite (232.3)

    a.   God's glory (232.3)

    b.   The incarnation (233.1)

    c.   God's love and authority (233.4)

Chapter 12: Divine Timelessness of Unlimited Duration?

I.   The clash between secular and biblical notions of time and eternity (235.1)

II.   Theological confusion about time and eternity (236.2)

III.   Secular views of time and eternity (239.1)

IV.   Traditional Christian views: timelessness or unlimited duration of God (239.4)

V.   Modern Christian rejections of divine timelessness (241.1)

VI.   The witness of Scripture (241.4)

    a.   Competing opinions (241.4)

    b.   Biblical starting points (249.1)

Chapter 13: The Modern Attack on the Timeless God

I.   Rejection of God's timelessness by philosophers and theologians (252.1)

    a.   Objections posed by theologians (252.2)

    b.   A departure from orthodox theism (253.3)

    c.   The limited contribution, and flaws, of process philosophy (254.3)

II.   Responses to theological objections to God's timelessness
        (256.3)
III.   Is God's timelessness a necessary truth? (258.3)
        a.   Augustine, Anselm, Aquinas (259.2)
        b.   Modern philosophers (259.3)
IV.   Evangeclial affirmations
        a.   Time is real and important (260.1)
        b.   God is not temporal (260.3)
        c.   Interaction with Eric Mascall (261.2)
V.   Philosophical defenses of God's timelessness (262.3)
VI.   Philosophical denials of God's timelessness (264.1)
VII.   Biblical terms for time must be carefully assessed (265.3)

Chapter 14: Divine Timelessness and Divine Omniscience
I.   God's timelessness is inferred from his omniscience (268.1)
II.   The nature of God's omniscience (268.2)
III.   Practical consequences of God's omniscience (270.1)
IV.   God's omniscience is timeless (270.2)
V.   Mistaken views of divine timelessness (271.1)
VI.   The biblical view (276.1)
VII.   God's knowledge of the future (278.1)
        a.   Predictive statements (278.1)
        b.   Divine foreknowledge and human freedom (279.2)
              i.   Divine foreknowledge and sin (283.1)
              ii.   Foreknowledge and foreordination (283.4)

Chapter 15: The Unchanging Immutable God
I.   Introduction: biblical statements of divine changelessness
        (286.1)
II.   Is the doctrine of divine immutability derived from Greek
        philosophy? (286.2)
III.   Divine changelessness is both moral and ontological (287.4)
IV.   Timelessness and changelessness go together (288.2)
V.   God is unchangeable in all his attributes and perfections
        (289.3)
VI.   Practical consequences of divine immutability (289.4)

VII.   Philosophical denials of divine changelessness: pantheism, personal idealism, process theology (290.1)
    a.   Whitehead (290.4)
    b.   Hartshorne (290.5)
    c.   Ogden (291.1)
    d.   Pannenberg (291.2)
    e.   Moltmann (291.3)
VIII.   Divine changelessness and the created universe (292.1)
IX.   Divinie changelessness and redemption through Christ (292.4)
X.   The changelessness of Jesus Christ (294.1)

Supplementary Note: Anthropomorphism and Divine Repentance
I.   Introduction: questions commonly posed (295.1)
II.   Process theology rejects immutability (295.5)
III.   Karl Barth's loose statements (296.1)
IV.   Anthropomorphisms
    a.   Different from zoomorphic motifs in pagan religion (296.1)
    b.   Rejected by Greek philosophers and Hellenized Jews (296.2)
    c.   Biblical use of anthropomorphisms
        i.   Old Testament (297.1)
        ii.   New Testament (298.1)
        iii. The incarnation of the Word of God (298.2)
        iv.   Different from modern philosophy (299.1)
V.   Divine "repentance"
    a.   Introduction: Calvin and Barth (300.1)
    b.   Biblical passages (300.4)
    c.   God's "repentance" different from man's (301.4)
        i.   God does not change as we do (301.5)
        ii.   Does God change his mind? (302.1)
    d.   Theological discussion
        i.   Inadequate theological positions (302.2)
        ii.   Divine "repentance" not inconsistent with immutability (303.1)
        iii. Comparison with human bodily change (304.3)
        iv.   Inadequate dialectical/paradoxical formulations (305.3)

Chapter 16: The Sovereignty of the Omnipotent God

I.   Reasons for the current questioning of God's sovereignty (307.1)

II.   Biblical teaching on God's sovereignty
   a.   Old Testament (308.1)
   b.   New Testament (309.2)
   c.   Church fathers (310.1)

III.   What does "omnipotence" mean?
   a.   Not "absolute" power (310.2)
   b.   Not just relational power (311.1)
   c.   Philosophical speculations (311.3)
   d.   Influence of the problem of evil (312.2)
   e.   Schleiermacher (313.1)
   f.   Evangelical view (313.5)
   g.   Unlimited possibility is unacceptable (314.1)
   h.   God's freedom is his power (317.2)
   i.   God's power is power over all powers (318.2)
   j.   God's moral nature defines his power (318.3)

IV.   Man's rejection of God's power
   a.   Humanist presumption (319.4)
   b.   Limitations of human power (321.2)

V.   God's power and the laws of logic (324.3)

VI.   God's omnipotence embraces all other attributes (325.3)

VII.   African diminutions of God's omnipotence (325.5)

VIII.   Yahweh and Kurios (Lord) as designations of power
   a.   Biblical usage (326.2)
   b.   Hindu *avatar* not an acceptable title for Christ (327.3)
   c.   Critique of rejections of the reliability of New Testament documents (328.3)
   d.   The lordship of the risen Christ (329.2)

IX.   God's purposes and Christ's kingdom are invincible (330.2)

Supplementary Note: Sovereignty and Personality

I.   Why some believe sovereignty and personality are mutually exclusive (331.1)

II.   Christian responses
   a.   God is both omnipotent and personal (332.1)

b.   But *not* as in either Plato or Aristotle (332.3)

c.   The living God of the Bible discloses his sovereign personality (333.1)

Chapter 17: God's Intellectual Attributes

I.   Introduction: God is the source of all intelligence and reason (334.1)

II.   The creative and revelatory Word of God (334.3)

    a.   God's Word and our thoughts (335.6)

III. The nature of ideas (337.4)

    a.   Early Western thought (338.4)

    b.   Modern Western philosophy (339.4)

Chapter 18: Shadows of the Irrational

I.   Modern secular irrationalism (359.1)

II.   Irrationalism in theology (360.2)

    a.   Kierkegaard (361.2)

    b.   Dialectical theology: Barth (365.1)

        i.   Earlier writings (366.1)

        ii.   Support for reason (366.2)

        iii. Limitations on reason (368.1)

III. The surrender of reason as a criterion of reality (373.2)

Chapter 19: The Knowability of God

I.   We cannot know God fully, but we can know him truly (375.1)

II.   Only the Bible is authoritative (376.3)

III. A false understanding of "mystery" (377.1)

IV.   Errors of evangelical theologians (379.3)

V.   The rational image of God in man (380.1)

VI.   The necessity of rational revelation (381.2)

Chapter 20: Man's Mind and God's Mind

I.   Man's mind is the image of God (382.1)

II.   The mind of the sinner and the mind of the saved (382.4)

III. God's reason makes man's reason possible (383.2)

IV.   The failure of naturalism to explain man's reason (385.4)

V.   The failure of secular science (388.1)

a. Behaviorism (390.1)

b. Marxism (392.1)

c. Atheism (393.1)

d. Moral relativism (393.2)

Chapter 21: Reflections on the Revelation-and-Culture Debate

I. The earlier debate about culture and revelation (395.1)

II. Introduction to the current debate (396.1)

III. Christian revelation was given within culture (396.2)

IV. Questions about the Bible and culture (397.5)

a. Modernism (398.1)

b. The evangelical response to modernism (400.2)

c. Recent critical thought (401.1)

d. The evangelical response (404.3)

e. Problems with the principle of relativity (404.3)

f. Semi-evangelical views (405.3)

g. Meaning is found in propositions (405.4)

h. The cultural limitations of the modern interpreter (407.3)

Volume VI

Chapter 1: Shall We Surrender the Supernatural?

I. Avoiding the term "supernatural" (11.1)

II. Distinguishing the "supernatural" from nature (13.1)

III. Modern theology (14.1)

IV. Emphasizing the immanence of God (14.1)

V. The transcendence of God (15.2)

VI. Views of existential, "futurist," and "process" theologians (20.2)

VII. God and other "spiritual" beings (21.3)

VIII. Loss of the transcendent (23.2)

IX. Modern loss of the immanence of God (25.2)

X. Modern secular philosophy (25.3)

XI. Four major theories (26.1)

XII. "Supernatural" must be clearly defined (28.3)

XIII. Modern naturalism (31.1)

XIV. The church must proclaim the supernatural God (33.1)

Chapter 2: God's Transcendence and Immanence

I.   Introduction (35.1)
II.   The transcendent God of the Bible (36.4)
III.   Modern philosophy rejects transcendence (37.3)
IV.   The biblical response to philosophy (39.1)
V.   Marxism and humanism (40.3)
VI.   False views within the church (41.2)
VII.   Karl Barth (42.1)
VIII.   Evaluating alternative views of transcendence (42.3)
IX.   Christology and transcendence (45.3)
X.   Transcendence and immanence (48.2)

Chapter 3: The Resurgence of Process Philosophy

I.   The rise of process philosophy (52.1)
II.   Is process theology "new"? (53.4)
III.   God and the universe (54.2)
IV.   Is God timeless and immutable? (61.1)
V.   God is concerned about this world (67.1)
VI.   Contrast between the Bible and Greek philosophy (68.2)
VII.   The love of God (69.2)
VIII.   The need for a biblical metaphysics (75.1)

Chapter 4: Election: The Freedom of God

I.   Is this doctrine necessary? (76.1)
II.   The biblical teaching about God's freedom (76.2)
III.   The importance of God's choice (77.3)
IV.   God's eternal choice (78.2)

Chapter 5: God the Sovereign Creator

I.   Creation is known by faith alone (108.1)
II.   The Bible rejected ancient views (109.4)
III.   God the sovereign Creator (110.3)
IV.   Christ and creation (111.3)
V.   The "process" of creation (112.1)
        a.   Six days? (112.2)
        b.   "Literal" interpretation of Genesis (116.1)
VI.   Science and the creation account (116.3)
VII.   Consequences of rejecting the biblical account of creation (118.2)

Chapter 6: Creation *ex Nihilo*

I.   Introduction: creation from nothing (120.1)

II.   Does the Bible teach creation from nothing? (121.2)

III. Uniqueness of the doctrine of creation from nothing (121.6)

IV.   "Creation from nothing" not a biblical phrase (122.1)

V.   Creation from nothing is implicit in the Bible (122.4)

VI.   Creation by God's Word (123.1)

VII. Misunderstandings about creation from nothing (123.2)

VIII. Only God is eternal (124.1)

IX.   Philosophical and scientific speculation (124.3)

X.   The Big Bang theory appears (124.4)

XI.   The steady-state theory (125.5)

XII. The oscillating universe model (126.3)

XIII. The Big Bang theory and science (126. 5)

XIV. What (or Who) caused the Big Bang? (129.4)

XV.   The Big Bubble theory (130.6)

XVI. Man's revolt against God as Creator (131)

Chapter 7: The Six Days of Creation

I.   The framework of the creation account (133.1)

II.   The meaning of the sequence of creation (134.3)

    a.   What is "light"? (134.6)

III. How should we view the Genesis account? (137.4)

    a.   Theistic evolution? (140.1)

    b.   Scientific creationism (140.6)

    c.   The "gap" theories (144.2)

IV.   Comparison of the Bible and evolutionary theory (146.3)

V.   Evolutionism and human rights (152.1)

VI.   Diversity of interpretations (153.2)

Chapter 8: The Crisis of Evolutionary Theory

Although this chapter was written more than fifteen years ago, it remains essentially correct. New books critical of evolution, such as Denton's Evolution: A Theory in Crisis; *Johnson's* Darwin on Trial; *and Behe's* Darwin's Black Box *have decisively refuted the scientific arguments for Darwin's theory.*

I.   The resurgence of evolutionary theory (156.1)
II.   The growing doubts about evolution (157.3)
        a.   The weakness of Darwinian biology (158.1)
        b.   The collapse of Darwinian paleontology (162.7)
        c.   Problems with natural selection (164.2)
        d.   Two key issues (166.1)
             i.   The mode of evolution (166.2)
                  1.   Life in outer space? (176.1)
                  2.   The odds against chance origination (177.0)
                  3.   Life from outer space? (178.10)
                  4.   The uniqueness of the earth (180.3)
                  5.   Seven false assumptions (182.2)
             ii. The role of metaphysical assumptions (184.2)
                  1.   Evolutionism is unscientific (188.1)
                  2.   The limits of science (190.2)
                  3.   A major shift in perspective? (194.1)

Chapter 9: The Origin and Nature of Man

I.   Introduction (197.1)
II.   Genesis 1 and 2 compared (199.1)
III.   Adam and Christ (199.2)
IV.   Animal ancestry and the biblical view (200.1)
V.   Four main views of the origin of man (205.1)
VI.   "Ancestors" of modern man? (206.1)
VII.   Is man of recent origin? (212.3)
        a.   The re-emergence of catastrophism (215.1)
             i.   A worldwide flood? (217.2)
        b.   What distinguishes man from hominids? (219.2)
        c.   Evangelicals debate the age of man (223.5)
VIII.   The uniqueness of man (226.2)

Chapter 10: Angels, Satan and the Demons, and the Fall

This chapter forms a bridge between the five previous ones on creation, and the ten that follow, all dealing in one way or another with God's victory over evil.

I.   The power behind all evil (229.1)

II.   Angels, Satan, and the demons (229.3)
      a.   The creation of angels (229.3)
      b.   Neglect of the doctrine of angels (230.1)
      c.   The priority of man in creation (233.4)
      d.   The origin, nature, ministry of angels (232.5)
      e.   Fallen angels (235.2)
      f.   The folly of neglecting Satan (238.3)
III.   The fall (239.4)
      a.   The creation of woman (239.4)
      b.   Sexual differentiation (242.3)
      c.   The fall into sin (244.3)
          i.   The tree of knowledge of good and evil (245.6)
          ii.   Adam the representative sinner (246.3)
          iii.   The consequences of the fall (247.1)
          iv.   The role of Satan in the world (249.3)
IV.   Conclusion: *Christus Victor* (250.4)

Chapter 11: The Goodness of God

After discussing Satan and the fall, Henry now deals with the goodness of God before turning to the problem of evil.

I.   God alone determines the good (251.1)
II.   The goodness of creation (252.2)
      a.   Goodness and beauty (252.4)
III.   The goodness of God's commands (253.2)
      a.   Opposition to command ethics (254.1)
      b.   The biblical view (257.2)
IV.   The goodness of God's salvation (258.1)
      a.   The Christian's good works (259.1)
V.   Humanistic views of good and evil (259.4)
      a.   Goodness in Chinese thought (260.2)
      b.   Science and the good (261.2)
      c.   Man's relationship to nature (262.2)
VI.   The only source for guidance in life (267)

Chapter 12: God and the Problem of Evil

As Henry says in his first paragraph, this chapter deals with the philosophical aspect of the problem of evil; the next chapter will address the more personal side.

I.   Introduction (269.1)
II.   Evil and God's omnipotence (269.2)
III.   The eternal punishment of evil (278)
IV.   Evil and free will (279.4)
V.   Philosophy gives no certain answers (281.4)

Chapter 13: Evil as a Religious Dilemma

In the previous chapter, Henry had discussed the philosophical problem of evil. Now he looks at the problem from the standpoint of the believer whose faith is shaken by the presence of suffering in the world or in his own life. The "dilemma" to which Henry refers is the apparent contradiction between God's love and his power, on the one hand, and the existence of suffering on the other.

I.   The problem of suffering for individuals (283.1)
II.   Explanations rejected by the Bible (284.1)
III.   The limits of the argument from experience (284.4)
IV.   Discussion and rejection of the views of those who would try to solve the problem of evil by limiting God (285.1)
V.   The incarnation and the problem of suffering (290.2)
        a.   Does God suffer? (290.3)
VI.   Does God allow meaningless suffering? (291.4)
        a.   God "creates" evil: Isaiah 45:6–7 (292)
        b.   God does not commit sin (294.3)
VII.   Unacceptable explanations of evil (294.5)
VIII.   God's wrath (295.3)
IX.   Facing the problem of evil and sin (295.5)
X.   We too are evil (296.3)
XI.   Learning from Job (297.2)
XII.   The undeserved suffering of Jesus (298.2)
XIII.   God's providence (299.5)
XIV.   Dealing with the question, "Why?" (301.4)
XV.   Hope and patience (302.4)
XVI.   Summary (304.2)

Chapter 14: The Fatherhood of God

I.   Introduction (305.1)
II.   Scripture alone tells us the meaning of God as Father (305.1)

III.   God as Father in other religions (306)
IV.   The Old Testament view (307.2)
    a.   God as Father to Israel (307.3)
    b.   God as universal King (309.1)
    c.   Father of individuals? (309.3)
V.   Judaism (310.1)
VI.   The New Testament (310.2)
    a.   The uniqueness of Jesus' teaching (311.1)
        i.   Abba (313.11)
        ii.   "My Father" (312.1)
        iii.   Is God the Father of all mankind? (314.3)
    b.   The Epistles: the new family (318.2)
VII.   Two important implications (320.1)
    a.   Both Father and Judge (321)
VIII.   God as lover (322.2)
IX.   Summary (323.1)

Chapter 15: The Holiness of God

Any true understanding of the relationship of good and evil in this world must include a clear concept of God's holiness, to which Henry now turns.

I.   The Holiness of God (324.1)
    a.   The priority of God's holiness (324.1)
    b.   Holiness is separation (324.3)
    c.   The centrality of the idea of God's holiness (325.3)
    d.   False ideas (325.5)
    e.   Jesus is holy (326.2)
    f.   A holy nation (326.3)
    g.   Holiness demands punishment (327.1)
        i.   The curse (327.2)
        ii.   Christ and the curse of God (327.4)
        iii.   Grief and sorrow (328.1)
        iv.   Enmity (328.2)
        v.   Wrath (328.3)
II.   God's redemption (324.1)
    a.   God provides the sacrifice (334.1)
    b.   Atonement as satisfaction (335.1)
III.   The holiness of Christians (335.3)
    a.   The necessity of obedience (335.3)

b. Justification by faith alone (336.2)

c. Life in the Holy Spirit (336.4)

Chapter 16: God's Incomparable Love

I.   A new idea of love (340.1)

II.   God is love (341.1)

III. Agape: love for the unlovely (342.3)

a. Two words for love (343.2)

b. Agape's different meanings (344.1)

IV.   Old Testament views of God's love (344.2)

a. Greek words for love (345.3)

b. The Pentateuch and history books (346.3)

c. The Prophets (347.2)

V.   New Testament views of God's love (347.4)

a. Jesus, God's gift of love (347.4)

b. John, the apostle of love (348.2)

c. Translation of Old Testament terms (349.1)

d. God's love is voluntary (349.2)

e. Jesus and God's grace (349.3)

VI.   God's love and His righteousness (350.1)

a. In the Old Testament (350.1)

b. In the New Testament (350.2)

c. Love and wrath (351.3)

d. Righteousness and love in the death of Jesus (354.4)

e. Justification by faith (356.4)

f. Reconciliation of God and man (358.1)

Chapter 17: The Ministry of the Holy Spirit

Having introduced the idea of life in the Spirit in chapter 15, and of God's love in chapter 16, Henry now discusses the ministry of the Spirit, who communicates God's love to his people and enables them to bear the fruit of love.

I.   Introduction (370.2)

II.   The Holy Spirit in the Old Testament (371.3)

III. The Holy Spirit in Jesus' life (373.1)

IV.   The promise of the Spirit (374.1)

V.   Between Calvary and Pentecost (375.1)

VI.   Pentecost (377.1)
    a.   The Spirit and prophecy (389.3)
VII.   The role of the Spirit in the life of the believer (384.1)
    a.   The baptism with the Spirit (385.1)
    b.   The fullness of the Spirit (386.10)
    c.   The gifts of the Spirit (388.2)
    d.   The gift of tongues (394.1)
    e.   The fruit of the Spirit (397.2)
    f.   Father, Son, and Holy Spirit (399.2)

Chapter 18: The God of Justice and of Justification

As he continues to explore the relationship of God to good and evil, Henry now looks specifically at God's justice in this and the following chapter.

I.   Justice in God and among men (402.1)
II.   Philosophical views of justice (404.3)
III.   God is impartial (405.3)
IV.   Justice: based on equality, merit, or need? (405.4)
    a.   God' judges according to our works (406.4)
    b.   Justice based on need? (407.2)
    c.   God's justice and mercy (410.1)
    d.   Confusing justice and love (410.3)
    e.   Our only hope (413.3)
V.   God demands justice among men (414)
    a.   Modern neglect of God's transcendent justice (414.3)

Chapter 19: Justice and the Kingdom of God

Henry continues his discussion of justice, as part of the larger examination of the relationship of God to good and evil in the world. This chapter contains an analysis of the relationship of human law to God's justice.

I.   God's justice and man's faith (418.1)
II.   Justice will eventually triumph (419.5)
III.   Justice has its roots in heaven (420.3)
    a.   Law comes from God (420.4)
    b.   Humanism: law is independent of God (421.2)
       i.   Natural law theory (423.2)
    c.   God's transcendent law (425.2)
    d.   The basis of human rights (426.1)

    e. Views of other religions (427.2)

    f. God's revealed law (429.1)

  IV. Jesus: the holy and just one (431.3)

    a. God's law is universal law (432.4)

  V. The role of believers in the world (433.1)

  VI. Rampant injustice in the world (433.3)

    a. The duty of the Christian to obey the law (434.1)

    b. Responding to injustice (434.4)

Chapter 20: God Who Stays: Divine Providence

This chapter continues the study of the relationship of God to good and evil in the world by expounding the doctrine of God's providence. In the process, Henry responds to various modern challenges to God's providence. The concluding three paragraphs eloquently describe the Christian's confident faith in God in the midst of a troubled world.

  I. God preserves the world he has made (455.1)

  II. Preservation is distinct from creation (456.3)

  III. God's goal in creation and preservation (457.3)

  IV. God's providence is specific (458.1)

  V. Providence and suffering (460.2)

    a. Jesus our example and hope (462.3)

  VI. Divine providence and public life (463.1)

  VII. Opposition to the idea of God's providence (463.8)

    a. Humanism (463.3)

    b. The shocks of modern history (465.1)

    c. Sociology (466.1)

    d. Science (468.2)

    e. The study of history (470)

      i. Opposition to just wars (473.3)

      ii. Marxism and capitalism (474.1)

      iii. The world of learning (477.1)

  VIII. Christianity's bold confidence in providence (477.2)

    a. The role of prayer (480.3)

    b. The only way to joy and peace (482.3)

Supplementary Note: Auschwitz as a Suspension of Providence

Henry here faces the criticism by Jews (and some others) that the Holocaust refutes the notion of God's providence.

I.   Auschwitz shatters Jewish faith in God (485.1)

II.   Another perspective on the Holocaust (487.2)

III.   The survival of the Jews (488.1)

IV.   The Holocaust and human sin (489.3)

Chapter 21: God Who Stays: The Finalities

In this final chapter Henry points toward the future, when God's goodness, majesty, holiness, wisdom, power, and righteousness will all be fully manifest.

I.   The unique teaching of Christianity (492.1)

    a.   History has a goal (493.1)

    b.   A new creation (493.6)

II.   Unanswered questions (494.3)

III.   Erroneous views of the end (495.1)

    a.   A desire for control (496.2)

IV.   Certainties given by God (497.2)

    a.   The personal return of Jesus Christ (498.1)

        i.   Jesus is God (499.1)

        ii.   The life to come (500.5)

        iii.   The coming of the kingdom of God (504.2)

        iv.   The new heavens and new earth (505.5)

        v.   Salvation for all? (507.2)

           1.   Eternal punishment (509.3)

        vi.   Reunion and renewal (512.2)

        vii.   Rest and joy (513.1)

V.   God knows and stays (513.3)

Bibliography

Abraham, William J. *The Coming Great Revival: Recovering the Full Evangelical Tradition.* San Francisco: Harper & Row, 1984.

Anderson, Ray S. "Evangelical Theology." In *The Modern Theologians: An Introduction to Christian Theology in the Twentieth Century*, edited by David F. Ford, 480–98. 2nd ed. Cambridge, MA: Blackwell, 1997.

Balmer, Randall Herbert. *The Encyclopedia of Evangelicalism.* Louisville: Westminster John Knox, 2002.

Beegle, Dewey M. *Scripture, Tradition, and Infallibility.* Grand Rapids: Eerdmans, 1973.

Behe, Michael J. *Darwin's Black Box: The Biochemical Challenge to Evolution.* New York: Simon & Schuster, 1996.

Bloesch, Donald G. *Essentials of Evangelical Theology.* 2 vols. San Francisco: Harper & Row, 1978.

———. *The Evangelical Renaissance.* Grand Rapids: Eerdmans, 1973.

———. *The Future of Evangelical Christianity: A Call for Unity amid Diversity.* Garden City, NY: Doubleday, 1983.

———. *Holy Scripture: Revelation, Inspiration & Interpretation.* Downers Grove, IL: InterVarsity, 1994.

Brand, Chad Owen. "Genetic Defects or Accidental Similarities? Orthodoxy and Open Theism and Their Connections to Western Philosophical Traditions." In *Beyond the Bounds: Open Theism and the Undermining of Biblical Christianity*, edited by John Piper, Justin Taylor, and Paul Helseth, 43–76. Wheaton, IL: Crossway, 2003.

Campbell-Jack, W. C., and Gavin J. McGrath, editors. *New Dictionary of Christian Apologetics.* Downers Grove, IL: InterVarsity, 2006.

Carson, D. A., and John D. Woodbridge, editors. *God and Culture: Essays in Honor of Carl F. H. Henry.* Grand Rapids: Eerdmans, 1993.

Chang, Lit-Sen. *What Is Apologetics?* Translated by Samuel Ling. San Gabriel, CA: China Horizon, 1999.

Colyer, Elmer M., editor. *Evangelical Theology in Transition: Theologians in Dialogue with Donald Bloesch.* Downers Grove, IL: InterVarsity, 1999.

Conn, Harvie M. *Contemporary World Theology.* 2nd rev. ed. Nutley, NJ: Presbyterian and Reformed Publishing, 1974.

Dembski, William A. *Intelligent Design: The Bridge between Science & Theology.* Downers Grove, IL: InterVarsity, 1999.

Denton, Michael. *Evolution: A Theory in Crisis.* Bethesda, MD: Adler & Adler, 1986.

Dockery, David S. "Millard J. Erickson: Theologian for the Church." In *New Dimensions in Evangelical Thought: Essays in Honor of Millard J. Erickson*, edited by David S. Dockery, 17–31. Downers Grove, IL: InterVarsity, 1998.

———, editor. *New Dimensions in Evangelical Thought: Essays in Honor of Millard J. Erickson*. Downers Grove, IL: InterVarsity, 1998.

Dulles, Avery Robert. "Donald Bloesch on Revelation." In *Evangelical Theology in Transition: Theologians in Dialogue with Donald Bloesch*, edited by Elmer M. Colyer, 61–76. Downers Grove, IL: InterVarsity, 1999.

———. *Models of Revelation*. Garden City, NY: Doubleday, 1983.

Edgar, William. "Christian Apologetics for a New Century." In *New Dictionary of Christian Apologetics*, edited by W. C. Campbell-Jack and Gavin J. McGrath, 3–14. Downers Grove, IL: InterVarsity, 2006.

Ellingsen, Mark. *The Evangelical Movement: Growth, Impact, Controversy, Dialog*. Minneapolis: Augsburg, 1988.

Erickson, Millard J. *Christian Theology*. 3 vols. Grand Rapids: Baker, 1983–85.

———. "Donald Bloesch's Doctrine of Scripture." In *Evangelical Theology in Transition: Theologians in Dialogue with Donald Bloesch*, edited by Elmer M. Colyer, 77–97. Downers Grove, IL: InterVarsity, 1999.

Evans, C. Stephen. "Approaches to Christian Apologetics." In *New Dictionary of Christian Apologetics*, edited by W. C. Campbell-Jack and Gavin J. McGrath, 15–21. Downers Grove, IL: InterVarsity, 2006.

———. *Pocket Dictionary of Apologetics & Philosophy of Religion*. Downers Grove, IL: InterVarsity, 2002.

Fackre, Gabriel J. *The Doctrine of Revelation: A Narrative Interpretation*. Edinburgh: Edinburgh University Press, 1997.

———. *Ecumenical Faith in Evangelical Perspective*. Grand Rapids: Eerdmans, 1993.

Ford, David F., editor. *The Modern Theologians: An Introduction to Christian Theology in the Twentieth Century*. 2nd ed. Cambridge, MA: Blackwell, 1997.

Frame, John M. *Apologetics to the Glory of God: An Introduction*. Phillipsburg, NJ: Presbyterian and Reformed Publishing, 1994.

———. *Cornelius Van Til: An Analysis of His Thought*. Phillipsburg, NJ: Presbyterian and Reformed Publishing, 1995.

Franck, John R. "Theologies of Scripture in the Nineteenth and Twentieth Centuries: An Introduction." In *Christian Theologies of Scripture: A Comparative Introduction*, edited by Justin S. Holcomb, 157–64. New York: New York University Press, 2006.

Gasaway, Brantley W. "As a Matter of Fact: J. Gresham Machen's Defense of the Metaphysical and Moral." *Fides et Historia* 41.1 (2009) 47–70.

Gay, Craig. M. *The Way of the (Modern) World, or, Why It's Tempting to Live as if God Doesn't Exist*. Grand Rapids: Eerdmans, 1998.

George, Timothy. "Carl Henry." In *Biographical Dictionary of Evangelicals*, edited by Timothy Larsen. Downers Grove, IL: InterVarsity, 2003.

———. "New Dimensions in Baptist Theology." In *New Dimensions in Evangelical Thought: Essays in Honor of Millard J. Erickson*, edited by David S. Dockery, 137–47. Downers Grove, IL: InterVarsity, 1998.

George, Timothy, and David S. Dockery, editors. *Theologians of the Baptist Tradition*. Nashville: Broadman & Holman, 2001.

George, Timothy, and Alister McGrath, editors. *For All the Saints: Evangelical Theology and Christian Spirituality*. Louisville: Westminster John Knox, 2003.

Gier, Nicholas F. *God, Reason, and the Evangelicals: The Case against Evangelical Rationalism*. Lanham, MD: University Press of America, 1987.

Grenz, Stanley J. "Fideistic Revelationism." In *Evangelical Theology in Transition: Theologians in Dialogue with Donald Bloesch*, edited by Elmer M. Colyer, 35–60. Downers Grove, IL: InterVarsity, 1999.

Grenz, Stanley J., and Roger E. Olson. *20th Century Theology: God & the World in a Transitional Age*. Downers Grove, IL: InterVarsity, 1992.

Grudem, Wayne A. *Systematic Theology: An Introduction to Biblical Doctrine*. Grand Rapids: Zondervan, 2000.

Halliday, Steve, and Al Janssen, editors. *Carl Henry at His Best: A Lifetime of Quotable Thoughts*. Portland, OR: Multnomah, 1989.

Hart, D. G., and John Muether. *Fighting the Good Fight: A Brief History of the Orthodox Presbyterian Church*. Philadelphia: Orthodox Presbyterian Church, 1995.

Henry, Carl F. H. *Aspects of Christian Social Ethics*. Grand Rapids: Eerdmans, 1964.

———, editor. *Baker's Dictionary of Christian Ethics*. Grand Rapids: Baker, 1973.

———. *Christian Countermoves in a Decadent Culture*. Portland, OR: Multnomah, 1986.

———, editor. *Christian Faith and Modern Theology*. Grand Rapids: Baker, 1971.

———. *The Christian Mindset in a Secular Society: Promoting Evangelical Renewal & National Righteousness*. Portland, OR: Multnomah, 1984.

———. *Christian Personal Ethics*. Grand Rapids: Baker, 1957.

———. *Confessions of a Theologian: An Autobiography*. Waco, TX: Word, 1986.

———. "The Concerns and Considerations of Carl F. H. Henry." *Christianity Today*, March 13, 1981, 18–23.

———. *The Drift of Western Thought*. Grand Rapids: Eerdmans, 1951.

———. "An Evangelical-Ecumenical Dialogue." In *Story Lines: Chapters on Thought, Word, and Deed: For Gabriel Fackre*, edited by S. F. Gibson, 39–44. Grand Rapids: Eerdmans, 2002.

———. *Evangelical Responsibility in Contemporary Theology*. Pathway Books. Grand Rapids: Eerdmans, 1957.

———. *Evangelicals at the Brink of Crisis*. Waco, TX: Word, 1967.

———. *Evangelicals in Search of Identity*. Waco, TX: Word, 1976.

———. *Faith at the Frontiers*. Chicago: Moody, 1969.

———. *Fifty Years of Protestant Theology*. Boston: Wilde, 1950.

———. *God, Revelation, and Authority*. 6 vols. Waco, TX: Word, 1976–83.

———, editor. *The Horizons of Science: Christian Scholars Speak Out*. Contemporary Evangelical Thought. San Francisco: Harper & Row, 1978.

———. *A Plea for Evangelical Demonstration*. Grand Rapids: Baker, 1971.

———. *The Protestant Dilemma: An Analysis of the Current Impasse in Theology*. Grand Rapids: Eerdmans, 1948.

———. *Remaking the Modern Mind*. Grand Rapids: Eerdmans 1948.

———, editor. *Revelation and the Bible: Contemporary Evangelical Thought*. Grand Rapids: Baker, 1958.

———. *Twilight of a Great Civilization: The Drift toward Neo-paganism*. Westchester, IL: Crossway, 1988.

———. *The Uneasy Conscience of Modern Fundamentalism*. Grand Rapids: Eerdmans, 1947.

Henry, Carl F. H., and Kenneth Kantzer, editors. *Evangelical Affirmations*. Grand Rapids: Zondervan, 1990.

Hill, Jonathan. *The History of Christian Thought: The Fascinating Story of the Great Christian Thinkers and How They Helped Shape the World as We Know It Today*. Downers Grove, IL: InterVarsity, 2003.

Hodges, Louis Igou. "New Dimensions in Scripture." In *New Dimensions in Evangelical Thought: Essays in Honor of Millard J. Erickson*, edited by David S. Dockery, 209–34. Downers Grove, IL: InterVarsity, 1998.

Holcomb, Justin S., editor. *Christian Theologies of Scripture: A Comparative Introduction*. New York: New York University Press, 2006.

Horton, Michael S. "Hellenistic or Hebrew?: Open Theism and Reformed Theological Method." In *Beyond the Bounds: Open Theism and the Undermining of Biblical Christianity*, edited by John Piper, Justin Taylor, and Paul Helseth, 201–34. Wheaton, IL: Crossway, 2003.

Hunter, James Davidson. *Evangelicalism: The Coming Generation*. Chicago: University of Chicago Press, 1987.

Johnson, Philip E. *Darwin on Trial*. 2nd ed. Downers Grove, IL: InterVarsity, 1993.

Johnson, William Stacy, and John H. Leith, editors. *Reformed Reader: A Sourcebook in Christian Theology*. Vol. 1: *Classical Beginnings, 1519–1799*. Louisville: Westminster John Knox, 1993.

Kantzer, Kenneth. "Carl Ferdinand Howard Henry: An Appreciation." In *God and Culture: Essays in Honor of Carl F. H. Henry*, edited by D. A. Carson and John D. Woodbridge, 369–77. Grand Rapids: Eerdmans, 1993.

Kelly, Douglas F. *Systematic Theology: Grounded in Holy Scripture and Understood in the Light of the Church*. Vol. 1: *The God Who Is: The Holy Trinity*. Fearn, Ross-shire, Scotland: Mentor, 2008.

Klein, William W., Craig L. Blomberg, and Robert L. Hubbard Jr. *Introduction to Biblical Interpretation*. Rev. ed. Nashville: Nelson, 2004.

Larsen, Timothy, editor. *Biographical Dictionary of Evangelicals*. Downers Grove, IL: InterVarsity, 2003.

Lewis, Gordon R., and Bruce A. Demarest. *Integrative Theology*. 3 vols. in 1. Grand Rapids: Zondervan, 1996.

Livingston, James C., and Francis Schüssler Fiorenza, with Sarah Coakley and James H. Evans. *Modern Christian Thought*. 2 vols. 2nd ed. Minneapolis: Fortress, 2006.

Marty, Martin. "Period 5: Recent Times (Since 1965)." In *Makers of Christian Theology in America*, edited by Mark G. Toulous and James O. Duke, 519–45. Nashville: Abingdon, 1997.

McGrath, Alister. *Evangelicalism and the Future of Christianity*. Downers Grove, IL: InterVarsity, 1995.

———. *A Passion for Truth: The Intellectual Coherence of Evangelicalism*. Downers Grove, IL: InterVarsity, 1996.

McKim, Donald K., editor. *Dictionary of Major Biblical Interpreters*. 2nd ed. Downers Gove, IL: InterVarsity, 2007.

McKnight, Scot. "Five Streams of the Emerging Church." *Christianity Today*, February 2007, 35–39.

McNeal, Thomas Reginald. "A Critical Analysis of the Doctrine of God in the Theology of Carl F. H. Henry." PhD diss., Southwestern Baptist Theological Seminary, 1986.

Mohler, R. Albert, Jr. "Carl F. H. Henry." In *Theologians of the Baptist Tradition*, edited by Timothy George and David S. Dockery, 279–96. Nashville: Broadman & Holman, 2001.

———. "Carl Ferdinand Howard Henry." In *Baptist Thinkers*, edited by Timothy George and David S. Dockery, 279–96. Nashville: Broadman & Holman, 1990.

———. "Evangelical Theology and Karl Barth: Representative Models of Response." PhD diss., Southern Baptist Theological Seminary, 1989.

Montgomery, John Warwick. *Faith Founded on Fact: Essays in Evidential Apologetics.* Nashville: T. Nelson, 1978.

Moore, Russell D. *The Kingdom of Christ: The New Evangelical Perspective.* Wheaton, IL: Crossway, 2004.

Nassif, Bradley, "New Dimension in Eastern Orthodox Theology." In *New Dimensions in Evangelical Thought: Essays in Honor of Millard J. Erickson*, edited by David S. Dockery. Downers Grove, IL: InterVarsity, 1998.

Noll, Mark A., and George A. Rawlyk, editors. *Amazing Grace: Evangelicalism in Australia, Britain, Canada, and the United States.* Montreal: McGill-Queen's University Press, 1994.

Oliphint, K. Scott. *Reasons [for Faith]: Philosophy in the Service of Theology.* Phillipsburg, NJ: Presbyterian and Reformed Publishing, 2006.

Olson, Roger E. "Carl F. H. Henry." In *Makers of Christian Theology in America*, edited by Mark G. Toulous and James O. Duke. Nashville: Abingdon, 1997.

———. *The Story of Christian Theology: Twenty Centuries of Tradition & Reform.* Downers Grove, IL: InterVarsity, 1999.

———. *The Westminster Handbook to Evangelical Theology.* Louisville: Westminster John Knox, 2004.

Osborne, Grant R. *The Hermeneutical Spiral: A Comprehensive Introduction to Biblical Interpretation.* Downers Grove, IL: InterVarsity, 1991.

Ovey, M. J. "Rationalism." In *New Dictionary of Christian Apologetics*, edited by W. C. Campbell-Jack and Gavin J. McGrath, 592–94. Downers Grove, IL: InterVarsity, 2006.

Patterson, Bob E. *Carl F. H. Henry.* Makers of the Modern Theological Mind. Waco, TX: Word, 1983.

Pinnock, Clark H. *Tracking the Maze: Finding Our Way through Modern Theology from an Evangelical Perspective.* San Francisco: Harper & Row, 1990.

Purdy, Richard A. "Carl F. H. Henry." In *Handbook of Evangelical Theologians*, edited by Walter A. Elwell, 260–75. Grand Rapids: Baker, 1993.

Ramm, Bernard. *After Fundamentalism: The Future of Evangelical Theology.* San Francisco: Harper & Row, 1983.

Smith, David L. *A Handbook of Contemporary Theology.* Wheaton, IL: Victor, 1992.

Sproul, R. C., John Gerstner, and Arthur Lindsley. *Classical Apologetics: A Rational Defense of the Christian Faith and a Critique of Presuppositional Apologetics.* Grand Rapids: Zondervan, 1984.

Studebaker, J. A., Jr. "Common Ground." In *New Dictionary of Apologetics*, edited by W. C. Campbell-Jack and Gavin McGrath, 161–65. Downers Grove, IL: InterVarsity, 2006.

Toulous, Mark G., and James O. Duke, editors. *Makers of Christian Theology in America.* Nashville: Abingdon, 1997.

Trembath, Kern Robert. *Divine Revelation: Our Moral Relation with God.* New York: Oxford University Press, 1991.

Trueman, Carl R. "Admiring the Sistine Chapel: Reflections on Carl F. H. Henry's *God, Revelation, and Authority.*" *Themelios* 25:2 (2000) 48–58.

Van Til, Cornelius. *A Christian Theory of Knowledge.* Phillipsburg, NJ: Presbyterian and Reformed Publishing, 1969.

———. "The New Evangelicalism." Unpublished paper, Westminster Theological Seminary, n.d.

Vanhoozer, Kevin J. "Theology and Apologetics." In *New Dictionary of Apologetics,* edited by W. C. Campbell-Jack and Gavin McGrath, 35–43. Downers Grove, IL: InterVarsity, 2006.

Ward, Graham, editor. *The Blackwell Companion to Postmodern Theology.* Oxford: Blackwell, 2004.

———, editor. *The Postmodern God: A Theological Reader.* Malden, MA: Blackwell, 1997.

Wells, Jonathan. *Icons of Evolution: Science or Myth? Why Much of What We Teach about Evolution Is Wrong.* Washington, DC: Regnery, 2000.

White, James Emory. *What Is Truth?: A Comparative Study of the Positions of Cornelius Van Til, Francis Schaeffer, Carl F. H. Henry, Donald Bloesch, Millard Erickson.* Nashville: Broadman & Holman, 1994.

Wilder-Smith, A. E. *Man's Origin, Man's Destiny: A Critical Survey of the Principles of Evolution and Christianity.* Minneapolis: Bethany, 1975.

Woodbridge, John D. "Carl F. H. Henry: Spokesperson for American Evangelicalism." In *God and Culture: Essays in Honor of Carl F. H. Henry,* edited by D. A. Carson and John D. Woodbridge, 378–93. Grand Rapids: Eerdmans, 1993.

Index of Names

Abraham, William, 119n1
Anselm, 42, 67, 207
Aquinas, Thomas, 33, 46, 57, 65, 67, 74,
  107n3, 130, 141–42, 151, 157–
  58, 161–62, 170, 203, 207
Athanasius, 65, 130, 138
Augustine (of Hippo), xii–xiv, 9, 17, 32,
  37–39, 41–42, 65, 67, 69, 74,
  111, 126, 130–145, 161, 164–65,
  207
Barna, George, 87, 90
Barr, James, 16, 28n6, 96, 194
Barth, Karl, 9, 12, 16–18, 20, 23–27, 29,
  30, 32–35, 49, 53, 56, 58, 59n34,
  65, 70, 73, 81, 82, 98, 103, 116,
  118, 122, 136, 142, 151, 161,
  162, 163, 166, 170–71, 174, 178,
  180, 182, 192–93, 200, 203–4,
  206, 208, 210, 212
Bavinck, Herman, 32
Behe, Michael, 76n29, 83n8, 101n30,
  213
Berkhof, Louis, 32
Bloesch, Donald, 9, 16–18, 34–35,
  73, 82n6, 86, 92, 101, 104–6,
  113n36, 116, 122, 204
Boice, James Montgomery, 32
Boyd, Gregory, 33, 88
Bright, John, 16
Briggs, Kenneth, 13
Brunner, Emil, 23–24, 171, 188
Bonhoeffer, Dietrich, 24, 29
Bultmann, Rudolph, 16, 24, 29, 30n9,
  96, 99, 157, 174, 182, 194
Buswell, Oliver, 33

Calvin, John, 15, 32–33, 37–40, 42, 45,
  50, 57, 65, 69, 74, 111, 123, 130,
  139, 142, 151, 165, 208
Carnell, E. J., 6, 33n17, 107, 190
Chafer, Lewis Sperry, 33
Chang, Lit-sen, 65, 69
Clark, Gordon, 5, 19, 32–33, 57, 61, 65,
  73, 87, 92, 95, 96n16, 105–7,
  118, 128, 142, 177
Conn, Harvie, 18, 50, 92n1, 107,
  108n11, 118, 127
Colson, Charles ("Chuck"), 15
Cullman, Oscar, 174
Demarest, Bruce, xiv, 14, 21n1, 32n13,
  33, 95, 104, 127–28
Denton, Michael, 76n29, 83n8, 100n30,
  213
Descartes, Rene, 42, 152, 154, 203
Edgar, William, 73–77
Edwards, Jonathan, 32, 38, 111, 130,
  138, 142
Ellingson, Mark, 82
Erickson, Millard, 14, 16, 33
Euclid, 105, 115
Fackre, Gabriel, 14, 92n1, 105
Falwell, Jerry, 36
Feuerbach, Gottfried Wilhelm von, 152,
  180, 206
Frame, John, 16, 32–33, 38, 41n13,
  67n11, 69, 70n16, 128–29
Gay, Craig, 83
Genco, Peter, 163
George, Timothy, 12, 14–16, 87, 90
Gerstner, John, 33, 67, 76
Gill, John, 33
Graham, Billy, 6, 8, 14, 65, 102

Grenz, Stanley, 13, 18, 21n1, 24n2, 33–34, 36, 73, 92n1, 93, 97–98, 106, 139, 140n2

Grudem, Wayne, 14, 33, 41n13

Hegel, Georg Wilhelm Friedrich, 152, 158, 161, 164–65, 181, 203, 206

Henry, Helga, 10, 131

Hodge, Charles, 32, 65, 83

Hodges, Louis Igou, 38, 96

Hume, David, 159, 161, 164, 166, 203, 206

Hunter, James, 87

Kant, Immanuel, 29, 42, 74, 153, 158, 161, 165–66, 182, 200, 203, 206

Kantzer, Kenneth, 9–11

Kierkegaard, Søren, 23, 153, 182, 210

Kelly, Douglas, 16, 32, 38

Kuhn, Thomas, 28

Kung, Hans, 35

Kuyper, Abraham, 69

Ladd, George E., 16, 181

Leibnitz, Gottfried Wilhelm, 153, 164,

Lewis, C. S., 67n10, 141

Lewis, Gordon, xiv, 14, 21n1, 32n13, 33, 95, 104, 127–28

Locke, John, 153, 164, 203

Luther, Martin, 32, 37–39, 42, 69, 130, 132, 138, 142, 153, 165

Machen, J. Gresham, 83

Marx, Karl, 26, 30, 75, 110, 153–54, 159, 188, 197–99, 206, 211–12, 220

McDowell, Josh, 33, 67, 141

McGrath, Alistair, 15, 65n3, 118

McNeal, Thomas Reginald, 106n3

Mohler, Albert, 6, 14–15, 28–29, 33, 35nn21–22, 51, 54n22, 63n49, 64n52, 105n1, 106n3

Moltmann, Jürgen, 25, 27–31, 58, 88, 122, 154, 171, 174, 208

Montgomery, John W., 32–33, 67, 141, 163

Morris, Leon, 16

Murray, John, 32, 38

Newbigen, Leslie, 65

Noth, Martin, 16

Nygren, Anders, 42, 166

Ockenga, Harold, 6

Oden, Thomas, 33

Ogden, Schubert, 171, 188, 208

Oliphant, Scott, 16

Olson, Roger, xi, 9n9, 13, 15, 17–18, 21n1, 24n2, 32–34, 36, 66n8, 73, 82n6, 85–87, 89, 92n1, 93, 97–98, 101, 105–6, 122, 139, 140n2

Ostling, Richard, 11n20, 13

Otto, Rudolph, 42, 67, 166

Ovey, M. J., 107, 109

Owen, John, 32, 38, 130, 138, 142,

Packer, James I., 32

Pannenberg, Wolfhart, 26–28, 30–31, 88, 154, 174, 208

Patterson, Bob, xiv, 18, 52, 95, 97, 103, 105–7, 109n22, 117n4, 120n16

Pinnock, Clark, 33, 34n20, 73, 86, 88, 92n1, 96n16, 105, 163, 190

Piper, John, 33

Plantinga, Alvin, 66n9, 69, 76

Plato, 42, 127, 140, 154, 164–65, 202, 205, 210

Rahner, Karl, 12, 26, 30–31, 35

Ramm, Bernard, 9, 16–18, 33–34, 73, 82n6, 83, 84, 86, 92n1, 94–98, 103, 105, 190

Rauschenbusch, Walter, 23

Ritschl, Albrecht, 22, 42

Ryrie, Charles, 33

Schaeffer, Francis, 69

Schleiermacher, Friedrich, 22, 42, 159, 209

Schweitzer, Albert, 16

Solzhenitsyn, Aleksandr, 90

Spinoza, Baruch, 42, 155, 161, 164, 203, 206

Sproul, R. C., 33, 67, 76, 141

Tertullian, 155, 161

Thiessen, Henry Clarence, 33

Tillich, Paul, 188, 201

Torrance, Thomas, 181

Trembath, K. R., 19, 94n11

Troeltsch, Ernst, 42, 166

Trueman, Carl R., 14–15

Voltaire, F. M. A., 206

von Rad, Gerhard, 96

Van Til, Cornelius, 5, 18–19, 32, 65,
        67n11, 69, 70n16, 95, 107, 118,
        127–29, 142
Warfield, Benjamin B., 32, 38, 83
White, James, 92n1, 109, 110n23, 228
Wiley, H. Orton, 33
Woodbridge, John D., 3n1, 9n10, 10

Index of Subjects

NOTE: *This index does not refer to references in the Macro Index or the Theological Index, but it does include terms found in the Outline.*

a priori views of religion, 56, 95, 151, 163–66
Adam and Christ, 52, 141, 151, 214–15
angels, 55, 139, 150, 151, 177, 214–15
apologetics
    "classical", 67–70, 72, 141,
    presuppositional, 68–70, 72, 113–14
apriorism, 74
Aquinas, Thomas,
    "proof" of the existence of God, 56, 70, 74, 141
Arminian, Arminianism, 17, 33, 38, 89
atheism, 211
authority, 107, 109, 126, 139, 167, 176, 187–88, 190–92, 196, 206
Barthianism (see also "dialectical theology"), 82, 103
Bible
    and Christ, 187–88, 191
    and culture, 188, 211
    and philosophy, 187, 212
    and science, 22, 28, 34–35, 69–70, 73, 76, 100, 136, 189
    and tradition, 193, 223
    application to all of life, 143
    as narrative, 82
    authority of, 26, 29, 39, 62, 74, 185, 187–88, 210
    canon of, see "canon"
    Carl Henry's use and view of, 5–7, 9, 18, 28, 28–34, 37, 43–47, 96–97, 102, 113–14, 128, 133, 136, 145
    contradictions in, see "Bible, problem passages of"
    exegesis of, see "exegesis, exegete"
    historical reliability of, both believed and rejected, 22, 24, 27, 31, 35–37, 60, 63, 70, 72, 87n20, 141, 174, 194
    inerrancy of, 9, 26–27, 63, 86–87, 190–91
    infallibility, 20, 28, 33, 63, 87n22, 102, 113, 136, 139, 169, 191–92, 194
    inspiration of, 43, 46, 51, 63, 87n20, 94, 101, 127, 134, 136, 139, 188–91
    interpretation of, 6, 16, 26, 36, 44, 60, 62, 77, 82, 95, 97, 99, 103n39, 163, 171–72, 188–89, 191–95, 211–13, 223–24, 226
    locus and focus of God's revelation, 3, 22, 29, 39, 42–43, 47, 49, 55, 62, 68, 113, 128, 142, 163
    problem passages of, 30, 63, 69, 195
    translations, 63, 185, 191–92, 218
    unity of, 169, 178, 195–96
    witness to revelation, 23, 25, 27, 58
    Word/words of God, 24, 27, 56, 58, 113, 185, 191
biblical criticism
    general references to, 18, 86, 102
    proper, 6, 62, 73, 86, 96–97, 99, 194

biblical criticism (*continued*)
  skeptical ("negative"), 22–23, 27, 34, 37, 63, 69, 72–73, 86–87, 94–96, 99, 102, 188, 194, 196
biblical theology movement, 196
Big Bang theory, 213
Calvinism, Calvinistic, 15, 50, 139
canon, canonical, 60, 63, 195–96
capitalism, 220
catastrophism, 214
Christ, see "Bible, and Christ"; "Jesus Christ"; "revelation, and Jesus Christ"
Christology, see "Jesus Christ, person of"
"common ground", 70–71, 142, 166, 227
creation, 25–26, 28, 31–32, 42, 45, 47–48, 53, 55–57, 61, 74, 76, 91, 100, 103, 125
creationism, 83
criticism, biblical, see "biblical criticism"
death, 48, 200
Devil, the, see "Satan and demons"
dialectic theology, dialectical-existential theology, 9, 29–30, 34, 161, 174, 210
empiricism, 72, 108, 111, 158, 159, 160, 166
epistemology, epistemological, 29n9, 37, 41, 49, 51, 82, 105n1, 139
eschatology, eschatological, see also "Jesus Christ, return of," 6–7, 26, 31, 48, 52, 54, 58, 63, 77, 94, 103, 177, 199, 215–16, 221
ethics, Christian, 7, 23, 29, 43, 50–51, 63, 76, 94, 134, 138, 215, 225
evidences, see "apologetics, classical"
evidentialism, see "apologetics, classical"
evil, problem of (see also "God, providence of"), 35, 37, 47–49, 64, 136, 139, 197, 209, 215–16, 220
evolutionary theory, evolutionism, 17, 63, 67, 76, 83–84, 100, 139, 159, 183–84, 213–14

exegesis, exegete, 26, 44, 62–63, 88, 95, 97, 99, 178, 188–89, 194, 197, 199, 203
existential, existentialism, existentialist, 23–24, 61, 85, 159, 204, 206, 212
fall, fallen, 23, 30, 45, 55–58, 70, 108, 112, 125, 139, 141, 162, 167, 171, 184, 214–15
feminism, feminist theology, 26, 87–88
Fundamentalism, Fundamentalists, 6, 14, 19, 35–37, 43, 55, 64, 75, 86n17, 91, 97–98, 101–103, 138, 226–27
God
  as source of guidance, 4, 55, 76, 215
  as sovereign Creator, 4, 21, 31–32, 41, 48, 52, 61, 88, 111, 124, 139, 142, 165, 167, 177, 182, 212–13
  as Spirit, 205, 211
  attributes of, 35, 139, 202–3, 207, 209–10
  changeless, immutable, 31, 88, 201, 207–8
  eternal, 30–32, 48, 50, 60, 77, 80, 88, 138, 175, 179, 185, 199, 205–6, 212–13
  fatherhood of, 23, 139, 216
  foreknowledge, knowledge of the future, 207, 212
  freedom of, 47–49, 136, 209, 212
  goodness of, 32, 76, 111, 139, 215, 221
  holiness of, 35, 139, 177, 217, 220–21
  immanence, 22, 24, 32, 211, 212
  immutable, see "God, changeless"
  infinite nature of, 27, 31, 123, 189, 205–6
  intellectual attributes of, 210
  justice of, 22, 55, 64, 137, 219
  king, kingdom of, kingdom of Christ, 23, 26, 30, 37, 48–50, 52–53, 64, 77, 91, 143, 167–68, 177, 209, 217, 219, 221, 227
  knowability of, knowledge of, 9, 21–24, 26, 28, 30, 32, 42, 45–47, 52–57, 59n34, 62, 68–70, 72,

91, 106n, 107, 110–13, 115–18,
120–21, 123–25, 136, 139, 141,
158, 165–67, 170–71, 179, 182,
187, 189, 201–3, 210, 212
living, 31, 49, 54, 88, 110, 112, 116,
126, 179, 184–85, 201–2, 210
love of, 22, 25, 35, 49, 55, 91, 137,
139, 203, 206, 212, 216–19
mind of, and man's mind, 37, 42, 53,
55–57, 66, 68–69, 106–7, 113,
119–20, 124–25, 141–42, 166,
174, 179, 210
names of, 59, 62, 122, 139, 171–73,
204
personal, 25, 27, 40–41, 45, 48, 53,
58–60, 62, 82, 87, 116, 120–21,
171, 179, 185, 203–205, 209–10
problem of evil, see "evil, problem
of"
providence of, 4, 32, 42, 48, 76, 139,
196, 216, 220
reality and objectivity of, 47, 56,
112, 119–21, 200, 202–3
timelessness of, 89, 206–7, 212
transcendence of, 22–25, 31–32,
40, 53, 57, 88, 111, 121, 124–25,
211–12, 219
triune, see "Trinity, doctrine of"
gospel, 6–7, 31, 40, 60, 66, 69, 70–71,
75, 77, 137, 143, 156, 176–77,
198
hell, 22–23, 49
Henry, Carl F. H., life and character,
3–12, 130–45
hermeneutics, 77, 88n24, 101, 193
historical-critical method, 96, 195
holiness, of Christians, 40, 49–50,
105n1, 143, 217
Holy Spirit (see also, "Trinity, doctrine
of")
internal testimony of, 33, 64
ministry of, 4, 39, 45, 64, 71, 218–19
role in church proclamation, 196
role in inspiration of Scripture, 39,
46, 62–63, 103n39, 177, 188,
192–93, 195
role in interpretation and
understanding of Scripture 4,
9, 71, 76, 103n39, 113, 126–27,
139, 192
idealism, philosophical, see "realism,
philosophical"
illumination, see "Holy Spirit,
role in interpretation and
understanding of Scripture"
image of God, of Christ, 30, 42, 43, 45,
55–58, 70, 74, 119, 124–25, 139,
142, 169–71, 180, 183, 197, 210
incarnation, see "revelation, and Jesus"
inerrancy, see "Bible, inerrancy"
infallibility, see "Bible, infallibility"
inspiration, see "Bible, inspiration"
interpretation, see "Bible, interpretation
of"
intuition, 30, 111, 142, 158, 202
irrationalism, 85, 89, 127, 210
Israel, 23, 27, 31, 50, 60, 173–74, 217
Jesus Christ
and Adam, 214–15
and creation, 212
changelessness of, 288
eternal, 205
Lord, 49, 209, 215
mediator, 60, 77, 80, 176
Messiah, 43, 177, 182
person of, 39, 41, 55–56, 178–79,
209, 212
priestly ministry, 168
redemption through, 217, 288
resurrection of, 25, 41, 60, 68, 141
return of, 3, 55, 138–39, 145, 215,
221
Son of God, 23, 71, 173, 179, 205
Son of Man, 173
suffering of, 23, 25, 60, 91, 139, 218
union with, 3, 10
view of Scripture of, 60, 176
Word [Logos] of God, 56, 80, 112,
139, 177, 179, 187
Jesus Movement, 80–81, 159–60
Judaism, 73, 176, 217
Judgment, Last, 43, 177, 216, 221
justification, 39, 43, 197, 218–19

kingdom of God, see "God, king"

language, 61, 75, 77, 87, 93n3, 123, 136, 139, 171, 181–85, 186, 189–91

last days, see "eschatology"; "Jesus Christ, return of"

liberalism, theological, viii, 7, 23–24, 29–30, 35, 37–38, 44, 71, 81, 82n6, 86, 95, 99, 101–2, 143, 162, 182, 196

liberation theology, 25–26, 29–30, 75, 199

logic, 34, 45, 56–58, 65, 67, 70, 76, 105, 107–8, 111, 116–20, 125, 133, 139, 141–42, 158, 163, 166, 179–81, 184, 204, 209

logical positivism, 28, 72, 111, 136, 140, 159, 181, 183, 186, 200

Logos (see also "Jesus Christ, Word of God"),
    and image of God, 42, 45, 55, 57, 61
    and language, see "language"
    and logic, 112, 119, 180
    and New Testament, 60, 179
    and Old Testament, 60, 179
    as mediator of revelation of God, 179
    eternal, 60
    general, 179–80
    love, human, 74, 81, 197, 218

man
    origin and nature of (see also "God, as sovereign Creator"; "Logos, image of God,") 7, 42, 48, 83n8, 100n30, 212–14, 238
    priority in creation of, 215

Marxism, Marxist, 26, 30, 75, 159, 188, 197–99, 211–12, 220

meaning, meaning of life, 31, 46, 60, 76–77, 119, 125, 136–37, 145, 160, 175, 180, 216

miracles, 21–23, 48, 55, 68, 175, 194

monotheism, 204–5

mystery and revelation, see "revelation, and mystery"

mysticism, 3, 158

myth, 24, 29n9, 31, 60, 72, 77, 79, 99, 157–58, 160, 181, 228

names of God, see "God, names of"

names of Jesus Christ as revelation of God, 59, 173

natural theology, 54, 70, 170

naturalism, 21, 108, 157, 166, 170, 210–11

neo-orthodoxy (see "dialectical theology"), 12, 23, 82, 98, 136, 180

noetic effects of sin, see "revelation, necessity of"

non-contradiction, law of, 117–19, 128, 196, 202

openness theology, open theism, 35, 48, 75, 88–89, 92, 127, 223, 226

paradox, 9, 30, 34, 53, 112, 184, 208

Paul of Tarsus, 3, 66, 125, 136, 142, 161, 188, 197

Pentateuch, 99, 194, 218

philosophy, see "theology, and philosophy"

post-modern, post-modernism, 34, 84–85, 95, 99, 108, 109, 112, 228,

prayer, 5, 10, 131, 220

process philosophy, process theology, 25, 35, 88, 89, 103, 201, 204, 206, 208, 212

proofs
    for the existence of God, 67, 116
    Scripture proofs, 74

propositional revelation, see "revelation, propositional"

providence, see "God, providence of"

rationalism, 19, 26, 34, 85, 89n29, 105–29, 159, 225, 227

realism, philosophical, 202

reason, human, 6, 21–24, 30, 33–34, 42, 44–46, 54–57, 65–70, 76, 80, 82, 84–85, 95, 105–129, 140–42, 157, 159, 161–63, 165–66, 170, 175, 179, 193, 204, 210, 225, 227

Reformed theology, 15–16, 19, 32–33, 38–50, 69, 166, 223, 226

revelation of God,
    and history, 27, 31–32, 46, 49, 57, 59, 63, 66n8, 68, 70, 72, 77, 80,

82, 87n20, 89, 136, 138, 170,
173–76, 181, 184, 193
and infinite nature of God, 27, 31,
54, 123, 189, 206
and Jesus Christ, 24–25, 32, 37,
55–56, 60–61, 69, 91, 122, 125,
127, 139, 175–77, 179–80, 188,
205–6, 208, 216
and mystery, 35, 50, 53–54, 111,
124, 168, 175, 210
and nature, 42, 50, 54, 56–57, 66n8,
80, 165, 169–70, 173, 211, 215
as Wisdom, 182
coherent, 30, 39, 56, 62, 67, 76, 95,
116–18, 128, 162–63
cognitive aspects, 56, 62, 105n1,
116, 121, 181–82, 186
comprehensibility, 57, 61, 71, 113,
116, 126, 178, 193
forms of, 74, 122, 139, 169, 171,
general, 54–55, 60, 160, 165–66,
169, 186
in Scripture, see "Bible"
limits of, 54–56, 178, 186, 190
modern errors about, 7, 44, 53, 60,
70, 75, 101, 163, 181, 194, 210
necessity of, 57, 66, 141–42
personal, 4, 23, 40, 47, 49n41, 53,
58–59, 60, 62, 82, 101, 116,
120–21, 171, 180, 185–86
propositional, 34, 61–62, 119–22,
185–87
purpose, 52–53, 165, 167
rational, reasonable, 57–58, 61, 112,
117, 125, 128, 140, 178, 182
responses to, 50, 53, 59, 61, 64, 82,
111, 114, 116, 125, 158, 160,
176, 184, 191, 227
unity of, 30, 54–56, 169–70, 173,
178, 182, 184, 195–96
varieties, 55, 58, 122, 169
salvation, doctrine of, see "soteriology"
"salvation history" school of theology,
174
Satan and demons, 119, 139, 214–15
science, 4, 6, 22–24, 28, 34, 47, 69–70,
72, 74, 82–85, 87, 94, 98–101,
115–17, 133–34, 136, 143, 156,
159–62, 165, 189, 197, 207, 210,
212–15, 220, 223, 225, 228
Scripture, see "Bible"
soteriology, 17, 23, 31–32, 42–43, 48, 50,
52–53, 55, 63, 77–78, 94, 136,
144, 170, 173, 199, 215, 221
suffering, and goodness of God, see
"evil, problem of"
theology
and philosophy, 7, 23, 29n9, 44,
76, 89, 99–100, 110, 140, 157,
160–61, 179, 183, 187, 200–208,
210–12, 216, 227
coherence (see also "revelation,
coherent"), 39, 44, 116, 118, 128
as science, 115–17, 162
method and criteria, 39, 162
theophany, theophanies, 122, 171, 205
Trinity, doctrine of, 25, 27, 31, 39,
48, 117, 139, 143, 173, 204–5
truth, 3, 7, 19, 22–25, 28, 30, 33, 36, 41–
42, 44–46, 52, 54, 56–58, 61–64,
66–72, 74–76, 79–80, 82–85, 91,
95, 97, 101–3, 106–13, 116–22,
124–27, 129, 136, 138–40, 156,
158, 161–63, 166–67, 171, 181–
83, 185–86, 188–89, 191–93,
198–99, 207, 226, 228
Western civilization, Western culture,
90, 187
women, 87, 188

Made in United States
Orlando, FL
22 August 2023

36308399R00137